No Small World

No Small World

Visions and Revisions of World Literature

Michael Thomas Carroll, Editor
New Mexico Highlands University

National Council of Teachers of English
1111 W. Kenyon Road, Urbana, Illinois 61801-1096

Acknowledgments

My thanks to New Mexico Highlands University students Carol Romero, Mollie Busbey, and Joan Snider, all of whom contributed valuable assistance. Thanks also to Marlo Welshons at NCTE.

Richard Greene Moulton's diagram of the "Literary Pedigree of the English-Speaking Peoples" is adapted from *World Literature and Its Place in General Culture* (Norwood, MA: Macmillan, 1911) and is used here by permission.

"The Intellectual and Pedagogical Value of Traditional African Literature in the Western Classroom" by Erskine Peters was published in *The Western Journal of Black Studies* (13.1 [1989]: 28–35) and is used here with their permission.

"2 mothers in a h d b playground," by Arthur Yap, is reprinted by permission from his *Down the Line* (Singapore: Heinemann Asia, 1980). Copyright © Arthur Yap 1980.

The first stanza of "Song of the Banana Man," by Evan Jones, is reprinted by permission from *The Penguin Book of Caribbean Verse in English,* ed. Paula Burnett (London: Penguin, 1986).

"Psalm" and passages from "Parousia," "Of Being Numerous," "The Little Hole," and "Route" are reprinted by permission from *George Oppen: Collected Poems* (New York: New Directions, 1975). Copyright © 1975 by George Oppen.

Manuscript Editor: Lee Erwin

Cover Design: Barbara Yale-Read

Interior Book Design: Tom Kovacs for TGK Design

NCTE Stock Number 33681

Library of Congress Cataloging-in-Publication Data

No small world : visions and revisions of world literature / Michael
  Thomas Carroll, ed.
    p.   cm.
  Includes bibliographical references and index.
  ISBN 0-8141-3368-1 (pbk.)
  1. Literature—History and criticism.   I. Carroll, Michael
Thomas, 1954–   .
PN524.N6   1996
809—dc20   96-11056
                                                                CIP

Contents

Introduction

National literature has little meaning today; the time has come for the epoch of world literature to begin, and everyone must now do his share to hasten its realization.

—Johann Wolfgang von Goethe

When one considers the unimaginably vast quantity of literature that has been produced since human beings first produced script some five millennia ago; when one considers the number of cultures that occupy (or once occupied) the globe; when one considers the various genres, movements, and experiments that have been attempted—when one considers all this, the term "world literature" will inevitably become, to say the least, questionable. And when one begins to speak of it not only as a theoretical problem, but also as an element of the educational curriculum, the problem becomes multiplied—or more accurately, artificially minimized. That is, given the immensity of the subject and the paucity of the curricular space it is afforded, some principle of selection and limitation is needed. For this reason, the term in question, one might argue, is best understood not as an academic discipline or a pedagogical imperative, but as a bit of terminological turf whereupon the conceptually infinite is asked to submit to cultural and institutional needs that are, unfortunately, all too finite.

When Goethe first coined the term *Weltliteratur* in 1827 (qtd. in Jost 16), his aim was to establish a literature that would, as Strich puts it, "serve as a link between national literatures and thus between the nations themselves, for the exchange of ideal values" (4). More idealized notions, as Strich argues, followed, as in A. Owen Aldridge's Arnoldian formulation of world literature as the "great classics of all times selected from all the various national literatures" (55), or E. D. Hirsch's Johnsonian formulation that an "almost timeless character" is the principal criterion for inclusion in the world's canon (82). Such formulations, however, fail to observe that Goethe's *Weltliteratur* has been reduced from a universal concept to a merely European one (not to mention male-dominated and informed by a narrowly conceived set of aesthetic criteria)—a most ironic turn of events, for as Boubia notes Goethe first coined the term in a discussion of a Chinese novel (83). All of this, of course, has affected not only scholarly discourse, but curricular practice as well, and thus as it has been presented in the educational curriculum world literature has been, for the most part, synonymous with a grandiose metanarrative of Western culture. Nonetheless, as a curricular agenda, it not only persists, but continues to evolve, as evidenced by a spate of new anthologies, all released within the past year, from Norton (Mack, et al.), Heath (Davis, et al.), and HarperCollins (Caws and Prendergast). The formation of a world literature curriculum, however, remains problematic, for however we may conceive of it it is one thing to proclaim, as did Goethe, the onset of an era of global literature; it is quite another to realize such a bold concept both in theory and in educational practice.

It is certainly not my intent (nor that of the contributors to this edition, if I may be permitted to speak for their many voices) to undermine and discredit world literature as a field of study. Rather, the purpose of this volume is, first, to more thoroughly map some of the conceptual and cultural problems that attend this view of literature; second, to suggest some new (or forgotten) genres and perspectives; third, to consider some specific curricular and pedagogical issues; and fourth and finally, to introduce "new" texts for consideration. This collection is organized according to these four dominant concerns.

The first section, "The Problem of World Literature," helps to lay the groundwork by posing some important questions about three of the most important factors contributing to the concept of world literature: history, translation, and anthologization. In "Richard Moulton and the Idea of World Literature," Sarah Lawall introduces us to a theorist whose ideas, though admittedly Victorian and nationalistic, nonetheless provide a valuable exploration of the problems of perspective and worldview as they relate to the canon. Indeed, Moulton's scholarly endeavors are perhaps the ideal point of departure for this anthology, for as Lawall points out, "Moulton's situation . . . resonates peculiarly with our own. Both periods are witness to massive institutional change, in which educational policy is seen as a matter of national politics." Moulton is also important in that, in spite of his erudition, he rejected the role of ivory-tower scholar: he was an advocate of extension education and a critic of the research-oriented university, and he was deeply concerned with educational policy.

If canon formation is at one end of the world literature problematic, then surely translation is at the other. It is therefore fitting that Marilyn Gaddis Rose, Director of the Center for Research in Translation at

SUNY-Binghamton, has provided us with "The Translator and the Voice of the Other," an essay demonstrating that "translators have been mobilized to use their skills as weapons in the conflict of cultures," a problem that many "would like to transform into a living mosaic through even-handed curricula." Rose's commentary on the various English editions of Jules Verne's *Twenty Thousand Leagues under the Sea* provides a provocative examination of literary translation as a cultural and political practice that warrants our deepest concerns as readers, teachers, and scholars. "Translating," Rose notes, "always involves usurping the Other's voice, and the need to make multicultural expressions maximally available means that those other voices will necessarily be altered. . . . What we cannot claim is that our intentions can ever be completely disinterested." The concerns that both Lawall and Rose so compellingly raise for us are echoed in José J. de Vinck's "Anthologizing World Literature," in which he asks one of the major questions posed by this collection: "Can world literature be translated and anthologized without destroying the differences within and among cultures?" The answer is a very tentative "yes," although, as de Vinck points out, we clearly need anthologies that evidence more critical thought in terms of "the rhetoric of representation."

The literature curriculum has long been organized by traditional genres (e.g., poetry, drama, and fiction), subgenres (e.g., the pastoral, the *bildungsroman*), and national literatures. Our second section, " 'New' Traditions, Genres, and Perspectives," contains three essays that help us rethink these categories. First, Paulo de Medeiros, writing on the "colonization of Portuguese literature," helps to correct some of our misconceptions about national literatures by pointing out that "the amalgamation of everything European into a fictive unity" is an unfortunate byproduct of the ongoing attack on Eurocentrism. There are, de Medeiros reminds us, "parts of Europe that 'Europe' itself tends to forget." In the essay that follows, Sharon Hileman examines perhaps the most unexpected of genres: women's prison narratives. Hileman demonstrates the ways in which writers like Domitila Barrios de Chungara, Joyce Sikakane, Barbara Deming, and Eugenia Semyonovna Ginzburg use self-writing to move beyond the self, creating narratives in which "the individual, communal, and political truly merge." Finally, we have Mackie J. V. Blanton's work on the sacred as a literary genre. Blanton roots meaningful literary endeavor in the quest for answers to life's unanswerable questions, an endeavor which has resulted in a narrative structure he refers to as the "sacred conversation," which involves a movement from the myth of creation, to revelation, ritual, sacrifice, and finally, the promise of eternity. Blanton's essay forcefully reminds us that we should not forget literature's relationship to "the persistent yearnings of human nature."

While many of the essays in this collection reveal a deep concern for pedagogy (Blanton's and Dodson's in particular), those that appear in the third section, "Pedagogical and Curricular Concerns," attempt to move pedagogy and curriculum from periphery to center, to borrow a phrase from Mariolina Salvatori. I am very pleased to include these essays, for I have long been concerned with the institutional schizophrenia that separates teaching from scholarship. In a recent essay, Jane Tompkins shares with us an experience that demonstrates the deep institutional roots of this problem. Recalling an experience at Swarthmore as she waited to hear from a scholarship committee, Tompkins notes the exact moment when she learned of a peculiar attitude which is, unfortunately, not uncommon in our profession:

> While I sat there in a state of abject terror, I overheard a conversation between two young men also hoping to convince the committee's greybeards to find them worthy of a fellowship. One of them said to the other—I no longer remember his exact words—that thinking about teaching was the lowest of the low and that anyone who occupied himself with it was hopelessly beyond the pale and just didn't belong in higher education. I'll never forget my surprise and dismay at hearing this opinion which had never occurred to me before, for I had previously thought (coming from a family of teachers) that teaching was an important part of what any college professor would do. As things turned out, I subsequently embraced the view I overheard . . . or rather, this view embraced me, for my antipedagogical indoctrination went on pretty steadily throughout graduate school. (655)

Perhaps Tompkins's awakening to her "indoctrination" signals a paradigm shift that is further evidenced by the concerns of the teacher/ scholars who have contributed to this anthology. Thus, in addition to suggesting a more polymorphic and pluralistic conception of literature (as have any number of critics, such as Nina Baym, Paul Lauter, and Houston Baker, over the past twenty years or so), the aim of this collection is to demonstrate ways in which scholarly and pedagogical discourse can be meaningfully juxtaposed, ideally to the benefit of both.

And so, this section begins with Ismail Talib, a professor of English at the National University of Singapore, who suggests that the English-speaking world needs to be more inclusive of literatures in forms of English other than what we find in "the United States, Great Britain, or other predominantly white Anglophone countries." We have thus far been concerned with world literature in translation; Talib points out that there is indeed a worldwide literature in English, a corpus of works which include writers as diverse as Chinua Achebe, Olive Senior, Wole Soyinka, and R. K. Narayan. Talib also steers us through some of the logistical problems that attend the formation of a syllabus that includes this rich new literature in "World English" as he simultaneously points out the far-reaching positive influence that such a curriculum might have on our students and on society at large.

Another essay that employs a specifically pedagogical strategy is Howard Fraser's essay on contemporary Latin American theater, for it successfully manages to combine issues related to language pedagogy, literature pedagogy, and the canon. Fraser introduces us to the "meta-theatrical" plays of, among others, Sergio Vodanović and Emilio Carballido, and he demonstrates ways in which a "directorial" pedagogy can enhance simultaneous language and literature learning. Fraser's essay should also remind those of us who teach in English departments that we share many methodological concerns with our colleagues who teach literature in other languages—and that our students should experience at least *some* literature in a language other than English.

Fraser's essay is followed by my own, which examines world literature (as a curricular practice) in terms of its institutional structure and its relationship to contemporary popular culture. It is my argument that world literature as a pedagogical imperative can be aided by what has usually been regarded as its mortal enemy—contemporary popular culture—and that by enlisting such aid we may help to tear down the cultural *cordon sanitaire* that separates the college curriculum from more familiar cultural forms. My essay is followed by the work of African studies scholar Erskine Peters, who, drawing on the theories of Frantz Fanon and John Mbiti, suggests that works from African traditions (specifically, *Sundiata: An Epic of Old Mali* and *The Mwindo Epic*) may serve to bring a new sense of esteem and value to African American students by helping to heal "the wounds of a peculiar psychological condition."

The fourth and concluding section, titled simply " 'New' Texts," contains essays that exhibit a continuing preoccupation with the problems of cultural nationalism, canonization, anthologization, translation, curriculum, and pedagogy, but with more of a focus on specific texts. The first essay, by Aron Aji and his student Katrina Runge, provides a parallel reading of Rushdie's *Haroun and the Sea of Stories* and the work of Jalal al-Din Rumi, a thirteenth-century Sufi mystic. This essay helps the reader to understand Rushdie in the context of a rich cultural tradition with which many of us are unfamiliar. Almost as important, Aji and Runge demonstrate the value of the student/teacher collaborative writing project, and thus this essay is of special importance to the aims of this collection.

In an essay that recalls some of the general points made by José J. de Vinck, Dennis Young takes a look at the poetry of George Oppen and the status of the objectivist poets in the curriculum. Young ponders over the exclusion of "poet's poets"—Louis Zukofsky, Charles Rezni-koff, and especially Oppen—from the poetry anthologies, and comes to the conclusion that a "tenacious New Critical mindset" may be the culprit. Next, Caroline McCracken-Flesher considers the fate of Sir Walter Scott, who, unlike the objectivists, is included in the canon—but in a rather backhanded manner: "Time and again, we find [the] self-conscious builders of novelistic tradition invoking Scott as a naive, flawed, yet authorizing precursor for some 'better' novelist." Thus, while Young calls for the inclusion of the excluded poet George Oppen, McCracken-Flesher's reading of Scott's *The Talisman* calls for a reev-aluation of a figure who is already within the canon, and yet remains seriously misunderstood. The next essay, by Charles B. Dodson, brings us back to some of the concerns of the contributors in Section 3 by providing an examination of *The Tale of Genji* that places it in the context of other heroic epics, such as *The Odyssey, The Song of Roland,* and *The Ramayana,* while also including some observations regarding the reception of such a work in an American classroom. As Dodson points out, "the sharp contrast that Genji . . . provides with the classic figure of the warrior hero they have inherited from the European cultural and literary tradition forces students to reconsider and perhaps even modify their response to that traditional figure. Some of them even end up admiring Genji."

This collection is rounded out and given tentative closure with Ranee Kaur Banerjee's study of Bharati Mukherjee, whose stories introduce us to a new subject in the global dominions—the postcolonial exile, whom Banerjee describes as follows:

> As our world becomes increasingly a-cultural, as the number of tribes traveling across traditions grows, as Bombay and New York become boroughs of the same moving city, itinerants like Bharati Mukherjee are creating their own nomad literature. Here is, finally, a literature that no national boundary can hold in and claim; a literature that reflects fragments from distant parts of the globe that have come together and collected within the nomad's body; a literature of kaleidoscopic rather than mirror images.

Have we finally, then, in the work of Bharati Mukherjee, fulfilled the promissory note handed to us by Goethe so long ago when he proposed a *Weltliteratur* that is unhampered by any boundaries? Or, are we thrown back to Richard Moulton's far-sighted suggestion that world literature is inevitably perspectival: "We must take our stand at the point where we find ourselves, and, looking from that point in all directions, we must bring perspective into play"? If the latter be true, then Mukherjee has not paid off the cultural debt incurred by Goethe; rather, she has contributed yet another viewpoint to what is surely not a singular world literature, but rather an amalgam of world literature*s* which are, fortunately, far too diverse to submit to the demands of any unitary theory.

—Michael Thomas Carroll,
New Mexico Highlands University,
June 1995

Works Consulted

Aldridge, A. Owen. *The Reemergence of World Literature: A Study of Asia and the West*. Newark: U of Delaware P, 1986.

Boubia, Fawzi. "Universal Literature and Otherness." Trans. Jeanne Ferguson. *Diogenes* 141 (1988): 76–101.

Caws, Mary Ann, and Christopher Prendergast, eds. *The HarperCollins World Reader*. New York: HarperCollins, 1994.

Davis, Paul, et al., eds. *Western Literature in a World Context*. 2 vols. New York: St. Martin's Press, 1995.

Guerard, Albert. *Preface to World Literature*. New York: Holt, 1940.

Hirsch, E. D., Jr., Joseph F. Kett, and James Trefil. *The Dictionary of Cultural Literacy*. New York: Houghton Mifflin, 1988.

Jost, François. *Introduction to Comparative Literature*. Indianapolis, IN: Bobbs-Merrill, 1974.

Mack, Maynard, et al., eds. *The Norton Anthology of World Masterpieces*. Expanded ed. New York: Norton, 1995.

Salvatori, Mariolina. "Pedagogy: From the Periphery to the Center." In *Reclaiming Pedagogy: The Rhetoric of the Classroom*. Ed. Patricia Donahue and Ellen Quandahl. Carbondale: Southern Illinois UP, 1989. 17–34.

Strich, Fritz. *Goethe and World Literature*. Trans. C. Sym. Westport, CT: Greenwood, 1971. (Translation of *Goethe und die Weltliteratur*. Bern: Francke Verlag, 1946).

Tompkins, Jane. "Pedagogy of the Distressed." *College English* 52.6 (Oct. 1990): 653–60.

I The Problem of World Literature

1 Richard Moulton and the Idea of World Literature

Sarah Lawall
University of Massachusetts at Amherst

Shortly after the beginning of the century, Richard Greene Moulton—Biblical scholar, "inductive" literary theorist, writer on ancient theater, and critic of Shakespeare—proposed a theory and practice of world literature. In *World Literature and Its Place in General Culture* (1911), Moulton claimed that world literature—in addition to being a collection of global masterpieces—was also a proving-ground for literary theory, an indispensable part of cultural studies, and a fundamental course for nationwide extension programs. Moulton is an interesting figure, and in many ways a precursor. He preaches the autonomy of literature and the need for an objective, intrinsic literary criticism well before New Criticism. He drew on the Great Books tradition and general theories of cultural identity to propose courses specifically in world literature when such courses were not yet on the books. Recognizing that readers are inevitably influenced by cultural perspective, he recommended using such perspective as an organizing principle, arguing that each tradition can lay claim to its own coherent view. Finally, he attacked research-oriented universities for ignoring their role as teaching institutions, and he advocated extension education nationwide.

Moulton is not well-known in discussions of world literature, perhaps because the Eurocentrism of his critical practice undermines an otherwise flexible theory. His "world literature from the English point of view" does not merely situate itself among a network of cultural possibilities; relying on canonical examples and a conventional world history, it sets up a hierarchy of values that favors a Judeo-Hellenic-Christian tradition and the idea of progress. His dislike of narrow philological criticism leads him to underestimate the play of language. His proposals are highly nationalistic. Yet many of Moulton's concerns reappear eight decades later: the desire to write a broader and more inclusive history of civilization; the preoccupation with cultural identity; the attempt to clarify and preserve cultural values; the insistence on

3

scientific method and perspectival analysis; and the vision of a mixed community whose educational needs must be met with broad and innovative programs. Reading Richard Moulton is an exercise in critical displacement, for this Victorian writer's interpretation of world literature and "cultural studies" elicits comparison with other studies of literature and culture today.

Moulton was born in England and received degrees from London University and Christ College, Cambridge, before moving to the United States in 1890; he received a Ph.D. from the University of Pennsylvania in 1891. This transplanted British scholar taught for twenty-seven years at the University of Chicago before returning to England upon his retirement in 1919. A former University Extension teacher for Cambridge University and the University of London, professor of literary theory and interpretation and head of the Department of General Literature at Chicago, he was a charismatic teacher and scholar who used examples from the Bible, ancient drama, and Shakespeare to substantiate new models for literary theory. His concept of world literature is rooted in comparative studies and what he calls the "comparative reading" of literature; he did not consider himself a comparatist, however, but rather a generalist and theoretician of literature. In 1885 he published *Shakespeare as a Dramatic Artist: A Popular Illustration of the Principles of Scientific Criticism,* which sets out a theory of inductive criticism. In 1911, he published *World Literature and Its Place in General Culture,* which links his inductive theory with concepts of global civilization, perspectivism, and world literature. The culmination of Moulton's work in literary theory came in *The Modern Study of Literature* (1915), part of which recapitulates the arguments of *World Literature and Its Place in General Culture.* The latter book's concluding chapter, "The Place of World Literature in Education," attacks current research-oriented institutions and proposes a new educational outreach system that would offer world literature as a foundation course chiefly because it transmits a shared understanding of cultural values. World literature, however, is not the primary focus of Moulton's inquiry; it is instead the example that illustrates his theories of literary study, of the evolution of civilization, and of humanistic value. Although he proposed teaching world literature on a broad scale, his discussion actually antedates the development and institutionalization of any courses by that title, the first of which were offered under Philo Buck at the University of Wisconsin in the late 1920s (Rosenberg 27; cf. Graff 134).

World literature as an established and flourishing academic course dates to the midcentury: to the postwar period, when higher education expanded, thousands of returning veterans entered college, and the curriculum was rethought to reflect America's new prominence in global affairs. "World literature" and "world civilization" courses were offered as general introductions to other cultures, and were usually part of the required humanities curriculum. World literature courses were offered in *conjunction* with world history or world civilization: in other words, imaginative literature was separated from history or philosophy as it had not been in the traditional Great Books course. Yet the value-oriented aim was the same: literature offered the vicarious experience of other worlds and could therefore be used to instruct young minds and prepare an enlightened and mature citizenry. Goethe's notion of *Weltliteratur* (1827), a future-oriented concept in which different nations would get to know one another through reciprocal reading of each other's works, had little to do with this curriculum. The world it envisaged was rather the scene of an evolving Western heritage—the ideals and values of the Greco-Roman-Judaic tradition in relation to which the rest of the globe served as context. How to represent the variety of world cultures figured chiefly as a statistical problem of global coverage, with occasional complaints from comparatists and foreign-language teachers that works in translation reduced the world to Anglophone perspectives or to "world literature from the English point of view."

The idealist Great Books model is important for Richard Moulton, and in fact it implicitly shapes his schema of world literature as the "autobiography of civilization." Nonetheless, it is not the focus of his attention. Instead, he devotes his efforts to proposing a new model of literary studies that is linked simultaneously to concepts of world-projection and to world literature.

Moulton is an interesting figure because he combines three areas that are still lively sources of debate: literary theory, cultural studies, and educational policy. Each of his world-literature proposals is colored by contemporary circumstances that are not quite the same as our own and yet are not entirely different either, so that the issues are often clarified for us by historical distance. World literature, he says, is dependent on literary theory; it is not merely an accumulation of texts from different parts of the globe. Linking literary theory and civiliza-tional studies, he defines world literature as the "autobiography of civilization" or more specifically "cultural studies." Finally, as an ardent proponent of university extension (today's adult or continuing educa-tion), he sees world literature as an agent of "general culture": it reaches out to the entire population to promote a sense of cultural identity and a continuing inquiry into human values.

In defining world literature as cultural studies, Moulton is also defining literary criticism as a combination of theoretical perspective and historical knowledge. He desires a scientific literary criticism in order to grasp the meaning—the philosophical and cultural burden—of major texts of world literature. By "scientific" criticism he does not mean philology (which he detests) or positivist literary history, for he argues that "in cultural studies few things are more barren than literary facts and information" (*World Literature* 296; hereafter *W*). Moulton is truly impatient with contemporary literary studies and emphasizes that "the study of literature, in any adequate sense, has yet to begin" (*W* 1–2). Here he is not speaking of formal analysis as an end in itself. He is more interested in devising adequate literary-critical techniques to discern meaning-structures otherwise distorted or overlooked. A Biblical scholar whose *Literary Study of the Bible* (1906) is subtitled *An Account of the Leading Forms of Literature Represented in the Sacred Writings,* he frequently illustrates the importance of structural awareness by pointing out the doctrinal error of those who repeat wise sayings from the Book of Job without considering that they are voiced by a character whose opinions are later criticized by God. From his original description of inductive criticism in *Shakespeare as a Dramatic Artist* (1885; hereafter *S*) to his culminating "synthetic view of the theory and interpretation of literature" (viii) in *The Modern Study of Literature* (1915; hereafter *M*), Moulton preaches an approach that foreshadows the work-centered strategy and even some of the vocabulary of New Criticism. Doubtless there are substantial differences, especially in his desire to link literature with cultural values and a particular pattern of literary history. Moulton's approach to world literature is nonetheless remarkable for its attempt to look at "world" texts from a "scientific" or "philosophic" point of view (which is also, he says, a "comparative" point of view), and for its insistence that any other perspective falls into a trap of cultural as well as aesthetic misprision. According to Moulton, interpretation in literature is "*of the nature of a scientific hypothesis, the truth of which is tested by the degree of completeness with which it explains the details of the literary work as they actually stand*" (*S* 25).

There are predecessors, of course. Moulton's concept of the unity, complexity, and autonomy of literature is openly indebted to the Schlegels, to Coleridge, and to Saintsbury. His map of world literature expands on Matthew Arnold's categories of Hellenism and Hebraism and he shares Arnold's determination to preserve the cultural heritage. Yet Moulton is a practicing teacher with a missionary interest in university extension—that is, in reaching a large and diverse audience outside academia. He wants to translate critical principles into pedagogic practice. He draws up syllabi, lectures on academic administration, and considers such questions as the range of material to be covered and the needs of his potential audience. Most of all, he examines the mechanics of literary study. The study of literature is to be distinguished from philology, from historical research that merely accumulates facts, and from the "judicial criticism" of reviewers or impressionistic critics who proceed by personal taste or conformity to canonical models.

Instead, literary theory and an awareness of the reader's own perspective are the proper tools of interpretation—or, better, of *analysis.* "Interpretation" for Moulton does not have the pejorative overtones that it will acquire in T. S. Eliot. Moulton sees it neither as impressionistic fiction nor as a "presentation of historical facts which the reader is not assumed to know" (Eliot 142), but rather as the logical result of the "inductive science of literary criticism" that he proposes in *Shakespeare as a Dramatic Artist.* Inductive criticism pursues the observation of details—the "facts" of the text—and reconstructs their inner relationships or the text's intention. This is not the "author's intention," and Moulton is far from falling into an "intentional fallacy"; instead, he draws on his understanding of scientific method to construct a theory of literary intentionality:

> Deep designs are traced in Shakespeare's plots, and elaborate combinations in his characters and passions: is the student asked to believe that Shakespeare really *intended* these complicated effects? The difficulty rests largely upon a confusion in words. Such words as 'purpose,' 'intention,' have a different sense when used in ordinary parlance from that which they bear when applied in criticism and science. . . . in science the 'purpose' of a thing is the purpose it actually serves, and is discoverable only by analysis. . . . In this usage alone can the words 'purpose,' 'intention,' be properly applied to literature and art: science knows no kind of evidence in the matter of creative purpose so weighty as the thing it has actually produced. (*S* 26)

In both literature and art, the "details of literary and artistic productions" are themselves the "phenomena which the critical observer translates into facts. . . . A picture is a title for a bundle of facts" (*S* 22–23). More than mere analysis or interpretation, inductive criticism reveals, as no other criticism can, the complex workings that embody artistic value.

Moulton's study of Shakespeare concludes by stating that judicial or evaluative criticism is paradoxically unable to grasp artistic value— to perceive, for example, how Shakespeare elevated the conception of plot from mere unity of action to "a harmony of design binding together concurrent actions from which no degree of complexity was excluded" (*S* 397). Judicial criticism cannot address Shakespeare's quality because it unconsciously uses standards from the past or present as criteria for judgment. If there is a tacit adherence to the past and a concomitant "secret antagonism to variations from received models," then new literary forms are required to "justify themselves, and so the judicial critic brings his least receptive attitude to the new effects which need receptiveness most" (*S* 37). The opposite bias may also hold true, and a progress-oriented critic may evaluate the past according to "the degrees in which past periods have approximated his own, advancing from literary pot-hooks to his own running facility" (*S* 38). Moreover, asks Moulton, "What if the idea of judging be itself a prejudice?" (*S* 7). Thirty years later, in *The Modern Study of Literature,* he is still affirming the importance of the inductive method and the intrinsic study of literature. "The criticism of inductive interpretation is the basis on which all other criticism rests: only as the reader verifies his conceptions by observation of the literature can he become a judge" (*M* 494).

The literary-critical vocabulary of this inductive theory is startlingly familiar. Moulton's science of inductive criticism is also an "intrinsic" criticism, in which the question is "not the origins of literature, but the literature itself" (*M* 490), and as such indicts a number of fallacies that detract from proper interpretation. There is an "allegorizing fallacy" (*M* 290), the "fallacy of the superior person" (292), the "fallacy of inconsistency" (291), the "author fallacy" (295), the "common-sense fallacy" (300), the judicial fallacy, which passes "from the idea of *values* to the idea of *valuation*" (318), and a "fallacy of kinds" that measures everything new against previous models (491). The "most fundamental of all fallacies," he declares, is the fallacy that ignores unity of impression and "the relativity of details in a work of art" (289). Other fallacies fall into various versions of extrinsic criticism. The "allegorizing fallacy" superimposes another structure of meaning; it leads one writer to "interpret the whole Book of Job as an astronomical treatise, Job and his friends being four stars in the constellation Boötes" (290). The fallacy of the "superior person" appears when a reader tries to make the literary work square with his or her more "advanced" views. The "author fallacy" represents "the inability of many readers to keep under observation a piece of literature without their attention wandering to its author" (293). This author fallacy, which clearly prefigures later "intentional" and "genetic" fallacies, "arises most usually in connection with the more complex examples of art." Often "common-sense" readers cannot believe that the poet "really meant" a particular complicated design, but Moulton responds in a sentence that could have come straight out of I. A. Richards's *Practical Criticism* (1929): "The conscious purpose of a poet—if he has one—belongs to his biography; what criticism means by 'purpose' and 'design' is the purpose particular parts are seen to serve in the poetic product when analyzed" (295).

What does Moulton's notion of inductive literary criticism have to do with world literature? For one thing, he uses it to separate the study of world literature from purely historical and philological studies. Literature is a category to itself; literary evolution is linked to historical evolution but has nonetheless its own set of relationships; the study of world literature depends on an awareness of relations and perspectives. This awareness is self-reflexive: it leads one to interpret not just the "record" of literature, but also "the conception of literature itself" (*M* 491) as well as one's own position as observer. The inductive literary critic tries to avoid habitual analysis or preset categories of judgment.

Undeniably there are more than a few cultural assumptions underlying Moulton's own schema of world literature, from his paradigm of five Literary Bibles to a "literary pedigree of the English-speaking peoples" that situates certain cultures as "extraneous" or "etc." He relies on "natural divisions of mankind, like races and nations" (*W* 31). The race of Abraham possesses a spiritual instinct that becomes "a force strong enough to determine the whole spiritual side of English and kindred civilizations" (*W* 432). There is a cultural "shrinkage" in the Dark Ages before the culmination of "modern civilization" in Europe (*W* 29, 27). The "special art of the modern world is the art of music," and the orchestra (including human voices) is "the great achievement of modern times" (*W* 50). More disturbingly, this Biblical scholar dedicated to the Hellenic-Hebraic tradition describes Islam as "a new religion, a perverted Hebraism" that appeals "to the more facile side of the moral nature" (*W* 32). Medieval Arabs, moreover, had "the main carrying trade in ideas, but they brought nothing of their own to the civilization of the future" (*W* 33). Moulton's sweeping survey of civilization falls short of the self-consciousness he recommends for inductive literary criticism, and ultimately distorts the outline of world literature that he equates with an "autobiography of civilization." Yet he spends considerable time opposing—in the name of literary theory and competent reading practices—ingrained habits of selection and judgment that influence our concept of world literature.

In Moulton's view, both literary theory and world literature make a distinction between accumulative, documentary knowledge and an awareness of framework and perspective: between "coverage," to use the terms of syllabus-design, and organization. He is basically suspicious of accumulating texts from around the world and calling them world literature. Such an accumulative procedure, which he finds appropriate for "universal literature" in its global variety, implies a never-ending quest for completeness that will ultimately prevent analysis. It leads to the "barren" image of literature as "mere information" (*W* 296). In contrast, *World Literature and Its Place in General Culture* "presents a conception of World Literature, not in the sense of the sum total of particular literatures, but as a unity, the literary field seen in perspective . . ." (*W* v). World literature involves not a "catalogue of works to read, but principles to guide individual choice" (*W* 408). Moulton is opposed to global booklists, even of "Best Books," because they contribute to the "naive idea that everything knowable is of the nature of information, sure to be found in the right compendium" (*W* 1). If the overriding idea of world literature is to demonstrate the variety and interconnectedness of human values in their most powerful literary form—what Moulton calls the "autobiography of civilization," or cultural studies through literature—then the chief task becomes to outline an appropriate perspective.

We have returned to the provocative concept of "world literature from the English point of view." Moulton undoubtedly meant the paradoxical phrase to draw attention to the idea of inductive criticism and to the inevitability of *having* a perspective. In an era of postcolonial criticism, it is hard not to see a self-proclaimed "English point of view" as one more display of Moulton's comfortable Anglocentricity, and many examples support this view. Yet Moulton is more aware than most of the inescapable positioning of any worldview; indeed, he makes it his point of departure:

> World Literature will be a different thing to the Englishman and to the Japanese: the Shakespeare who bulks so large to the Englishman will be a small detail to the Japanese, while the Chinese literature which makes the foreground in the one literary landscape may be hardly discernible in the other. World Literature will be a different thing even to the Englishman and the Frenchman. . . . More than this, World Literature may be different for different individuals of the same nation . . . it may be that the individuality of the student, or of some teacher who has influenced him, has served as a lens focusing the multiplex particulars of the whole in its own individual arrangement. (*W* 7)

And he adds:

> We must take our stand at the point where we find ourselves,
> and, looking from that point in all directions, we must bring
> perspective into play... (*W* 435)

Moulton's study of world literature is thus openly positioned. It does
not assume a single universally valid canon of books drawn from
different parts of the globe. It draws on "whatever of universal literature,
coming from whatever source, has been appropriated by our English
civilization, and made a part of our English culture" (*W* 297). It is
national but not British, since he says that before the medieval period
"the real English culture is the culture of Europe," and "nine-tenths
of the history of English civilization and culture" falls outside Britain
(*W* 434).

To a certain extent, this view of world literature as a historical
phenomenon draws on Goethe's future-oriented concept: that different
nations will get to know and understand one another through reading
one another's literature, and by producing newly cosmopolitan works.
There is a distinct echo of Goethe, too, in Moulton's statement that
"it is a feature of the present age that the leading peoples of the world
are drawing nearer to one another, as if making a common reading
circle to which the best products of each people will appeal" (*W* 427).

Like Goethe, Moulton emphasizes nationality as a basic principle
of world literature. The two basic principles on which his theory of
world literature rests are "the National Literary Pedigree," by which he
means "the train of historic considerations that connects the reader's
nationality with its roots in the far past, and traces its relationship with
other parts of its field" and, second, "Intrinsic Literary Interest" (*W*
8). Let us not misunderstand "intrinsic literary interest": this is not a
qualitative criterion (Moulton is not interested in aesthetic judgment),
but an instrumental one. Only by paying attention to literary structure
can one grasp the significance of major cultural documents, whether
the Bible, ancient Greek drama, or other works included in Moulton's
outline of world literature. Inductive literary criticism is a tool in
elucidating world literature, which is itself another tool in establishing
a common culture: "just what is needed to draw together the scattered
parts of humanity studies" (*W* 453).

"World literature from the English point of view" turns out to have
a very Arnoldian cast, although Moulton does complicate Arnold's
Hellenic-Hebraic dualism in a chart with the rather off-putting title
"Literary Pedigree of the English-Speaking Peoples" (see Figure 1).

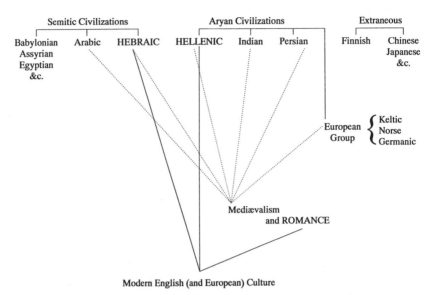

Figure 1. Moulton's "Literary Pedigree of the English-Speaking Peoples." Adapted from *World Literature and Its Place in General Culture* (Norwood, MA: Macmillan, 1911), 52.

As the chart makes clear, "Modern English (and European) Culture" is rooted in "Semitic Civilizations" (broken down into "Babylonian, Assyrian, Egyptian, &c.; Arabic; HEBRAIC"), "Aryan Civilizations" (broken down into "HELLENIC; Indian; Persian" and a younger "European Group" of "Keltic, Norse, [and] Germanic"), with a subsequent third component which enters as "Mediaevalism and ROMANCE" with ties to Arabic, HEBRAIC, HELLENIC, Indian, and Persian civilizations as well as to the European Group. To one side on the chart are "Extraneous" civilizations ("Finnish; Chinese, Japanese, &c."), whose somewhat awkward *et cetera* position is explained through their being "extraneous to the evolution of which we are the product" (*W* 13). Lumped together, they form "not a related group, but merely a total of the races other than Semitic and Aryan, which have exercised a correspondingly small influence upon history, as history affects ourselves" (*W* 11).

There are obvious objections to packaging complex civilizations as individual contributing units—objections that remain even if we give the author credit for adding historical texture to the by-then conventional dualism of Hellenic and Hebraic cultures (cf. Arnold 109–27). Moulton's careful (and, it must be said, somewhat "judicial") discussion of literary-cultural history does not avoid the value judgments that so easily follow distinctions between "our pedigree" and "the rest of the world." Recapitulating the qualities of Hellenism and Hebraism as the "originating elements of our civilization," for example, he decides that they "seem to hold a summarizing position in reference to the main civilizations of the world"; later, that these "two ancient civilizations which are the component factors of our own seem to represent the flower of the civilizations of the world" (*W* 11, 13). This slippage from the "English point of view" to the statement that its components represent the high point of all world civilizations only demonstrates again how difficult it is to define a perspective without giving it priority. It is a problem that continues to face those drawing maps (or syllabi) of world literature.

Once the "Literary Pedigree of the English-Speaking Peoples" has been outlined, Moulton proceeds to analysis of specific literary works based on the cultural history he has just provided. The "Survey of World Literature" that constitutes the rest of the book presents ten chapters devoted first to five "Literary Bibles" and then to diverse literary-critical perspectives on world literature. The sequence of "Literary Bibles" constitutes a set of cultural reference points throughout Western world literature. Although the Bible itself is the subject of the first chapter,[1] subsequent "bibles" are composed of more than one text, reflecting Moulton's concept of a bible as a cluster of works that possess "high significance of matter," "some sense of literary unity," and visible importance for modern culture (*W* 53–54). Separate chapters are devoted to classical epic and tragedy, to Shakespeare, Dante, and Milton, and to versions of the story of Faust.

The remaining five chapters take up such topics as "Collateral Studies in World Literature" (significant works outside the Hebraic-Hellenic tradition), "Comparative Reading" (clusters of works that shed light on one another through common themes), and "Strategic Points in Literature" (groups of correlated works to be read for their mutual relationships or the way they crystallize moments of historical change). Moulton's adherence to comparative literary studies is made clear in "Comparative Reading," which begins with the optimistic assertion that comparative literature is a "middle stage between the purely departmental treatment of literature, which has prevailed in the past, and that which is surely coming—the study of literature as an organic whole" (*W* 351). His comparatist readers have "acquired a habit of mental grouping," a habit that organizes a particular world-literary unity for each "miscellaneous reader" (352). Moreover, "the study of world literature" develops "the comparative habit of mind, which acts as a lens to bring together resemblances and contrasts from all parts of the complex civilization" (36).

While we may subscribe to Moulton's comparatist strategy and his recognition that each reader organizes the world from a slightly different point of view, his own groupings are highly canonical and display the unspoken influence of the Great Books list. Under "Comparative Reading" there is an "Alcestis Group," a "Bacchanals Group," and "Minor Groups" that include the Hebrew and the Indian Song of Songs. "Strategic Points in Literature" are occupied by Plato and Lucretius; Aristophanes; the medieval *Romance of the Rose, Reynard the Fox,* and *Everyman*; "Malory's *Morte d'Arthur* and Chaucer's *Canterbury Tales*"; the *Faerie Queen,* for its "universally recognized position as a common meeting-ground for Classical, Romantic, and Puritan"; Froissart's *Chronicles* and Cervantes's *Don Quixote*; Erasmus and Bacon; Rabelais; Molière, Racine, and Shakespeare; Walter Scott and Sienkiewicz; Balzac and Hugo; Wordsworth and Byron.[2] Clearly this list is precisely the traditional catalogue of "dead white men" that contemporary cultural studies have criticized for a limited view of the world. Moulton's "cultural studies" have selected these authors to be the literary representatives of significant epistèmes: turning points of history that foreshadow modern European civilization. His original concepts of perspective and positioning have been imperceptibly domesticated, until a tacit definition of modern society dictates what to look for in earlier (and related) literatures. It seems appropriate that the title of his last full chapter, "World Literature as the Autobiography of Civilization," should evoke the form of a subjective linear narrative reaching into the present. We have moved away from the "inductive science of literary criticism" to world literature as its own autobiography, or "civilization presented by itself" (*W* 37).

Yet there is a third side to Moulton's enterprise, and it is political engagement in the task of mass education. The author of *World Literature and Its Place in General Culture* saw his work as part of educational outreach, and he ends the book with a discussion of "the place of world literature in education." Moulton was a dedicated and charismatic teacher, an activist who sensed that educational and social institutions were undergoing a profound change and who wished to help mold the future. Most of his books are addressed to the general public and they often contain suggestions for teaching; *World Literature and Its Place in General Culture* contains an appendix with a "syllabus" outline of material in the book, and an annotated list of works and translations.

When studying at Cambridge University in the 1870s, Moulton became part of the developing university extension movement. He returned to teach extension courses at London University for a year after receiving his Ph.D. from the University of Pennsylvania, and when he joined the new University of Chicago in 1892 he taught both regular and extension courses for a time. Unlike T. S. Eliot, who disliked teaching extension courses, Moulton was an ardent proponent of a diversified general education to be taught by itinerant (but university-sponsored) teachers throughout the country—in fact, he helped found the American Society for University Extension. Printing, Moulton noted, was the first university extension, and "the time has now come to send teachers to follow the books" ("University Extension" 9; hereafter "UE"). The conclusion to *World Literature and Its Place in General Culture* draws heavily on an early lecture on university extension that he gave at the Johns Hopkins University in 1890 (one of many he gave in America that year). In the lecture, Moulton outlined three waves of religious, political, and educational change that have shaped modern history: first, the Reformation; second, a series of revolutions that helped bring about self-government; and last of all, a recent shift in which "the conception of an isolated learned class" gives way "before the ideal of a national culture." ("UE" 12). Education for the whole nation, and a concomitant understanding of one's own national culture in its broadest context, form an integral part of Moulton's scheme of world literature.

Society as a whole—that is, national society—is to profit by educational reform. Rebuffing in advance accusations of "educational communism, on a par with benevolent schemes for redistributing the wealth of society," he wishes to enlist "the whole nation without exception . . . shop-assistants, porters, factory-hands, miners, dock or agricultural laborers, women with families and constant home duties" into extension classes. Here, they will come into contact with the great works that have shaped modern society and will gain a better understanding of English cultural identity. Moulton wishes to catch a society in transition and persuade it to incorporate education as one of the "permanent interests in life," like religion and politics ("UE" 2–3). A propitious moment has come, he believes, in which the general population is open to the idea of higher education for everyone. If educators meet the demand it will be as if there is a "University of England" or "University of America," for "educationally the whole adult population will be just as much within the university as politically the adult population is within the constitution" ("UE" 12).

The utopian overtones of this vision cannot obscure its dual role—
its breadth is as ambiguous as the "strategic points" recommended for
the study of world literature. Just as the strategic points were defined
through canonical European works written by men, Moulton's university extension is defined by a specific (and class-conscious) vision of
society. General (or "extension") education is aimed at a specific British
audience and its presumed work patterns, and this education proposes
to fill their leisure with the "English point of view" on the world.
Moulton's picture of English society echoes Matthew Arnold, in fact,
in his insistence on the human obligation to find leisure time for
cultural pursuits:

> But if a man or woman is so entangled in routine duties as never
> to command leisure. . . . Such an individual . . . is a slave. It may
> be cruel circumstances that have thus absorbed him in business,
> but that does not alter the fact: slavery was a misfortune rather
> than a fault to those who suffered it, but in any case to be content
> with slavery is a crime. ("UE" 4)

The benevolent intentions of this passage do not conceal the peculiar
rhetoric of slavery, or the fact that the physical reality of slavery is far
removed from Moulton's image of an Anglo-Saxon race whose "genius . . . leans towards self-help" ("UE" 13). In short, Moulton's populist
sympathies, and his reformist plan to center world literature in general
education, are already colored by a traditionally "English point of
view" on the nature and needs of his audience.

No one today, I believe, would claim Richard Moulton as a prede-
cessor. The solutions he found are too often flawed, either by logical
inconsistency or by incompleteness. Defending the text "in itself" as
an object of study, he discounts the importance of original languages
and philological exactness; in fact, he thinks of language as a transparent
medium for ideas that are easily translated. He does not seem to
recognize the presence of a preemptive "judicial criticism" in his own
"inductive" discussions of world masterpieces. His arguments for
recognizing the importance of perspective are undercut by the visibly
insular nature of his "English point of view." Describing world literature
as the "autobiography of civilization," he distracts attention from the
fact that many different people write that *auto*biography. Yet he remains
an interesting figure in many ways: as an academic activist who tried
to reform educational policy to fit current social needs; as a scholar
with his own view of comparatism and world literature; as a literary
theoretician whose work-centered approach foreshadows much New
Criticism without quite extricating itself from traditional literary history.

Let me recapitulate some of the issues Moulton addressed that retain their academic and political relevance. He raised the question of blind obedience to the canon, and criticized "judicial" or traditionally evaluative criticism for being unable to assimilate new or unfamiliar works. He asserted the importance of *positioning* in literary and cultural studies, noting that the outline of world literature (and the image of the world) will look different to people from different societies and even within the same society. He took up one of the touchiest questions of today's literary curriculum—its relationship to community needs— by seeking to define a common heritage in "world literature from the English point of view." He recognized the fact that the student body was changing, and devised pedagogic strategies with that in mind. In spite of the monolithic blocs, dotted-line relationships, and collateral and extraneous readings of his chart of world literature, he worked to diversify the conventional "English point of view" and had the courage to present it *as a perspective* in pedagogical practice.

Moulton's situation, so much embedded in his own time, resonates peculiarly with our own. Both periods are witness to massive institutional change, in which educational policy is seen as a matter of national politics. Demographics, economics, and the technological revolution are redefining the way we talk about issues of class, canon, and curriculum; they influence literary theory and propel cultural studies; they restructure our academic institutions. We have the benefit of hindsight in assessing Moulton's strategies for coping with educational and social change, and there is a certain fascination in observing the overlapping paradigms of his work. It is less easy to observe our own overlapping paradigms, and even harder to foresee the impact of social pressures on the institution of education in this country: whether, for example, it will be subtly reorganized to conform to a more centralized vision, or split into highly diverse units that reflect various forms of local control; whether world literature will be researched as canonical information ("what every American needs to know") or explored as patterns of shifting perspective. In each era, however, as Richard Moulton shows, the idea of world literature is a catalytic concept that opens up literary, cultural, and personal horizons.

Notes

1. Moulton wrote in *The Literary Study of the Bible* that the Bible is the "worst-printed book in the world" (9), nearly incomprehensible because of the medieval arrangement of a run-on text into short verses that obscure its

dramatic form. From 1895 to 1913, he edited the various books of the Bible "in modern literary form" with introduction and notes, under the general title *The Modern Reader's Bible.* A passage from his *A Short Introduction to the Literature of the Bible* explains the principles of these specially printed editions: "The literary study of the Bible thus seeks new light which will come into any passage of Scripture when it is read in accordance with its exact literary form" (6). "Though the Bible is proclaimed to be one of the world's great literatures, yet if we open our ordinary version we find that the literary form is that of a scrap book: a succession of numbered sentences, with divisions into longer or shorter chapters, under which all trace of dramatic, lyric, story, essay, is hopelessly lost" (9).

2. It is assumed that all non-English works are read in translation. Moulton enthusiastically supports Emerson in his preference for translations (*W* 5), recommends specific translations in his appendix, and says firmly that "what the Englishman needs is world literature brought to him in his own English tongue, in which he can reach the literary effect of what he is reading, undistracted by interruptions of linguistic puzzles, and the mechanism of grammar and dictionary" that "excludes the interpretation of perspective on which literary culture depends" (*M* 456).

Works Consulted

Aldridge, A. Owen. *The Reemergence of World Literature: A Study of Asia and the West.* Newark: U of Delaware P, 1986.

Arnold, Matthew. *Culture and Anarchy: An Essay in Political and Social Criticism; and Friendship's Garland: Being the Conversations, Letters, and Opinions of the Late Arminius, Baron von Thunder-ten-Tronckh.* New York: Macmillan, 1924.

Brandt Corstius, J. C. "Writing Histories of World Literature." *Yearbook of Comparative and General Literature* 12 (1963): 5–14.

Brown, Calvin S. "Debased Standards in World Literature Courses." *Yearbook of Comparative and General Literature* 2 (1953): 10–14.

Eliot, T. S. *Selected Essays.* New York: Harcourt, 1950.

Graff, Gerald. *Professing Literature: An Institutional History.* Chicago: U of Chicago P, 1987.

Guerard, Albert. *Preface to World Literature.* New York: Henry Holt, 1940.

Hirsch, E. D., Jr., Joseph F. Kett, and James Trefil. *The Dictionary of Cultural Literacy.* New York: Houghton Mifflin, 1988.

Moulton, Richard Green. *The Ancient Classical Drama: A Study in Literary Evolution Intended for Readers in English and in the Original.* Oxford: Clarendon P, 1890.

———. *The Literary Study of the Bible: An Account of the Leading Forms of Literature Represented in the Sacred Writings.* 1895. Rev. ed. Boston: D. C. Heath, 1906.

———. *The Modern Study of Literature.* Chicago: U of Chicago P, 1915.

————. *Shakespeare as a Dramatic Artist: A Popular Illustration of the Principles of Scientific Criticism.* 3rd rev. ed. Oxford: Clarendon P, 1897.

————. *A Short Introduction to the Literature of the Bible.* Boston: D. C. Heath, 1901.

————. "University Extension and the University of the Future." *Education, History, and Politics,* III–IV. The Johns Hopkins University Studies in Historical and Political Science, Vol. 9. Baltimore: Johns Hopkins UP, 1891. 1–14.

————. *World Literature and Its Place in General Culture.* Norwood, MA: Macmillan, 1911.

Richards, I. A. *Practical Criticism.* San Diego, CA: Harcourt, 1929.

Rosenberg, Ralph P. "The 'Great Books' in General Education." *Yearbook of Comparative and General Literature* 3 (1954): 20–35.

Schulz, H. J. and P. H. Rhein. *Comparative Literature, the Early Years: An Anthology of Essays.* Studies in Comparative Literature 55. Chapel Hill: U of North Carolina P, 1973.

Strich, Fritz. *Goethe and World Literature.* Trans. C. A. M. Sym. Westport, CT: Greenwood P, 1971. Trans. of *Goethe und die Weltliteratur.* Bern: Francke Verlag, 1946.

Wellek, René, and Austin Warren. *Theory of Literature.* New York: Harcourt, 1949.

2 The Translator and the Voice of the Other: A Case in Point

Marilyn Gaddis Rose
Translation Research and Instruction Program
State University of New York at Binghamton

How does one speak for the Other as a matter of course, when doing so is regarded as epistemologically impossible and ethically prohibited? This is the problem of representation and re-presentation in translation. And yet, if translation is to occur at all, the translator must assume the Other's voice in order to repeat it. This ventriloquial act requires presumption—Douglas Robinson would say "guts" (5)—or at best a neutrality that needs conscious examination and, occasionally, explanation. Emanuel J. Mickel's recent retranslation of Jules Verne's *Vingt mille lieues sous les mers* (*Twenty Thousand Leagues under the Sea*) serves as my metonymic conceit, for its unobtrusive translation strategy caused me to rethink this problem. Verne's novel—in which "submerged" characters have the choice of rationalization, resistance, or capitulation—causes one to wallow, perhaps drown, in Otherness, and is thus, along with its English translations, a good point of departure for an investigation into the problem of translation and Otherness.

One of the best-known image sequences in *Twenty Thousand Leagues* occurs toward the end of the novel when an attacking octopus jams the helix of the *Nautilus* with one of its tentacles. Captain Nemo, members of his multinational crew, and his three prisoner-passengers rush out and up to disengage the helix by slashing the tentacle. With seven tentacles amputated, the octopus uses the one remaining to seize the sailor occupying the vanguard position protecting Nemo. Professor Aronnax, Verne's chief spokesman, relates the event:

> Quelle scène! Le malheureux, saisi par le tentacule et collé à ses ventouses, était balancé dans l'air au caprice de cette énorme trompe. Il râlait, il étouffait, il criait: "À moi! à moi!" Ces mots, *prononcés en français,* me causèrent une profonde stupeur! J'avais donc un compatriote à bord, plusieurs, peut-être! Cet appel

déchirant, je l'entendrai toute ma vie! (474–75; emphasis in
original)

And, after the octopi phalanx has been routed and the submarine is
back up to speed, Aronnax ranks the moments of horror and terror in
his record:

> Pour moi, au milieu de cette lutte, c'était le cri de désespoir
> poussé par l'infortuné qui m'avait déchiré le coeur. Ce pauvre
> Français, oubliant son langage de convention, s'était repris à
> parler la langue de son pays et de sa mère, pour jeter un suprême
> appel! Parmi cet équipage de *Nautilus,* associé de corps et d'âme
> au captaine Nemo, fuyant comme lui le contact des hommes,
> j'avais donc un compatriote! (476)

As you may recall, Aronnax (a French marine scientist), Conseil
(his valet-taxonomist), and Ned Land (the Canadian ace harpooner),
essentially begin the novel as victims of the *Nautilus,* rescued and
incarcerated by the ship's crew. (They might be considered prisoners
of war since they were on board Admiral Farragut's frigate *Abraham
Lincoln,* seeking out the presumed monster whale that was making the
seas unsafe.) Their collective polylingualism—French, English, and
German—is no asset in effecting their release: they are land-dwellers
speaking "natural" languages, while the *Nautilus*'s crew, men of the
sea, speak an "artificial" language (Nemo, at some point prior to the
beginning of the novel, created a new language for his crew). However,
we assume that French, the medium of the narrative, becomes the
medium of communication for the speaking characters since Aronnax
is French, Conseil is Belgian, and Ned is Canadian, while Nemo knows
all major world languages.

There are four inferences to be made regarding the Otherness of
languages in these two passages, all of which are related to the translator's
inescapable presumption of speaking for the Other. First, one infers
from Nemo's characterization as a ruthless genius that he had forced
his language on his crew—had taken their tongues and given them one
unheard (of) on earth. Second, Aronnax and his two friends, speaking
French only among themselves and with Nemo, and not hearing others
speak French,would have supposed that French was a foreign language
for the crew. Therefore they would have assumed that they could speak
French in front of them without being understood, for inasmuch as
the *Nautilus*'s language would have been a special excluding code, so,
for the purposes of the three captives, would have been French. Third,
Aronnax with his two fellow captives have a we/they relationship and
attitude toward Nemo and his crew, and this separation is reinforced
by language use.[1]

Our fourth inference is language-bound and therefore opens up to a whole host of complexities. We note that Aronnax, a bachelor like his two companions Conseil and Land, is stricken by the instantaneous realization that in life-and-death distress the French sailor spontaneously called out in the language of *son pays et sa mère* (not *sa langue maternelle,* "his mother tongue," but "the language of his country and his mother"). We note that the ways in which the two languages structure the message are diametrically different. English specifies the action: "Help!" French specifies the object: *"À moi!"* "Come to me!" And we note further Verne's choice of idiom; we would usually expect *"Au secours!"* for "Help!" Thus, the sailor asks his mother, as it were, to come to him.[2]

Grammatical gender can be intriguing in Verne's works, where, by implication and apparent absence, woman is Other, where romance and love are overt only in *Le Château des Carpathes* (*The Carpathian Castle*)[3] and where, consequently, only those reading Verne's French note that key nouns are feminine: e.g., *la science, la nature, la machine, la mer* (sea), *la mort.* Generally in a Verne novel men and boys are engaged in solving problems for mankind, but they are immersed and surrounded by the feminine, using the resources of *la science* and *la machine* to enlist *la nature* in the struggle for *la victoire* of *la vie* against *la mort* on behalf of *l'humanité.*

While I would hesitate to say that the feminine principle has a voice in the French language, at the same time we all recognize that this implicit, covert, nearly automatic shading will not be carried into English. The men of Dickens, Hawthorne, even Melville—to mention only a few of Verne's contemporaries—may need the help of women, but in the English-language Verne, the fellows do what must be done by themselves. Any English translation of Verne will inescapably omit the helpful and nurturing female voice in the text, whether Same or Other. There is no record, it is true, that Verne consciously sought out feminine nouns. And I think it can be assumed that gender compensation never entered the mind of Verne's first and determinative translator, Lewis Page Mercier. Emanuel J. Mickel's careful and first-ever integral translation of *Twenty Thousand Leagues,* in fact, allows us to see how much Mercier, a Church of England cleric translating Verne to the obvious satisfaction of Victorian book buyers, knew what the Other—all the Others—wanted said. (The closeness of the two translations also shows how much control Verne exerts over a translator.) In the era of high Western imperialism, translation was a tool, a function, an activity, almost a weapon of cultural aggrandizement, and Mercier, it would seem, used it to lasting effect. In French, Verne

(1828–1905) is at best an ambivalent romantic, and in fact is wistfully nostalgic for the time when he thought progress was within reach of *l'intelligence* and *l'industrie*. After all, Verne can be claimed by science fiction, but not by fantasy fiction. He was not out to show that there are more resilient mysteries than can ever be explained in ways congenial to Enlightenment rationalism; rather, he (or his narrators and tragically flawed superheroes) was out to show that what appeared to be resilient mystery was largely explicable in rational terms. In short, Verne the romantic inventor of plots replete with symbolism coexisted with Verne the realist/positivist editor. Mercier's more realistic Aronnax/Verne is subtly more at home with himself—and insensitivity to grammatical gender may have had as much to do with that fact as a judgmental attitude.

Mercier's chief aggression was excision. His 303-page translation contains roughly 144,000 words. Verne's novel contains roughly 226,800 words. My calculation for Mickel is 192,000 words, but I noted no omissions. (The Verne edition has no illustrations. The Mercier contains the original illustrations but does not include them in the numbering. Mickel's translation numbers the illustrations. A typical Mickel page has 480 words; however, the critical apparatus is so extensive that there are few typical pages.) For Mercier, Aronnax as Other clearly did not need to say so much; more particularly, he did not need to describe the underwater world in such great detail. Therefore, Mercier cut out the parts we are tempted to skip—like the cetological taxonomy in *Moby Dick*. For Mercier, readers were also Other, but he identified with them, rather than with Aronnax or with Verne. They—Mercier and the readers—were Others together, and Mercier as the clergyman who knows what is good for his parishioners decided how much of the sea world was pertinent for this adventure. Because of this abridging, Verne's English readers, we can assume, are younger and less sophisticated than his French readers and would not have appreciated Aronnax/Verne's ambivalences. Moreover, since Mercier had, after all, looked up all the words, his translations probably dominate subsequent English translations. Even Mickel's meticulous revision keeps much of Mercier intact.

Discounting Mercier's excisions, his Verne translations are not poor. They are matter-of-factly Victorian in sound and spelling. His errors, as cited by Miller in the annotated edition, are few, and Mercier can surely be excused for referring to North America's *mauvaises terres,* for example, as a "disagreeable region" instead of as the Badlands. Verne's French is of sufficient formality and impeccability that it cues a similarly correct standard English, with the result that Mickel's

retranslation uses the same register and diction and thus does not
sound different from Mercier's. Since Mickel appears to follow the
Société Jules Verne's no-nonsense approach, eschewing reading across
the text, he has the apparent aim of neutrality: just let Verne speak
through Aronnax as he would have spoken had he, Verne, been writing
in English. Of course, neutrality is a strategy with its choices, if not so
many or so noticeable as an a priori interpretation, neither domesticating
nor foreignizing, but straddling a fluctuating middle border. In Aronnax's recollection of the octopus who strangled the French sailor, the
1870 Mercier and 1991 Mickel translations are virtually identical:

> Mercier:
> What a scene! The unhappy man, seized by the tentacle, and
> fixed to the suckers, was balanced in the air at the caprice of this
> enormous trunk. He rattled in his throat, he was stifled, he cried,
> "Help! Help!" These words, *spoken in French,* startled me! I had
> a fellow-countryman on board, perhaps several! That heartrending
> cry! I shall hear it all my life. (275)

> Mickel:
> What a scene! The unhappy man, seized by the tentacle, and
> fixed to the suckers, was balanced in the air at the caprice of this
> enormous trunk. He rattled in his throat, he was stifled, he cried,
> "Help! Help!" These words, *spoken in French,* startled me! I had
> a fellow countryman on board, perhaps several! That heartrending
> cry! I shall hear it all my life. (462)

And in the second section of our quotation:

> Mercier:
> For me it was the despairing cry uttered by the unfortunate man
> in the midst of the struggle that had torn my heart. The poor
> Frenchman, forgetting his conventional language, had taken to
> his own mother tongue to utter a last appeal! Amongst the crew
> of the *Nautilus,* associated in body and soul with the captain,
> recoiling like him from all contact with men, I had a fellow-
> countryman. (275)

> Mickel:
> For me it was the despairing cry uttered by the unfortunate man
> in the midst of the struggle that tore my heart. The poor French-
> man, forgetting his conventional language, had taken to his own
> mother tongue to utter a last appeal! Among the crew of the
> *Nautilus,* associated in body and soul with the captain, fleeing all
> contact with men, I had a fellow countryman. (473)

In the penultimate chapter, however, Mercier's identification with
Aronnax and against Nemo comes to the foreground. The *Nautilus*
has sunk a mystery battleship by using itself as a torpedo and piercing

the enemy vessel, drowning its hundreds of men. Aronnax's ambivalence toward Nemo abruptly ends; he joins Conseil and Ned Land in their escape plot. Aronnax realizes, "Ce n'était plus mon semblable, c'était l'homme des eaux, le génie des mers" (511). Mercier's Aronnax is superior: "He was no longer *my equal* [emphasis mine], but a man of the waters, the genie of the sea" (299). Conversely, Mickel's Aronnax is horror-struck: "He was no longer a fellow human being, but the man of the waters, the genie of the sea" (494). In short, as is often the case with literature in translation, readers are ill-advised to rest their case on the translation.

As translators, our own appropriation of the Other may be more subtly domesticating or more openly foreignizing. We may inflict futile apologies on those who read our translator's notes. We may envy the Victorians their confidence and their nerve. But since they knew what literature was and how it should sound, since they knew what was good for their readers, they knew what to choose and how to translate it. For us it is different: our insecurity, uncertainty, and uneasiness—if not unwillingness to presume—leads to an impasse which simply calls for rerouting and going on. Speaking for the Other is an inevitable fact of translating. I am not sure that it qualifies as a dilemma: perhaps it is simply a condition of the activity. Or should I say an encompassing complex of conditions as unavoidable as *la mer* and *la langue de sa mère* in *Twenty Thousand Leagues*? The translator is the Self and the self-same. The text and all its impulsions, and intentions, and patrons both instigating and receiving the translation are Other. The language of the source text is the Other's language. The language of the target text is for the use of others, and the translation text, once expressed, is outside or Other.

I am not quite proclaiming that the question of the Other is moot, but I am suggesting that among moderately self-aware writers, translators, and readers, it can be managed. It can be offset in the classroom by stereoscopic reading, where the text is available in both the author's language and that of the class (at least for the instructor). It can be obviated in reception by the translator's admission of the interpretation developed and the strategy employed. In this respect as well, Mickel's Verne is exemplary. Traveling below the text in footnotes are his exegeses. He tells us what he thinks the import of a passage is. We are free to skip the footnote, but the *caveat* principle has been observed.

Aronnax ends with the claim that he and Captain Nemo alone have seen what hitherto has been only suspected. As the writer/recorder he has taken upon himself Nemo's role, the "No man" or "Nobody" in Latin who claimed "I can do and undo everything and transform 'yes' into 'no.'" This claim belongs deservedly also to the translator. I mean not only Mickel—but, yes, Mercier, as well.

Translating always involves usurping the Other's voice, and the need to make multicultural expressions maximally available means that those other voices will necessarily be altered. When we read popular press interviews with 1992 Peace Nobelist Rigoberta Menchú, whose native language is a special variety of Quiché, we needed a printed proviso to inform us that not only were we reading a translation, but also that in speaking Spanish to the interpreter, Menchú was probably first translating her own thoughts into Spanish. However, since we wanted to know approximately (rather than not at all) what Menchú was thinking, we were prepared to risk the distortion. And we probably should have allowed a little distortion also for the editorial policy of that particular newspaper.

What is always true in any translation project is that there is some kind of purpose behind it and that translators must accede to that purpose, which always includes some component of decision making for two Others—the source author and the target audience. Most generally we, both translator and "patron" (a term I will discuss later), have decided that the Other needs something: the author needs a wider audience; the target audience needs exposure, if not persuasion, to different values, goods, attitudes, motivations, different information, whether true, false, or mixed. Our intentions are not necessarily malefic, but as I have insisted, they are always to some extent presumptuous. And what we cannot claim is that our intentions can ever be completely disinterested. Unwitting, inadvertent perhaps—but innocent? Never. Even conscientious, conscious neutrality is a purposeful choice.

Anna Lilova, an eloquent and elegant Bulgarian who headed the Fédération Internationale des Traducteurs in the 1980s, claimed that translation was a link between cras, civilizations, and peoples. She was always careful to close at this point, leaving her audience of translators with the impression that linkage of this sort always had a positive value, and we always left with a very good feeling about our mission. As long as Madame Lilova's spell lasted, we felt, even believed, that communication always had beneficent effects, and that if there were *more* and *better* translators, the world would be a much better place. It is enough to state such premises to refute them. The best we can truthfully aver is that the world would probably be no worse for more and better translators.

We must now recognize that some of the most formidable translation projects have been mounted on behalf of inherently conflicted causes. For example, in the East the U.S.S.R. had its most talented writers organized and systematized to translate. After all, it was more prudent for Boris Pasternak to translate Shakespeare than to write *Doctor Zhivago,* and when Efraim Etkind even made an allusion to that situation, he was thankful to be allowed to emigrate to France. One explicit grand design at which the Russian translators were, it now seems, fated to fail was the integration of the separate heritages of the constituent republics into a common, shared culture through translation.

In the West, the United Bible Society, through its affiliates, still supports a worldwide network of evangelical Protestant translators who are committed to preserving and stabilizing many of the world's 5,300 discrete languages by converting their implicit grammars to writing systems. Of course, along the way, they have brought those preliterate cultures the Bible and Judeo-Christian ethics, including Western material culture and all that it entails. Their translator corps are trained by Western standards: they study preliterate grammars in a grid of Western grammars (specifically, Graeco-Latin, Franco-German, and Anglo-American) to transcribe texts as their Western-trained ears hear them. This, as Lauren Leighton has painstakingly documented, was true of the Russian translators as well.

In the mid-1970s the Polysystem group in comparative literature/ translation studies—which includes scholars from Amsterdam, Antwerp, and Tel Aviv[4]—introduced the term "patronage system" to designate the constraints imposed by whatever persons or groups authorize a given translation. The patronage system can designate an overt centralized system of control over what can be translated and published. This can be seen in the Foreign Language Publishing House in the People's Republic of China, or in the U.S.S.R.'s censorship system prior to 1991, or in other prereform Eastern Bloc censorship systems (Milan Kundera's *The Unbearable Lightness of Being* recounts such an incident in Czechoslovakia, when the physician begins his material descent by citing Oedipus in a newspaper). The patronage system, of course, can be so covert as to be nearly invisible, as in the U.S. system, where the economics of publishing (including advertising and market analysis) determines what gets published and hence what gets translated. "Market" here includes the government, organized religions, and so-called public service/public interest groups, from pro-life to pro-choice, from the NRA to Handgun Control. Since market analysis and the taste of key people in that market are determined by various socioethical values, this patronage system is open to majority domination and can be oppressive, although in the United States the small press, little magazine, and university press establishments to some extent counteract this monolithic tendency.

What may be paradoxical is that the Polysystem proponents—who unmistakably imply that the standards of taste imposed by the publishing system under corporate capitalism risk deforming literature— have for the most part learned English or French well enough to use those languages for their own publishing. With the exception of Susan Bassnett (of Warwick University), the Polysystem proponents are generally from countries with small language bases, and they are only too aware of the handicap of venue. Bassnett, in the afterword to her revised, tidy, *and* Western introduction *Translation Studies,* writes that she is going to make comparative literature a subfield of translation studies rather than the other way around. However, when into translation and creative writing on their own, the members of this group aim at publication with publishers such as Grove Press, the University of Chicago Press, Routledge, and Sun and Moon, and their products follow the norms of publishing economics—and do not sound like translations.

In the 1990s the vanguard position in translation studies is being assumed by Lawrence Venuti. His supporters (myself included) have yet to acquire a label, but we can take a cue from his essay "The Translator's Invisibility," and call our project "visible translation." The dilemma of dealing with the Other makes this group of "visibles" want to do more than mark texts as translations and foreground the translator. This group wants translators to be open about their ideological and stylistic strategies: honest with themselves, first of all, and, second and repeatedly, with their readers and patrons.

Here again, the *responsibles,* as the French would say, are not necessarily evil hypocrites; they can be benign activists. The benevolent and sincere can be found everywhere. But whatever our individual convictions regarding benevolence, sincerity, openness, and the relativity of such values, these *responsibles* do make decisions on behalf of the Other. If we translate, neutral as we often claim to be, we are either making such a decision or acceding to one. Let us, at least for our purposes here, avoid the most obvious and overt instances—of which I have next-to-firsthand knowledge because I know translators with the Summer Institute of Linguistics, which sends linguist/missionaries along the Amazon or in the remote villages of New Guinea. Let us not take issue with their decision that these peoples need Westernizing. As translators, let us look into our own consciences.

Let us look at instances of decision making for the Other which I wholeheartedly endorse. Mickel's retranslation is such a decision, for he recognized that the existing English translation was incomplete and contained some inaccuracies. Of course, Verne is in our Western tradition, so the presumption level, if I may put it that way, is slight. A more overt example of deciding what the others need or what the Other has to say comes with Francophone literature. For example, if A. James Arnold of Caraf Books thinks that the American English audience needs to hear the French Caribbean voice, he is making such a needs analysis. Carrol F. Coates, associate editor of *Callaloo,* a journal of Caribbean and African American literature, makes such decisions on a weekly basis.[5] In such matters we are no more self-reflective than Anna Lilova, whom I cited earlier: we simply believe that we *here* need to experience as tellingly as we can the lives and insights of those *there*.

Furthermore, once the decision to translate has been made, other decisions are in order. These decisions are likely to make neutrality either impossible—and/or undesirable. In the first place, like members of a jury who presumably are not supposed to have read newspapers or watched television for several months prior to being called to duty, translators cannot really claim not to know anything about the subject nor to have no preformed judgments; indeed, someone with no prior information and no shared opinions would not be qualified to do the translation. (Anyone retranslating Verne, for example, has already discovered the flaws in the prior translations, and has a conviction that Verne is worth serious critical attention.) This is no paradox. Translators are not practitioners of the traditional Western scientific method. They are, rather, more like critical theorists, for they must both share bias and be aware of it while processing their material.[6] In this regard, their competence depends on knowledge of both the source and target languages as well as knowledge of the subject matter, including knowing where and how to research the background.

Furthermore, more insidious decisions inevitably arise during translating, depending upon what response is desired from the readers. The spectrum is usually between target-language acceptability and source-language fidelity, and as a result the translator must face a number of hard questions. Should some integrity of the original be sacrificed to make sure that readers pay attention to it? Should the giveaways, such as strained effects, odd syntax, peculiar words be altered? Will the response be greater if it sounds as if the author wrote in English? There is a related problem: often, through either more extensive knowledge or highly convincing role playing, translators find errors in fact, sense lapses in register; in short, they find that the text needs "improvement."

It is a presumptuous decision, and yet may have to be made simply to ensure publication.

On the other hand, the contrary may look just as convincing. Perhaps we should let readers look at the Other face to face, thus hearing some of the text's alienating resonances. Perhaps we should allow the text to present itself. This is what Mickel did for Indiana University Press, because university presses are moving toward this new literalism. (The popular press still wants style to conform to Anglo-American norms.) In this way, readers know that this is a translation, a voice from another culture or another era. Indeed, a study of translating over the past five years shows that power centers and power languages (e.g., New York and English, Paris and French) are engaged in power struggles with the periphery. Even though in French literature the center has moved from Paris to sites on the periphery, it is we in the center (however that center may be constituted) who decide what is read and heard, what the rhetorical standards will be, what traditions will be followed, and what will be profitable. Translation always reacts to the center, whether through serving it (by bringing what is fashionable somewhere else over to English), or through countering it (by bringing in something the center would prefer to ignore or exclude).

It is, quite *literally,* inexpressibly convenient to be born into a dominant language milieu. While official bilingualism may undermine monolingual privilege, translation in an officially bilingual community like Canada—or a quasi-officially bilingual community like Haiti— maintains privilege. In Canada, translators can reduce creative language usage by their need to standardize expression and hence keep language the tool of conformity. Unapologetically, in Canada and on the continent, you speak French correctly or you speak something else, and Termium, the Canadian Secretary of State's formidable database in the praiseworthy pursuit of nonambiguity in information exchange, makes this effort machine-readable.

This kind of standardization emanates from the center and keeps the periphery in a neat circle. In Canada, the translation office is a subdivision of the Secretary of State. In Quebec, a state agency and a civic agency in Montreal try to monitor language—yet they do not concern themselves with the Algonquin minority at its border. Many a nation-state we envy (Sweden) or like to visit (France) makes an official effort to protect usage and hold the line on borrowings. Indeed, it is time that someone noted for the record that the rise of linguistic nationalism within the past thirty years heralded the resurgence of political nationalism. And before politicians, translators were confronting the concomitant resurgence of linguistic nationalism and world-language learning; that is, groups were bending their efforts to learn the colonizers' languages, voluntarily this time around, while committing themselves to the defense and illumination of their own language(s). The motives have been complex, even conflicted.

Whatever the motives may have been, translators have been mobilized to use their skills as weapons in the conflict of cultures—a conflict many would like to transform into a living mosaic through even-handed curriculum. With such we try to give the Other's words, not so much our own (although that will be inescapable), but words the Other would have used.

Of course, what we decide those words would have been is a matter of judgment, compounded of intuition, experience, and immersion. This judgment will be personal and subjective. In all translation there is a complex, multilayered, subjective factor. Various branches of applied linguistics (computational, descriptive, neural, and terminological) have been able to limit the subjective element in nonliterary language. Canada and the European Community have been able to limit the subjective element to such an extent that for sheer information transfer, there is a fair degree of reliable automatism in translating. Editing, obviously, is still necessary, so a degree of subjectivity remains, even in nonliterary translation. And in literary translation the subjective must take precedence.

In the final analysis, it is evident that literary translation is part of literature. Hence not only is translation appropriately deconstructed or explicated by literary criticism but also, and more important, literary translation is a response to the literary taste of an era, for what is accepted by the target audience determines, consciously or unconsciously, the decisions translators make.

When we encounter new literary translations that sound somewhat stilted and antiquated or, conversely, suspiciously smooth, it is likely that the translators have not been reading the target literature. What makes Mickel's retranslation of *Twenty Thousand Leagues* so persuasive is that as a specialist in the nineteenth century Mickel knows Anglo-American literature well enough to keep his Verne credible. Comparative, chronological charts (such as those made by the Leuven School under José Lambert) can show us what can happen lexically, syntactically, and grammatically in the interval separating the Mercier and Mickel translations. The passages from these translations that I have herein cited show minimal change. A time lapse of 121 years, a space distance of the Atlantic Ocean, and the considerable cultural differences between a nineteenth-century Oxford cleric and a twentieth-century Bloomington academic resulted only in the removal of a hyphen in the phrase, "fellow countryman." The tenses, mood, and voices stayed the same. Word order was preserved. Cognates were used confidently.

Mickel's decision to stay neutral and let the readers, all of us Others, see as nearly as possible what Verne would have written had he used English, was the best one. It mandated a certain rhetorical formality, fittingly associated with nineteenth-century novels, and in this form his *Twenty Thousand Leagues* reenters the multicultural curriculum with integrity.

Translators, then, are not unlike Professor Aronnax—although they may feel at times like the unfortunate, nameless French sailor. They cannot rescue the original just as it is. But they can transcribe and attempt to render *cet appel déchirant . . .* "that heartrending cry!"

Notes

1. There is no indication that Nemo, who speaks French natively, is a native speaker; Verne had originally planned to make Nemo a Pole, but his editor had too large a Russian market to permit the implication that Russian repression was responsible for Nemo's inhumanity. My Russo-Ukrainian colleague Georgui Derlugian informs me that in the Russian translation Nemo is a Hindu wronged by British colonialism.

2. Given Verne's passion for opera, "À moi!" almost certainly echoes Faust's call to Mephistopheles in Gounod's libretto. This would suggest that the sailor wants his mother but is calling on the devil, i.e., the diabolical Nemo. It is probably also no coincidence that "Nautilus" was the name of Robert Fulton's submarine model, which had a successful trial run in France in 1800.

3. Here there is affection and devotion between the affianced innkeeper's daughter and the game warden. But the eroticism is displaced. The castle owner, long exiled from this section of Transylvania presumably for his political activism, has returned with a charlatan who manipulates color slides and a recording to simulate the deceased opera singer whom the chatelaine loved. Simultaneously the opera singer's grieving fiancé and his valet pass through the area on a walking trip.

4. The leading proponents are José Lambert, André Lefevre, Itamar Even-Zohar, and Gideon Toury. For a brief guide to the Polysystem see Lefevre's "Beyond the Process."

5. Coates's Haitian issues of *Callaloo* received the Council of Journal Editors' 1992 monograph award, so such "presumption" was judged both valuable and attractive.

6. See the results of my survey of translators in "Seeking Synapses: Translators Describe Translating." Also relevant is my taxonomy of translator-text relations in "Crossroads or Spectrum: Translators' Range of Relations to a Text."

Works Consulted

Bassnett, Susan. *Translation Studies*. Rev. ed. London: Routledge, 1991.

Coates, Carrol F., ed. *Callaloo*. Special issues on Haitian literature, 15.2 (Spring 1992) and 15.3 (Summer 1992).

Kundera, Milan. *The Unbearable Lightness of Being*. New York: Harper-Collins, 1988.

Lefevre, André. "Beyond the Process." In *Translation Spectrum*. Ed. M. G. Rose. Albany: State U of New York P, 1981. 52–59.

Leighton, Lauren. *Two Literatures, One Art*. De Kalb: Northern Illinois UP, 1991.

Robinson, Douglas. *The Translator's Turn*. Baltimore: Johns Hopkins UP, 1991.

Rose, M. G. "Seeking Synapses: Translators Describe Translating." In *Translation Theory and Practice: Tension and Interdependence*, ed. Mildred L. Larson. ATA Series 5. Binghamton: Center for Research in Translation, 1991. 5–11.

———. "Crossroads or Spectrum: Translators' Range of Relations to a Text." In *Languages at Crossroads*, ed. Deanna Lindberg Hammond. Medford, NJ: Learned Information Systems, 1988. 297–303.

Venuti, Lawrence, ed. *Rethinking Translation*. New York: Routledge, 1992.

———. "The Translator's Invisibility." *Criticism* 28:199–202.

Verne, Jules. *Vingt mille lieues sous les mers*. Edition intégrale. Simone Vierne, ed. Paris: Garnier-Flammarion, 1977. The Mercier edition is *Twenty Thousand Leagues under the Seas* (Boston: James R. Osgood and Company, 1875); the annotated edition of the Mercier was compiled by Walter James Miller (New York: Thomas Crowell, 1967). The Mickel edition is *Twenty Thousand Leagues under the Sea* (Bloomington: Indiana UP, 1991).

3 Anthologizing World Literature

José J. de Vinck

> The petit-bourgeois is a man unable to imagine the other. If he
> comes face to face with him he blinds himself, ignores and denies
> him, or else transforms him into himself.
>
> —Roland Barthes, *Mythologies*

Can world literature be translated and anthologized without eliding the
differences within and among cultures? The production of accessible
anthologies of world literature has become more urgent as the globe
has become more closely linked; however, the editors of these anthologies need to think critically about the rhetoric of representation. For
example, *The Norton Anthology of World Masterpieces* defines world
literature in terms of the Western masterpiece and so imposes Western
models of the world, and of literature, on its representations of all
other cultures. In this essay I will briefly examine the essentialist
dialectic of Occidentalist and Orientalist discourse in the *Norton* and
then suggest alternate strategies of representation.

Said argues that "no one is likely to imagine a field symmetrical to
[Orientalism] called Occidentalism" (50). He furthermore claims that
Occidentalism could be a coherent discourse within non-Western cultures, but that is not the sense in which I will use the term. In this
essay "Occidentalism" refers to the ways in which Western cultures
and traditions are imagined *within* the West. This discourse of identity is inseparable from the discourse of difference. And, as Bhabha,
Mohanty, Parry, and Suleri argue, the discourses of self and other have
a complex, mutually deconstructive interrelationship.

Said himself recognizes that the diffuse and heterogeneous discourses
of the Western self—often unconscious and seemingly natural ways of
speaking and being—are inseparable from the more limited and homogenous discourse of Orientalism. In other words, the play of identity
is inseparable from the politics of difference. However, this dynamic is

often imagined as an essentialist dialectic of self and other. In this context the encounter of self and other does not result in the engagement of differences, but in the reinforcement of a presumed idealized identity over against a presumed idealized difference. It is this imagined essentialist dialectic, within Western culture, that the epigraph from Barthes evokes and which I propose to examine in the *Norton* series.

The first edition of the *Norton* was published in 1956; the fifth, in 1985; the sixth, in 1992; and an "expanded" edition made its first appearance in 1995. I will focus on the preface to the fifth edition since it articulates the presuppositions of the editors most clearly, and I will also briefly comment upon other texts in the series.

The preface to the fifth edition states: "From its first edition in 1956 it has been planned whole, each of its parts designed and executed by a recognized authority in that field, but changing steadily with the times . . ." (xiv). The *Norton's* form is determined by its didactic function as a "teaching instrument" (xiv). It attempts to represent "the ever-broadening cultural tradition that in these latter years of the twentieth century we all share" (xiii). The rhetoric of the preface employs different strategies of legitimation—organicism, expertise, didacticism, relevance, and tradition—to naturalize the *Norton's* representation of an Occidental culture that "we all share." However, a second look at the preface to the fifth edition reveals that its discourse not only represents the identity of the West—it *re-invents* this identity.

What is a "world masterpiece?" The designation refers to texts of "depth and subtlety" (xiv). The term "representative" often substitutes for the term "masterpiece" (xiv). An implicit Hegelian model of literary history operates throughout the *Norton*. History is divided into distinct periods, each with its own "complex sensibility" (xiv). The masterpiece represents the spirit of its age, which is at the same time a universal Spirit that remains forever pertinent.

The *Norton,* however, is more than a collection of representative texts—it is greater than the sum of its parts. The fifth edition is structured like the Bible: the first volume, or the Old Testament, begins with *Genesis* and ends with *Paradise Lost;* the second volume, or the New Testament, begins with the apostles of the Enlightenment and ends, nervously, with potentially apocryphal modern works. "The closer we come to contemporary times, the more disagreement there is over what is to be called a 'masterpiece'" (1907). In a sense, the editors have reconstructed a new, secular Bible, but who is this god called *Norton*?

The *Norton* reinvents and relegitimates the canonical tradition of the West through an essentialist dialectic of identity and difference. A

few selections from Africa, Japan, and India are included within the
anthology, and these relatively homogenous representations of otherness
authorize the heterogeneous representations of self. Of course the editors
of any anthology of world literature face the practical limitations of
space, but the choices of what to include and what to exclude are
instructive.

The most dramatic example of this dialectic of inclusion and
exclusion can be found in the *Norton*'s "Companion Volume" (see the
title and facing pages). That volume is significantly titled *Masterpieces
of the Orient* (1961; rev. 1976).[1] These are not "world" masterpieces,
but masterpieces of that vast homogenized territory of the "Oriental"
other. In a brief four hundred pages, compared to the four thousand
two hundred and seventeen pages of the two volumes of *World
Masterpieces,* the literature of the Near East, India, China, and Japan
is represented. *Masterpieces of the Orient* inherits the tradition of
"anthologizing" the Orient which Said suggests began in 1806 with
Sacy's *Chrestomathie arabe* (128). The modern *Masterpieces of the
Orient* includes longer selections, but is in every other way reminiscent
of Sacy.

The essentialist dialectic of Occidentalism and Orientalism, in terms
of identity and difference, is perfectly expressed by the first sentence
of the first edition of *Masterpieces of the Orient,* in which we are
informed that "*Masterpieces of the Orient* is a companion volume to
World Masterpieces . . ." (vii). The Orient is thus a companion to the
World Master. The preface continues:

> Its editorial principles are in the spirit of the original anthology.
> Imaginative literature is emphasized, though with the literatures
> of both the Near and the Far East it is difficult to make the
> distinction between intellectual writing (especially when it is
> concerned with philosophy or religion) and belles lettres. (vii)

This rhetoric brings to mind all the Occidentalist/Orientalist imagery
of the faithful colonial companion—from Enkidu to Gunga Din. The
work of Said, Bhabha, Mohanty, Parry, and Suleri, amongst others, has
made the political implications of this rhetoric familiar. *The Norton
Anthology of World Masterpieces* is the original—in the sense of
originating—text: the next paragraph refers to it as the "parent volume"
(vii). *Masterpieces of the Orient* is the child—in the sense of childlike—
text: even the philosophical and religious texts of the "Orient" are
indistinguishable from belles lettres. The dialectic of identity and
difference is clear: the father recognizes and accepts the childlike fictions
of his faithful companions.

The Occidentalist/Orientalist discourse of the 1961 preface to *Masterpieces of the Orient* is substantially revised in the edition of 1977, but it also slips into cultural stereotypes as it describes the "intricate language" of the Arab, the "stately splendor" of the Persian, the "pervasive religious element" of the Indian, the poetic "didacticism" of the Chinese, and the "instinctive sense of beauty" of the Japanese (x). To be sure, the discourse of the 1961 and 1977 prefaces to the "companion" *Anthology* is dated. Said's groundbreaking study was only published in 1978, and the various editors of the Norton series have already tried to respond to the changing times.

The *Norton* has recently generated from its rib another companion volume, *The Norton Anthology of Literature by Women: The Tradition in English* (1985). According to the title these texts are neither examples of world literature, nor masterpieces. They belong to a separate "Tradition in English" created by women. The exclusion of the word "masterpiece" from the title points to the gendered sense of the term. In this way this particular anthology serves as an important corrective to the *Norton,* but it does so in a way that reinforces the essentialist dialectic of identity and difference. Like *Masterpieces of the Orient,* this volume is as much a product of exclusion as it is of inclusion. It gives women writers their own space without disturbing the existing order of the ideal, and for the most part patriarchal, Western masterpieces. And between these companion volumes a literary third world, within the first world, is created.

The preface to the sixth edition (1992) explicitly raises the question of "canonicity" and "multiculturalism," but, as the binary opposition suggests, the question only serves to legitimate the essentialist dialectic of self and other:

> Looking out on the controversies now raging between advocates of "canonicity" and "multiculturalism," we find it useful to remember that a sound democracy, like an effective orchestra, needs diversity and consensus equally. (xix)

The preface to the sixth edition is sensitive to the controversy, and yet all the presuppositions of the preface to the fifth edition remain intact. The essentialist dialectic of Occidentalism/Orientalism, self/other, is now even more explicitly legitimated by what might be called an aesthetic liberal pluralism. This solution to the controversy is still underwritten by a Hegelian idealism and still enacted by a strategy of inclusion: texts are added in the sixth edition, but the order of the-world-according-to-Norton remains undisturbed.

The expanded edition of *Norton* (1995) seems to raise the same issues. For example, the publication announcement for the expanded edition claims that it will offer

> the best of the literatures of India, China, Japan, the Middle East, Africa, the Caribbean, and native America alongside the masterpieces of the Western tradition.

Once again the pluralistic strategy of inclusion is pursued within the essentialist dialectic of self and other. The "best" literature of other cultures is placed "alongside" the "masterpieces" of the West. While the table of contents indicates a more inclusive anthology, the rhetoric of the publication announcement falls back on the same unconscious ideological presuppositions of the earlier editions.[2]

The editors of the *Norton* series have led the way in making important texts available, and several generations of students and teachers are in their debt. Following Norton's lead, a new anthology from St. Martin's Press—*Western Literature in a World Context*—continues to wrestle with the problem of anthologizing world literature. The title of its preface states its intent: "Placing Western Literature in a World Context." However, the table of contents shows that the first section of "The World Context" only begins on page 787.

The Norton and St. Martin anthologies are valuable contributions to the study of world literature; however, the editors of any new anthology need to make questions of representation integral parts of their texts. Instead of relying on unexamined universals like the "masterpiece," "classic," or "great book," and instead of imagining an essentialist dialectic of identity and difference, the editors of a new anthology of world literature might discuss the history and politics of canonical and apocryphal writing in the light of the substantial research on this subject. These editors would also do well to abandon the very category of literature so as not to superimpose relatively recent Western aesthetic traditions and criteria on other cultures and their varied kinds of writing. For example, while it is perfectly legitimate to read the Bible and the Koran as literature, it is not legitimate to elide the questions raised by such a dramatic reorientation to these religious testimonies.

In the future, editors would do equally well to avoid the pasteurizing rhetoric of the "text." It would not be much of an improvement to replace the *Norton*'s aestheticization and homogenization of world "literature" with a postmodern textualization and pasteurization. The study of literature has only recently shifted "From Work to Text" (Barthes), and yet perhaps the time has already come for another shift to "discursive practices" (Foucault).

Instead of the universal categories of "literature," "work," or "text," the editors of the future might highlight the distinct discursive practices of various documents belonging to different times, places, cultures, and peoples. They might emphasize the variety of ways of constructing meaningful representations of particular worlds. They might explore the differences within cultures as well as between cultures. They might consider the political contest within and among hegemonic, popular, subcultural, and resistant forms of discourse. Instead of reinscribing the unexamined rhetoric of the masterpiece and its attendant idealist discourse of identity and difference, an anthology of distinct discursive practices from around the world might serve as an invitation to students to pursue ethnographic analyses of their *own* varied discursive practices *in relation to* those of others. In contrast to an imagined essentialist dialectic students might be asked to engage in an imaginative nonessentialist dialectic: a dialectic of difference.

Notes

1. Although this text was last revised in 1976, it is still in print, available, and in use at a number of universities and colleges. [Ed.]

2. It is, however, worth noting that the editors of the expanded *Norton* do address some of these ideological issues. In particular, Sarah Lawall (whose work appears elsewhere in this volume), in her introduction to "The Twentieth Century" in Volume 2, presents a revised definition of "masterpiece"—a work that "continues to be relevant because it constitutes a coherent structure of reference and representation that is neither easily exhausted nor tied to a single context" (1376). Such a definition, while reflective of the Johnsonian "test of time," and the modernist valorization of "complexity," nonetheless accommodates a more inclusive vision. [Ed.]

Works Consulted

Anderson, G. L., ed. *Masterpieces of the Orient.* New York: Norton, 1961. Rev. ed., 1976. Expanded ed., 1977.

Barthes, Roland. *Mythologies.* New York: Farrar, Straus and Giroux, 1972.

———. "From Work to Text." In *Textual Strategies.* Ed. J. Harari. London: Methuen, 1979. 73–81.

Bhabha, Homi K. "The Other Question: Difference, Discrimination and the Discourse of Colonialism." In *Literature, Politics, and Theory.* Ed. F. Barker et al. London: Methuen, 1986.

Davis, Paul, et al., eds. *Western Literature in a World Context.* 2 vols. New York: St. Martin's Press, 1995.

Foucault, Michel. *The Archaeology of Knowledge.* London: Harper Colophon, 1972.

Gilbert, Sandra, and Susan Gubar, eds. *The Norton Anthology of Literature by Women: The Tradition in English.* New York: Norton, 1985.

Mack, Maynard et al., eds. *The Norton Anthology of World Masterpieces.* 5th ed. 2 vols. New York: Norton, 1985. 6th ed., 2 vols., 1992; expanded ed., 2 vols., 1995. (The one-volume "Continental" editions exclude British and American authors, and, like the "Oriental" edition, are still available.)

Mohanty, S. P. "Us and Them: On the Philosophical Bases of Political Criticism." *Yale Journal of Criticism* 2.2 (1989): 1–28.

Parry, Benita. "Problems in Current Theories of Colonial Discourse." *Oxford Literary Review* 9 (1987): 27–58.

Said, Edward. *Orientalism.* New York: Random House, 1978.

Suleri, Sara. *The Rhetoric of English India.* Chicago: U of Chicago P, 1992.

II "New" Traditions, Genres, and Perspectives

4 Beyond the Looking Glass of Empire: The Colonization of Portuguese Literature

Paulo de Medeiros
Bryant College

The study of literature in the West has traditionally assumed a predominantly, if not exclusively, Western perspective masked under the guise of universalism or neutrality: consequently, non-Western works have either been ignored, dismissed as inappropriate, or simply made to fit Western patterns, down to the convenient but negative classification of "non-Western." With an increased awareness of the ideological binds intrinsic to such a process—an awareness undoubtedly fostered both internally and externally in the wake of the various European colonial systems and the rise of transnational capitalism—came efforts to eliminate, or at least adjust, such a skewed perspective.

The dream of (forced) homogeneity through Western hegemony has largely given way to a diversified understanding of culture and its various products. Within the general attack on Eurocentrism, however, there are two related flaws: first, the amalgamation of everything European into a fictive unity that, even if it might have some correspondence to the dream of homogeneity, has no real counterpart in a fragmented and divided Europe, more often than not torn against itself and amongst its constituent members; second, the forgetting exactly of those parts of Europe that "Europe" itself tends to forget, its own, anything but central, dominated others.

Case in point: a book on French literature in Belgium begins with the flat assertion that "Belgian literature does not exist. This is generally accepted in educated Belgian circles" ("La littérature belge n'existe pas. Dans les milieux cultivés de Belgique cette thèse est généralement admise" (qtd. in Vlasselaers 139). Clearly, the process of exclusion within Europe is not a peculiarity of Portuguese literature; it extends to all nondominant European literatures. Portuguese literature might even enjoy more visibility than Belgian since it has its own language and it too was used as a norm to be imposed on other people. Yet, as with Belgian literature, its existence can also be denied through a kind of vicious circle of exclusion. If a country appears outside of the mainstream, its cultural production tends to become isolated, is depreciated outside of its borders, and generally ceases to have any currency whatsoever. In this sense, Portugal's decentering dates at least to the beginning of the demise of its imperial pretensions, when it was temporarily annexed by Spain (1581–1640). With the waning of its political and economic role within the framework of an expansionist Europe, any culture produced in Portugal became ever more nearly invisible to European eyes, becoming confused with Spain or forgotten altogether along with its language. The reemergence of Portuguese culture only occurs, and then already as a mere oddity, when political circumstances warrant it—during Napoleon's invasions (1807–11) and during the standoff with (and ultimate capitulation to) England over competing claims in Africa (1890). The real diminishing of political influence immediately translates into a perceived diminishing of cultural relevance, which in turn leads to a lack of reception, until it becomes impossible to distinguish between perceived and real irrelevance—a process culminating in exclusion.

In other words, consideration of Portuguese literature becomes more and more difficult as its perceived irrelevance hinders critical reception and translation, the two processes whereby it could hope for recognition as part of world literature. As a consequence, even within a strictly European context it becomes possible to deny the existence of Portuguese literature out of ignorance. Whenever European letters are mapped Portuguese literature can be, and usually is, elided simply because of its invisibility. For instance, its exclusion from *Textual Liberation: European Feminist Writing in the Twentieth Century* (an otherwise excellent collection of nine essays dealing with British, Scandinavian, German, Eastern European, Russian, French, Spanish, Italian, and Turkish feminist writers) is symptomatic. There can be no doubt that either a priori, because of its focus on feminism and thus on counterhegemonic strategies, or in its breadth, extending to Eastern Europe and Turkey, an effort has been made to move away from a privileging of dominant, Western European, central literatures and traditional valuations. In this context, the lack of any mention, even casual, of Portuguese feminists such as the authors of the *New Portuguese Letters* makes clear the extent and pervasiveness of the exclusionary process.

A related form of exclusion—but more important and at the same time more difficult to pinpoint than denial through ignorance—is categorical denial. It reinforces ignorance while stemming precisely from an attempt to combat ignorance. As a case in point, Aubrey Bell's 1922 *Portuguese Literature* is still the only history of Portuguese literature available in English and thus not only a privileged example but the only one, its uniqueness reinforcing its unwitting success and failure. Bell's express purpose is the correction of critical neglect and the dissemination of knowledge of, and appreciation for, Portuguese literature; yet his own introduction, when read today, reveals a paternalistic logic that completely undermines its project and is in fact a form of categorical denial. The book's success as "authoritative" and normative goes hand in hand with its failure to bring about a renewal of interest in its subject matter.

Bell's desire to establish his text as foundational, declaring itself as the first systematic, comprehensive treatment of the topic is accomplished at the expense of his predecessors. These are seen as unsystematic and provisional (Teophilo Braga), or limited to single periods (Fidelino de Figueiredo). What is striking about this is not so much Bell's attempt to justify his enterprise, but rather the dislocation of other "histories," which has the effect of turning his outside perspective into the first realized (comprehensive, methodical, scientific) codification of the "native" (Portuguese literature). Referring to yet another previous history (by Mendes dos Remedios), Bell allows that it is "the only completely methodical [history] . . . since it contains that rarity in Portuguese literature: an index," but qualifies it as "a brief manual" that excludes living authors and, further, questions its chronological accuracy. The one of his predecessors Bell values highly, noting how "she has, indeed, laid the Portuguese people under an obligation which it will not easily redeem" (15n3), is German (Bouterwerk).

Allied to this controlling process, indeed inseparable from it, is the construction of Portuguese literature—the literature of the one European nation with the oldest fixed national structure and borders—as a "new" and "emergent" literature. Although Bell at one point goes so far as to consider that Portuguese literature also includes extensive works in Latin and Spanish ("over 600 names") by Portuguese authors from various periods, he starts his "Introduction" with the categorical assertion that "Portuguese literature may be said to belong largely to the nineteenth and twentieth centuries" (13). Clearly, what allows Bell to make such a remark is a twofold process of invisibility, whereby many important works had been ignored until the philological interest of the nineteenth century brought them back to light, and that ignorance was exacerbated by the lack of interest outside Portugal in its literature.

Bell does mention some works resuscitated by Portuguese scholars, but for the most part his listing of the discovery of manuscripts and their publication tends to give the impression not only that Portuguese literature, for all its antiquity, has been "produced" principally since the nineteenth century, but also that, strangely enough, this production has taken place, first and foremost, outside of Portugal and at the hands of others. After the declaration that "Europe can boast of no fresher and more charming lyrics than those which slept forgotten in the Vatican library until the late Professor Ernesto Monaci published *Il Canzoniere Portoghese* in 1875" follows a small but impressive list of similar recuperations in which foreign initiative is notable. For instance, Bell notes that Gil Vicente, Portugal's most important dramatist, was "almost unknown before the Hamburg (1834) edition, based on the Göttingen copy of 1562," and that "in prose, the most important *Leal Conselheiro* of King Duarte was rediscovered in the Paris Bibliothèque Nationale and first printed in 1842 . . ." (13–14). In this view Portuguese literature is a sort of sleeping beauty who depends on the saving kiss of the foreign prince to return to life—except that in many respects one can even doubt whether the princess is Portuguese at all.

The reasons Bell adduces for the greatness of some works and the "originality" of the literature in general are a mixture of an idealized projection of Portugal as a backward but attractive *locus amoenus* ("absence of great cities"; "pleasant climate" [19]) and a consideration of Portugal's maritime enterprises and historical role as natural providers of literary material. In fact, Bell's views here both exoticize Portugal and reflect Portugal's own assumption of those "differing" qualities in a move designed to retain some sense of "positive" identity. Bell's benevolent paternalism leads to a moral chiding of the Portuguese for their own lack of capacity to exercise judgment as regards their own (?) literary creation:

> The excessive number of writers, the excessive production of each individual writer, and the *desleixo* [abandon, moral lassitude] by which innumerable books and manuscripts of exceptional interest have perished, are all traceable to the same source: the lack of criticism. A nation of poets, essentially lyrical, with no dramatic genius but capable of writing charmingly and naturally without apparent effort needed and needs a severely classical education and stern critics, to remind them that an epic is not rhymed history nor blank verse mangled prose, that in bucolic poetry the half is greater than the whole, and to bid them abandon abstractions for the concrete and particular and crystallize the vague flow of their talent. (20–21)

There is obviously a perverse, almost schizoid, tension in these comments whereby Bell's obvious devotion to Portuguese literature clashes with his perception of its "faults" and shortcomings. The arrogance of the "outside" observer who brings his reason (criticism) to bear on the charm and simplicity of "nature" is inescapable. This characterization of Portuguese literature as "excessive" and "natural" is virtually indistinguishable from other European (Portuguese included) colonial attitudes toward colonized peoples and cultures: "noble savages" incapable of even appreciating or preserving their values without the discerning rule of the colonizer. In a curious metonymy, Portugal is viewed as "a nation of poets" and its prose naturally "of lyrical character, personal, fervent, mystic" (20). Consequently, Portuguese philosophy is deemed all but impossible. Bell's three examples only serve to deny themselves as examples: Spinoza, "the greatest if not the only Portuguese philosopher . . . left Portugal as a child," while Francisco Sanchez "lived in France and wrote in Latin," and Dr. Leonardo Coimbra contributed what is only "a notable but somewhat abstruse work. . . ." (20). Ultimately, the colonizing attitude made evident in these remarks is best encapsulated in a categorical denial of the value of Portuguese literature: "Had one to choose between the loss of the works of Homer, or Dante, or Shakespeare, and that of the whole of Portuguese literature, the whole of Portuguese literature must go . . ." (19).

Before proceeding, it is necessary to take a step beyond—lest all that is accomplished is a demonization of Bell, a dubious enterprise in itself and much more so from hindsight and seven decades after the fact. If the view from outside serves only to deny the view from inside (which would tolerate mediocrity, according to Bell), one must ask what the view from inside might in fact be. If Portuguese literature only obtains a reflection on the outside as inferior, what might be the view from the other side of the looking glass?

This question can be approached in two ways: one is to concentrate on a search for excellence, the "originality" of Portuguese literature, which might thus be redeemed of its perceived inferiority or of its debt towards the rest of Europe, as the influential critic Jacinto do Prado Coelho did in *Originalidade da literatura portuguesa*. The other way is best represented in the interiorization of a perceived inferiority and subsequent explicit or implicit privileging of the outside view as superior and normative. Such interiorization can take many forms. In its implicit state it can assume the form of defining literary movements, in their entirety, as characterized principally by their tardiness in reference to the rest of Europe. This is the case specifically of Portuguese romanticism as viewed by another prominent critic, Carlos Reis, in a 1990 survey. The explicit form of such interiorization of inferiority is perhaps nowhere better expressed than precisely in the translation of Bell's *Portuguese Literature* into Portuguese and its continuous reprinting.

The preface, added to the Portuguese translation and written by the translators themselves, is appallingly clear in detailing the "indebtedness" of Portuguese culture to a normative, outside, perspective. The terms of this preface furthermore insert such a rhetoric squarely in the field of a literary economy completely derived from Goethe's notion (as given particular expression in his letter to Eckermann of July 15, 1827) of the "corrective" value of the outside perspective (qtd. in Strich). After listing Bell's contributions to Portuguese studies and reserving the right to disagree on particular interpretations, the translators state:

> A capital point cannot, however, suffer from contradiction or even reticence on our part: the gratitude that Portugal owes to one of the foreign experts [*sábios*] who in the present century have given greater attention to the study of its literary genius. This study has a double advantage: it makes Portugal's literary genius known and appreciated outside, at the same time that it projects to this side of the border a clear and serene critical light, greatly favorable to the just gradation of our ways of being, which risk building deformations of reality. The myopia of abandon [*desleixo*] and the easily aberrant perspective of patriotism can be corrected with great profit by the impartial perspective of the alien gaze when sharp and educated. (xi)

This internalization of the rationalist discourse that discredits one's own claims of cultural emancipation is symptomatic of a colonizing process. For the colonized elite, self-identification with the colonizer appears as an easy way of escaping its own marginalization. This view, however, runs counter to that of Eduardo Lourenço, a prominent intellectual who has devoted many studies to the related questions of national identity and the interactions between Portugal and Europe. Although Lourenço clearly maintains that "our famous complex of cultural culpability did not originate solely from the gaze, more or less ignorant, disdainful, or condescending, that hegemonic nations or cultures projected over our creations or our knowledge" ("Nós e a Europa" 55), he still prefers to view the situation of Portugal (together with Spain) as a unique case. Specifically, when addressing the relations between French and Portuguese literature, Lourenço is at great pains to avoid considering the Portuguese situation in terms of cultural colonization. For Lourenço, cultural relations imply a mutuality characterized as much by the superiority of one of the agents as by the lacks and needs of the other. Consequently, to add to this basic assumption "a supplement of incomprehension" that would view the history of cultural relations as a "typical example of a colonizing cultural hegemony" would be unnecessary and fruitless ("Portugal-França" 129).

Obviously, any process of relation includes some form of exchange. When there is an a priori imbalance, however, such a relation can be termed unilateral. And when the processes of inequity become inescapable one can speak of colonization. No one doubts that the importation of chocolate, coffee, and potatoes from the New World radically changed Europe; but no one doubts as well that the exportation of cultural norms and, initially, technology, is what assured European domination. Lourenço bases his denial of the colonization of Portuguese literature on the "fact" that French hegemony was not planned as such by the French (129) nor forced upon the Portuguese (130). This defense remains at a level of naiveté that is discordant with the rest of his arguments, for literary colonization does not necessarily require forced territorial occupation. When Lourenço points to the exportation of people and talent that characterizes Portugal from the beginning of its imperial enterprise he attempts to see in that still an expression of being European in the extreme—as if Portugal's eccentric situation in Europe would not constitute its marginalization but rather its exaltation ("Nós e a Europa" 27).

What allows Lourenço to invert the process of valuation, ultimately, is not only a necessary if momentary blindness to the conditions underlying such an export of talent—religious and political persecution, cultural suffocation, and economic annihilation—but an unfinished processing of Portugal's relation to the idea of Empire. To Lourenço as to Boaventura de Sousa Santos, Portugal's imperial past is the key to an understanding of Portugal's marginal situation. But whereas Lourenço still clings to a view of the Portuguese as "creators" of a Latin American reality (27), Sousa Santos tends to put Portugal's past in a more critical light, defining Portugal as a semiperipheral nation that was at the center "in relation to its own colonies and [at] the periphery in relation to England" (14). On April 25, 1974, when the Revolution precipitated political democracy and the end of empire, Portugal was "the least developed country in Europe and at the same time sole possessor of the largest and longest lasting European colonial empire" (14). Given this condition, it is no surprise that outside views emanating from a European center such as Bell's would carry special weight in informing the "inside" views of the Portuguese.

When Sousa Santos declares that Portugal was "simultaneously a colonizing and colonized country," he obviously has in mind both complete colonization—Portugal's political, military, religious, and economic occupation and exploitation of vast territories outside of Europe—and cultural colonization—the major role played by foreign (chiefly French) culture in shaping Portugal's cultural expression, which as a result assumes a subaltern position: minor, dependent, and imitative. This view of cultural dependency can and should be related to the notion of territoriality itself. Portugal has not only been dependent on foreign tastes; its territorial integrity, either as a European nation or as a European empire, was successively challenged from the onset.

On the one hand, one could refer to European opinion on the status of the Portuguese nation. E. J. Hobsbawm, for instance, while delineating nineteenth-century ideas of nation, calls attention to the " 'liberal' concept of the nation" and its stress on the necessity of a country's possessing a "sufficient size to form a viable unit of development" (30). Accordingly, Hobsbawm continues, such a notion "seemed too obvious to require argument. . . . The *Dictionnaire politique* of Garnier-Pagès in 1843 thought it 'ridiculous' that Belgium and Portugal should be independent nations, because they were patently too small" (30). On the other hand, Portugal's independence, beyond any real or imagined Iberian affinity, had been constantly challenged by Spain and once even effectively annihilated for sixty years (1580–1640). During this period, Portugal's identity was forcefully submerged under a Spanish one and its imperial claims and territories became the target for systematic expansionist strategies, mainly on the part of England and Holland. Furthermore, the recovery of independence in 1640 was illusory, for Portugal's colonies in South America, Africa, and Asia remained in part under foreign control or were in the process of being wrested away. Indeed, Portugal continued for a long period to be involved in open war or engaged in direct military confrontation with France, England, Holland, and Spain. For instance, Dutch infiltration in Brazil was not halted until 1653, and peace only achieved in 1661. The succeeding decades also failed to bring any permanent normalization. In spite of renewed treaties and alliances, as well as royal marriages, Portugal remained immersed in various wars within Europe, continually losing parts of its empire either as a result of concessions to its allies or through force. 1697 marks both the publication of a Portuguese translation of Boileau's *Art poétique* and the French occupation of Amapá in Brazil. By 1710 a Portuguese fleet is still fighting a French one for the possession of Rio de Janeiro. In effect, then, Portugal's territorial identity as a European nation and as a colonial empire was significantly questioned for over a century to an extent that makes the question of cultural colonization much more than a rhetorical one.

The deterritorialization of Portugal as empire assumes yet another unique facet, one which raises interesting problems in terms of the relationship between center and periphery in cultural as well as political terms. With the imminent threat of a French invasion in 1807, the Portuguese court fled to Brazil. From 1808 to 1821, when D. João VI returned to Lisbon, Portugal and its empire were ruled from one of its colonies. It should be stressed that this evasive action on the part of the Portuguese Crown was not simply a way to avoid being imprisoned by Napoleon's armies, for after the third and final expulsion of the French troops from Portugal in 1811, the Court decided to remain in Brazil and only returned to Portugal when political revolt there made it imperative.

Even a sketchy look at some of the immediate consequences of this transfer of the Court will illustrate beyond a doubt that the establishment of the seat of the empire in Brazil did imply in effect a reversal of power and not just a nominal alteration. Brazil, which had already had insurrectionary movements of note, starting with the "Inconfidência Mineira" of 1789, was elevated to the category of Kingdom in 1815, just one year before the Prince Regent was crowned as João VI. With the arrival of the Crown in 1808, Brazil, which until then had suffered from strict censorship and did not even have a single printing press, saw the creation of one newspaper, the *Gazeta do Rio de Janeiro,* and the importation of another, the *Correio Brasiliense,* published in England. In 1810, only fourteen years after the creation of the "Real Biblioteca Pública de Lisboa," the "Biblioteca Nacional do Rio de Janeiro" opened its doors. Perhaps even more symptomatic was the establishment of a central bank, the "Banco do Brasil," in 1808, whereas the first metropolitan bank, the "Banco de Lisboa," was only founded in 1821, precisely when the Court returned to Portugal. Immediately following that event, in 1822, Brazil claimed its independence. Significantly, Brazilians did not opt for republican government, choosing instead to crown D. Pedro IV of Portugal (the son of D. João VI) as emperor. At the same time, José da Silva Lisboa's *Império do Brasil* ("The Brazilian Empire") was published there.

Subsequent developments in Portugal and Brazil make it even more nearly impossible to delineate which is the center and which the periphery. With the death of D. João VI and the assumption of the Brazilian Crown by D. Pedro IV, a power vacuum ensued in Portugal. While Portugal was being governed by one of his daughters, D. Isabel Maria, D. Pedro, who had remained in Brazil, was in fact for a brief period both King of Portugal and Brazilian Emperor. A solution was obtained in 1826 with his abdication of the Portuguese Crown in favor of his other daughter, D. Maria da Glória, who was seven years old and with him in Brazil. She was then married *in absentia* to her father's brother, D. Miguel, who had been exiled to Austria because of his previous attempt to usurp the Crown. In 1831, when these convoluted arrangements failed (due to D. Miguel's absolutist coup), D. Pedro abdicated the Brazilian Crown and left for Europe with D. Maria da Glória in order to launch an invasion that would restore her to power. Consequently, in 1832 he assumed the Regency of Portugal in his daughter's name and arrived in Lisbon in 1833. In 1834 the struggle for control culminated in D. Miguel's expatriation, D. Pedro's death, and the beginning of D. Maria's reign.

Given such a political conflation between center and periphery, metropolis and colony, it becomes especially difficult to determine with any precision what constitutes colonial or postcolonial literature. Clearly, noted authors of the period just before Brazil's independence, such as Tomás Aquino Gonzaga (1744–1810) are claimed by both countries. Or one could even go further back in time and consider the case of António José da Silva (1705–1739), who had been born in Brazil but went to Portugal, where he authored the period's most important plays—only to be executed by the Inquisition.

Taking the notion of "the concern with place and displacement" as a "major feature of post-colonial literatures" that Ashcroft, Griffiths, and Tiffin advocate (8), one would have to include many "Portuguese" texts as postcolonial. Even those that have been used to promote colonialism, such as Camões's celebrated *Os Lusíadas* (1572), are already implicated in the alienation produced by imperialism. Camões's poem is at once a national epic and already a lament for the forced effects of deterritorialization brought about by colonial expansion. If one turns to the romantic period in Portugal, one of its most salient features has to have been the impact made on Portuguese literature by those authors, chiefly Almeida Garrett and Alexandre Herculano, who had been forced into exile. Their introduction of a literary revolution came as a consequence both of their expatriate condition and their received foreign influence, and of their desire to resist foreign political intervention. Garrett's poem *Camões* (1825), which is generally credited with inaugurating romanticism in Portugal, was written in England

and published in France, and has to be seen as directly involved in the political turmoil that I have just outlined. While the Renaissance poet is the explicit topic, the poem's themes revolve precisely around the concept of nation and the condition of deterritorialization, which Garrett identifies in *Camões,* in himself, and in their nation.

In the contemporary period deterritorialization is even more acutely a determining factor in much of Portuguese literature. The end of the dictatorship and the final dissolution of the empire in 1974 led to a renewed search for identity based on the possibility of freely expressing such a concern. The need to rethink the nation in light of its having been returned to its original European territory became imperative. Portugal, no longer capable of perpetuating a self-aggrandizing self-image, had to contend immediately with its Europeanness, that is, with its peripheral situation. Sousa Santos notes, for instance, that although in the euphoria of the revolution it was possible to think of Portugal as going beyond Europe, economic and political realities in the form of the International Monetary Fund quickly brought the nation back to reality (14). While some authors eschew these realities, some of the more prominent—António Lobo Antunes, Lídia Jorge, José Cardoso Pires, José Saramago—have consistently pursued postcolonial issues in their novels.

In some cases Portugal's past is revisited specifically to demystify it and to provide an alternative view of history. In this regard one of the most influential texts is José Saramago's *Memorial do Convento* (1982; translated as *Baltasar and Blimunda,* 1987). This novel bases one of its main characters on a Brazilian who went to Portugal, distinguished himself by creating a rudimentary flying machine and other inventions, and was finally executed by the Inquisition. In another of Saramago's novels, *O Ano da Morte de Ricardo Reis* (1984; translated as *The Year of the Death of Ricardo Reis,* 1991), Portugal's most celebrated modernist poet, Fernando Pessoa, is reworked through the character of Ricardo Reis, one of the poet's heteronyms. Whereas Pessoa had created the fiction of Reis leaving Portugal for Brazil, Saramago has Reis returning to Lisbon to search for Pessoa. In *A Jangada de Pedra* (1986) Saramago treats deterritorialization forcefully by having the whole Iberian Peninsula magically separating from the rest of Europe at the Pyrenees, thus literalizing a series of metaphors related to Portugal's condition with regard to Europe. Drifting in the Atlantic the Peninsula becomes itself a trope for the Portuguese condition.

José Cardoso Pires, who has always written what can be termed a literature of resistance, provides a scathing indictment of life under the dictatorship in *A Balada da Praia dos Cães* (1982; translated as *Ballad of Dog's Beach,* 1986). António Lobo Antunes, in a series of novels, takes as his theme the problems of colonialism, particularly as they relate to the war Portugal led against the various African movements of liberation and the irrevocably changed nature of Portuguese society. In one of his most important works to date, *Fado Alexandrino* (1983; translated, 1991), Lobo Antunes mercilessly details the 1974 revolution as well. Lídia Jorge relentlessly pursues the issues of the colonial war (*O Cais das Merendas,* 1982) and of the revolution (*O Dia dos Prodígios,* 1980), while focusing on Portuguese society from a feminist perspective.

All these texts share two features: first, they can be regarded as political interventions—even after 1974—given the level of intensity with which they attempt to unmask the conditions of Portuguese society and rework its past and present; second, they are intricate metafictional narratives in which the complexity of content is readily matched by that of form. Lídia Jorge's *O Dia dos Prodígios,* for instance, insistently foregrounds its textuality and the problematics of polyphony, constantly mixing in different voices and even graphically accentuating that effect with running glosses on the main narration. In many respects these texts can be considered both postcolonial and postmodern. As such, they further reflect Portugal's semiperipheral condition and the combined needs or desires to decolonize Portuguese literature, to reterritorialize it as always already deterritorialized, and to challenge its continued invisibility.

Writing in Portuguese, then, is, in a sense, a practice of invisibility. Moreover, Lusophone literatures suffer from a double invisibility, with gender and race serving as additional veils of concealment. For instance, from all the examples of contemporary Portuguese literature that I have mentioned only those by Lídia Jorge have not yet been translated into English. Or one could point to *The New Portuguese Letters,* which, in spite of its momentary popularity, quickly went out of print and is rarely discussed. Works by Afro-Brazilians, especially women, remain buried under numerous layers of invisibility, not only lacking translations but remaining largely unknown even in Brazil and Portugal, where the literary market appears almost entirely closed to them.

While Portugal's entry into the Common Market has made its cultural production more recognizable, effective decolonization of Portuguese literature would necessitate further translations, critical studies, and curricular inclusion. Beyond specialized articles and monographs, moreover, the processes of exclusion outlined above have started to change. Books such as *Toward Socio-Criticism: Selected Proceedings of the Conference "Luso-Brazilian Literatures, A Socio-Critical Approach,"* edited by Roberto Reis, serve as agents of that change. Of special note is Phyllis Reisman Butler's "Writing a National Literature: The Case of José Luandino Vieira." Also noteworthy are Alfred J. MacAdam's *Textual Confrontations: Comparative Readings in Latin American Literature,* in which the Brazilian Euclides da Cunha is treated together with Carlyle, Hardy, and Vargas Llosa, and Earl E. Fitz's *Rediscovering the New World: Inter-American Literature in a Comparative Context,* which sets out fully to compare the diverse literatures of North and South America as an integral unit. Furthermore, many Portuguese texts could be used in general, genre, thematic, and period courses, and offerings in women's studies, autobiography, narrative poetics, or even postmodernism could integrate such texts as *The New Portuguese Letters.* Courses in world literature, nationalism, or politics and literature would also find important sources in much of the contemporary Portuguese and Lusophone literatures.

The interest in curricular change should go beyond a simple replacement of this or that canonical text by one written in Portuguese, and focus on how those issues are presented from a decidedly different perspective, one always informed by deterritorialization and the issues of the semi-peripheral. The question that still remains, however, is whether, and to what extent, attempts to integrate Portuguese literature might still be a process of false reterritorialization. That is, in attempting to show how Portuguese literature has been consistently colonized and made invisible, while writing or teaching on this side of the Atlantic, one could still hopelessly repeat the inscription of Portuguese literature into a forced context. I would like to think, however, that such a process might rather correspond to Saramago's gesture in *A Jangada de Pedra*—pulling Portugal into an Atlantic drift.

Works Consulted

Antunes, António Lobo. *Fado Alexandrino.* Lisbon: Dom Quixote, 1983.
———. *Fado Alexandrino.* Trans. Gregory Rabassa. New York: Grove Press, 1991.
Ashcroft, Bill, Gareth Griffiths, and Helen Tiffin. *The Empire Writes Back: Theory and Practice in Post-Colonial Literatures.* London and New York: Routledge, 1989.
Barreno, María Isabel, María Teresa Horta, and María Velho da Costa. *Novas Cartas Portuguesas.* Lisbon: Futura, 1974.
———. *The Three Marías: New Portuguese Letters.* Trans. Helen R. Lane. Garden City, NY: Doubleday, 1975.
Bell, Aubrey F. G. *Portuguese Literature.* Oxford: Clarendon Press, 1922.

————. *Literatura Portuguesa.* Trans. Agostinho de Campos and J. G. de Barros e Cunha. Lisbon: Imprensa Nacional, 1971.

Bennington, Geoffrey. "Postal Politics and the Institution of the Nation." *Nation and Narration.* Ed. Homi K. Bhabha. London and New York: Routledge, 1990. 121–37.

Boubia, Fawzi. "Universal Literature and Otherness." Trans. Jeanne Ferguson. *Diogenes* 141 (1988): 76–101.

Butler, Phyllis Reisman. "Writing a National Literature: The Case of José Luandino Vieira." *Toward Socio-Criticism.* 135–42.

Chamberlain, Bobby, Jr. *Portuguese Language and Luso-Brazilian Literature: An Annotated Guide to Selected Reference Works.* New York: MLA, 1989.

Coelho, Jacinto do Prado. *A Originalidade de Literatura Portuguesa.* Lisbon: Instituto de Cultura e Língua Portuguesa, 1977.

Eagleton, Terry, Fredric Jameson, and Edward W. Said. *Nationalism, Colonialism, and Literature.* Minneapolis: U of Minnesota P, 1990.

Fitz, Earl E. *Rediscovering the New World: Inter-American Literature in a Comparative Context.* Iowa City: U of Iowa P, 1991.

Forsøs-Scot, Helena, ed. *Textual Liberation: European Feminist Writing in the Twentieth Century.* London and New York: Routledge, 1991.

Garrett, Almeida. *Camões.* [1825]. Porto and Braga: Chardron, 1880.

Hobsbawm, E. J. *Nations and Nationalism since 1780.* Rev. ed. Cambridge: Cambridge UP, 1990.

Jorge, Lídia. *O Dia dos Prodígios.* Lisbon:Europa-América, 1980.

————. *O Cais das Merendas.* Lisbon: Europa-América, 1982.

Lawall, Sarah. "The Alternate Worlds of World Literature." *ADE Bulletin* 90 (1988): 53–58.

Lourenço, Eduardo. *Nós e a Europa ou as duas Razões.* Lisbon: Imprensa Nacional, 1988.

MacAdam, Alfred J. *Textual Confrontations: Comparative Readings in Latin American Literature.* Chicago and London: U of Chicago P, 1987.

Pires, José Cardosa. *Balada da Praia dos Cães.* Lisbon: Dom Quixote, 1982.

————. *Ballad of Dog's Beach.* Trans. Mary Fitton. London: J. M. Dent and Sons, 1986.

Reis, Carlos, ed. *Literature portuguesa moderna econtemporânea.* Lisbon: Universidade Aberta, 1990.

Reis, Roberto, ed. *Toward Socio-Criticism: Selected Proceedings of the Conference "Luso-Brazilian Literatures: A Socio-Critical Approach."* Tempe: Center for Latin American Studies, Arizona State U at Tempe, 1991.

Saramago, José. *Memorial do Convento.* Lisbon: Caminho, 1982.

————. *Baltasar and Blimunda.* Trans. Giovanni Pontiero. New York: Harcourt Brace Jovanovich, 1987.

————. *O Ano da Morte de Ricardo Reis.* Lisbon: Caminho, 1984.

————. *The Year of the Death of Ricardo Reis.* Trans. Giovanni Pontiero. San Diego: Harcourt Brace Jovanovich, 1991.

————. *A Jangada de Pedra.* Lisbon: Caminho, 1986.

Serrão, Joel. *Cronologia Geral de História de Portugal.* 3rd ed. Lisbon: Iniciativas Editoriais, 1977.

Sousa Santos, Boaventura de. "11/1992 (Onze Teses por Ocasião de mais uma Descoberta de Portugal)." University of Coimbra: Oficina do CES (Centro de Estudos Sociais) no. 21 (1990): 1–28.

Strich, Fritz. *Goethe und die Weltliteratur.* 2d rev. ed. Bern: Francke Verlag, 1957.

Vieira, José Luandino. *Luuanda.* [1964]. Lisbon: Edições 70, 1981.

———. *Luuanda.* Trans. Tamara L. Bender and Donna S. Hill. London: Heinemann, 1980.

Vlasselaers, Joris. "Belgian Literature? Some Reflexions on Socio-Cultural and Geopolitical Identity." *Proceedings of the 12th Congress of the International Comparative Literature Association.* Ed. Roger Bauer, Douwe Fokkema, and Michael de Graat. Vol. 4. Munich: Iudicium Verlag, 1990. 139–44.

5 "Yes, I Can": Empowerment and Voice in Women's Prison Narratives

Sharon Hileman
Sul Ross State University

In her poem "Requiem," Anna Akhmatova presents herself as observer and chronicler of Stalinist abuses and terrors. The poem is prefaced by an explanation of how it came to be written:

> ...I spent seventeen months in the prison lines of Leningrad. Once, someone "recognized" me. Then a woman with bluish lips standing behind me, who, of course, had never heard me called by name before, woke up from the stupor to which everyone had succumbed and whispered in my ear (everyone spoke in whispers there):
> "Can you describe this?"
> And I answered: "Yes, I can." (2:95)

In diverse ways, the writers of political prison narratives accept the same challenge. Whether coming to voice angrily or meditatively, immediately or years after incarceration, these authors construct a variety of literary forms and *topoi,* shaped by the historical, social, and political circumstances of their lives.

Prison literature as a genre has existed for centuries and is anthologized in collections such as *The Great Prisoners,* whose table of contents reads like the traditional European canon: Socrates, Boethius, Sir Thomas More, Daniel Defoe, Fyodor Dostoevsky, Honoré de Balzac, Paul Verlaine. The American prison experience has been discussed and anthologized by H. Bruce Franklin in a two-volume work, *The Victim as Criminal and Artist: Literature from the American Prison.* Franklin demonstrates that most American prison narratives have their roots in African American culture and history. French women's prison writings from the eighteenth to the twentieth century are discussed in Elissa Gelfand's *Imagination in Confinement,* and a general anthology of women's prison writings, *Wall Tappings,* was edited by Judith Scheffler in 1986. (The last fifty pages of Scheffler's work provide an invaluable annotated bibliography.)

Criticism of prison literature begins with Albert Camus's *L'Homme révolté.* Camus regards the prisoner as a social rebel, one who challenges society, and he furthermore contends that modern literature *in toto* is a literature of rebellion, a literature that rejects the world and expresses a desire for destruction and transcendence. Contemporary critics who study prison narratives believe that male prison authors still construct images of transcendence and rebellion (Scheffler 17; Gelfand 20), while such accounts written by women inmates explore different issues. Women focus on questions of self and identity, often contrasting present and former selves, and investigate the relationships that the "incarcerated self" enters into with fellow prisoners as well as with prison personnel. Women are also interested in the prison environment, depicting it both realistically and imagistically. Although women's prison writings before the twentieth century tended to be confessional narratives, the voice now speaking from the woman's prison narrative blends the solipsistic and communal into unique autobiographical discourse. Further enriching the blend is the element added when the writer is a political prisoner, aware of conditions in the larger society that structure individuals' lives and restrict groups' options. Marginalized as a woman, as a member of an ethnic, racial, or political group, and then as a prisoner, such a writer maintains a perspective at once distanced and engaged.

This cross-cultural study of political prison narratives written by women during the 1960s and 1970s will investigate the blending of the individual, the communal, and the political into the very different voices that emerge to articulate prison experiences. We will focus primarily on Domitila Barrios de Chungara's *Let Me Speak!,* a Bolivian activist's description of the exploitation of mineworkers in her country; Joyce Sikakane's *Window on Soweto,* a black South African's account of apartheid and imprisonment under the Terrorism Act; and Barbara Deming's *Prison Notes,* a white activist's chronicle of a freedom walk through Georgia to demand civil rights for blacks. An excellent point of departure for these more recent narratives is Eugenia Semyonovna Ginzburg's two-volume depiction of her lengthy imprisonment during the Stalinist purges of the 1930s and 1940s.

Ginzburg is the most naive of the authors in this study, not realizing in 1934 that her arrest was a real possibility and that advice to flee Moscow should be seriously considered. As a loyal Communist and party member, Ginzburg, like thousands of others, was an unsuspecting victim of the Stalinist "personality cult." The fact that Ginzburg spent eighteen years in prison, moving from solitary confinement to penal servitude in labor camps, also sets her experience and narrative apart from those of the other women in this study.

Ginzburg's narrative seems closer to fiction than to memoir, perhaps because of its panoramic scope. As the narrative progresses from its starting point near Moscow to its termination thousands of miles away in Kolyma, vivid descriptions of historically famous prisons are provided; dialogue from interrogations is fully rendered; and ongoing relationships are charted, including the protagonist's love affair with a camp doctor, which leads to marriage. Only the repeated coincidences in Ginzburg's life are unbelievable, and she remarks several times that they are too improbable to include in any fictional text.

Because the lines distinguishing autobiography and fiction are blurred in any approach to the two genres, Ginzburg's narrative serves as a reminder of the problem of authenticity or veracity in a work that claims to be based on fact. Any retrospective account, whether in a political prisoner's narrative or a canonical author's autobiography, is subject not only to the vagaries of memory but also to the shaping impulse that exaggerates, omits, and patterns in any literary undertaking.

Yet Ginzburg evidently had a phenomenal memory. She explains how she would recite Pushkin's poetry to her fellow prisoners, once even being accused of having a book (a forbidden object) from which she must be reading. Early in her prison experience she was suddenly able to visualize an entire page of Véra Nikoláevna Fígner's explanation of the code to interpret wall tappings. According to Ginzburg, she was able to recall perfectly what she had read years earlier (*Journey* 71). So when Ginzburg says that she is making a special point of remembering her experiences in order to set them down on paper later (*Within* 418), her ability to do so may well exceed that of the ordinary person. Unconcerned with the question of memory's reliability, critics have compared Ginzburg's work to fictional accounts. Harrison Salisbury, reviewing *Journey into the Whirlwind* for the *New York Times Book Review,* remarked, "Not even Alexander Solzhenitsyn's *One Day in the Life of Ivan Denisovich* matches it" (4). The fictional Denisovich, like Ginzburg's narrated self, "Genia," is an individual whose simple physical survival seems to have a symbolic significance that extends beyond the pages of the text. Perhaps Salisbury's comment is an indirect acknowledgment of the narrative and symbolic power residing in an account that chronicles eighteen years of survival as opposed to that of a single day. What Ginzburg documents more fully than the other prison writers in this study is the process of change that accompanies survival. Physical change is inevitable, and Ginzburg describes the unique moment in which it is viewed by women who have long been denied access to mirrors: "Hundreds of anxious, mournful eyes, all searching for their own reflection in the bluish glass . . . I recognized myself only by my resemblance to my mother" (*Journey* 315).

Accompanying physical change is a psychological or behavioral change that can render an individual unrecognizable to those who knew her before incarceration. Ginzburg believes that the camps, not prison, transformed "normal" people into brutal and self-serving wardens, willing to accept bribes and impose death sentences to ensure their own survival.

In prison cells, on the other hand, Ginzburg perceives a spiritualized transformative power. She compares her own solitary confinement to that of a nun or monk in a monastic cell. The small and silent space of her cell at Yaroslavl provided opportunity for meditation, reading (once library privileges were restored), and total self-immersion. Yet because of continued zealous sentencing, the number of prisoners soon surpassed the amount of space available to contain them. Ginzburg's solitary confinement was countermanded, but, even so, she acquired a cellmate with whom she could conduct philosophical discussions.

This idyllic life gave way to a very different environment when the prisoners were moved. From this point on in the narrative, Ginzburg describes cells where women could sleep only by taking turns using the available bed and floor space. Later, when seventy-six women were crammed into a railway car for transport across Russia, they were incredulous that an additional thirty prisoners were to be thrust into their car. Yet this initial hostility and resentment gave way to acceptance when the car's residents noted the "new" prisoners' shaved heads. Seeing others' degradation transformed Ginzburg's cadre into compassionate and welcoming hosts.

But Ginzburg does not idealize relationships among prisoners. Arguments and name-calling abound, especially when members of different parties and factions are forced to share space. One woman, an inveterate smoker, would not smoke Ginzburg's cigarettes because she believed it would compromise her integrity as a Social Revolutionary to accept gifts from a Communist (*Journey* 112–13).

Ginzburg's narrating of such factionalism and her description of several prisoners who persisted in suspecting others of being agents show that such divisiveness was foolish at best. All prisoners, regardless of guilt or sentence, were equally mistreated.

Even though Ginzburg is articulating her own story in an almost traditional autobiographical format, her voice clearly testifies to the experiences and sufferings of the numerous other prisoners she encountered over the years. Ginzburg makes space in her narrative for the voices of these other women, incorporating their spoken exchanges and speeches. Because her book is written retrospectively, Ginzburg can add parenthetical comments to explain what happened to many of these prisoner-comrades. Within each cell-group, women had memorized the names and addresses of one another's relatives in order to transmit news of the sender's existence and whereabouts should an opportunity to do so ever occur. Ginzburg's text brought to the print medium the oral commitments made in the crowded cells and doubtlessly provided information for families that might never have obtained it otherwise.

Ginzburg's narrative, then, has a dual purpose: it tells the story of the "I," its first-person protagonist, but it is also the "eye" that Anna Akhmatova became for "Requiem." The eye observes and records for future generations; Ginzburg, in fact, imagined she was writing for her grandson. But she was also jubilant that reforms made by several Party Congresses made it possible for her work to reach a larger audience of Russians than had already read parts of the manuscript in its *samizdat* (underground) forms.

It may be that Ginzburg also sought to justify herself before an audience, demonstrating both her own innocence and the Stalinist regime's inordinate excesses. Such a desire is marked in the text by the refrain, "The Moor has done his duty; the Moor can go." Genia and her comrades gleefully repeated this maxim each time a prison administrator, party mogul, or former interrogator suddenly became the accused instead of accuser. One such man, coming face to face with Ginzburg after his fall from power, murmured contritely, "Can you forgive me?"

What such anecdotes reveal is the tenuous line between prisoner and imprisoner in Stalinist Russia. While no other narrative in this study describes a similar fluidity, Barbara Deming's *Prison Notes* explores the fluctuating and ambivalent relationships between the incarcerated and their jailers in Albany, Georgia. She even includes "all those who put us in there" on the list of people to whom the book is dedicated. Unlike Ginzburg and most other political prisoners, Deming chose to go to jail. U.S. civil rights activists of the 1960s believed that conducting fasts during jail sentences would publicize their cause and perhaps serve as a catalyst for change. Deming begins her narrative with a reference to her first incarceration two years previously. And at the end of *Prison Notes,* when the group has successfully achieved its goals and been released, a temporary misunderstanding about passing out literature on the streets of Albany brings the physically and emotionally exhausted protesters to the point of risking jail again.

Exhilarated at being free, they are nonetheless ready to repeat the entire cycle if the action seems necessary to advance the cause of civil rights.

Such a repetitive pattern also characterizes the lives of the inmates who share the general Albany jail facilities and sometimes even the actual cells of the political prisoners. People who have been arrested for violence and drunkenness will be arrested again, and when "Ruth" and "Flo" are released,their phrasing of farewells attests that they will be back.

This rendering of the prison experience gives Deming's book itself a cyclical rhythm. Being in jail is not a climactic or life-altering experience as portrayed in her narrative; for political activists, going to jail is a tactic deliberately chosen to achieve a specific purpose, part of a larger strategy of nonviolent resistance. This is not to deny that Deming's experience is transformative and significant. Her daily, dated chronicle of the physical and emotional changes wrought by fasting is as frightening as anything described by Ginzburg. Given the frailties and health problems of Deming and several of her group, not to mention the unwillingness of the prison doctor to treat prisoners as "un-American" as these, it is quite possible that jail fasting could have resulted in several deaths.

Even against such a negative backdrop, however, Deming, like Ginzburg, finds a prison cell a place for contemplation. Pursuing thoughts generated in her prison cell, Deming elaborates upon the distinction between being inside and outside prison. She reinvokes an eighteenth-century image of prison as Hell and further defines prison as an institution whose existence implies there is something wrong with people's lives. Prisons, she contends, are built to exclude, to deny the humanity of prisoners, and for this reason prison guards tend to treat prisoners as animals or nonrational beings.

Throughout Deming's narrative, guards, matrons, the sheriff of Albany, the prison doctor, and all prison staff become the "other" against whom the prisoners will struggle to define themselves. What is especially difficult is that these activists want to communicate with and eventually change the attitudes and beliefs of their jailers.

To this end, the fasting prisoners deliberately objectify themselves, turning the institution's privacy-invading devices back upon themselves. The gaze of the incarcerators is forced to witness a display of fasting bodies and the fast's effects: weakness, dizziness, scurvy, diarrhea, and eventual immobility. The assistant police chief

> lingers in spite of himself, peers silently, in turn, at each one of us . . . perhaps he doesn't know how to define to himself a certain

> look about her [Yvonne Klein, a thirty-year-old professor from
> the University of Minnesota]. She lies there smiling at him
> strangely. . . . [Her smile] makes a complicated mixture of an-
> nouncements, to others and perhaps to herself. It announces: I
> am ready for the venture. It asks: How are you going to cope
> with me? (34–35)

Michel Foucault points out that the evolution of punishment techniques belongs not to the history of law or ideas but to "the history
of the body" (3–31). In prison, the body is depersonalized to become
part of a network of power and control. If "control over the body" (6)
is the issue in prison, as Judith Scheffler contends, Deming and her
group deliberately employ the body as a sign of their power. The
Albany police chief, fully aware that the physical body is the locus of
power in this struggle, reiterates threats to forcibly feed the protestors
should their fasts become life-threatening.

Again, it is important to realize that the Albany prisoners themselves
chose to use their physical bodies to exhibit signs of deprivation and
suffering. This element of choice is atypical of most political prisoners'
circumstances. More commonly, the body is unwillingly subjected to
hunger, physical searches, rape, and torture.

Perhaps because choice has been an element of her experience,
Deming can be analytical rather than fearful in describing the effects
of the fast. "One begins to be a stranger to oneself," she comments,
referring to new mental and physical sensations which include mind/
body dissociation. A little later she asks, "Am I sure it is I? How much
of me can waste away and my self remain?" (147–48). For Deming,
the self is very much a cerebral construct, but what she seems to be
suggesting is that the erosion of the body also limits the mind's capacity.
If her mind rambles out of control, she will no longer be a thinker or
writer, no longer be able to claim an identity.

Deming, perhaps more than any of the other authors in this study,
is aware of the power inherent in writing. Ginzburg recited lines of
poetry to cheer herself and her comrades; Deming inscribes William
Blake's lines on the walls and ceiling of her cell to affirm the need for
physical and intellectual freedom. One chapter of *Prison Notes* calls
attention to its status as a written document by appearing as a letter.
Its salutation, "Dear _____," enables Deming to address the critical
or hostile reader as well as her hypothetical audience, an audience that
does not understand the philosophy of nonviolent action and does not
believe that the twenty-six Albany protesters can make a difference in
race relations.

By placing one form of writing within another, Deming may hope to intensify her arguments, refuting her addressee while she confirms her own points. Certainly this chapter articulates most fully the necessity of communicating with "the enemy." However, Deming deliberately rejects the terms "enemy" and "outsider," terms which she believes the nuclear age has made obsolete. Part of her group's struggle is to convey this knowledge of commonality to their own hostile audience:

> Confronted by people who were treating us as though we were not human, one of us has managed, by a look or a word or a gesture, to assert: I am human; treat me as though I were—and has succeeded in making the others do just that. (58)

Later Deming describes such an event as a "magic moment" (60) and compares it to the Quaker concept of "speaking to that of God in another man" (61). If people recognized one another as human beings and as godlike, then labels, racist slurs, and stereotypes would not create dual systems for blacks and whites in the American South.

Of course, Deming's whole point is that barriers or boundaries do exist, not only between races but also between "insiders" (prisoners) and "outsiders" (guards and community). But Deming's prison experience, in many ways the opposite of Ginzburg's, shows that the barriers can be broken down from the inside out. Deming's narrative, which ultimately becomes very much like Ginzburg's, moves from its meditative, repetitive format into rising action that will culminate in a climax of political triumph for the protesters.

Being released from prison, though, is an ambivalent and ironic experience. Deming describes the sense of estrangement the group feels after being removed from their cells: they look back at the inmates who remain and see them not as individuals but as a group in a cage. It seems that the very bars of the cell immediately create the dehumanizing effect the group has itself been subjected to and fought to overcome. Deming concludes the narration of the actual imprisonment with characteristic musing and questioning: "If, after all these days spent in a cage myself, I can feel this distance, how can I hope that others will learn to cross it?" (173).

Deming's voice is philosophical, not angry or resentful. Prison has given her the opportunity to explore what it means to be "inside," and she is free to resume her life "outside" once she walks through the prison's doors. There is no such "outside," however, for Joyce Sikakane, a black woman who has grown up in apartheid South Africa. Although her "crime" is not very different from Deming's, Sikakane is jailed under the Terrorism Act and eventually forced to leave South Africa.

Sikakane's voice is not philosophical; it is both angry and matter-of-fact. She uses citations from newspapers and reference books to document her description of life in Soweto, "the largest single modern ghetto in Africa" (8). These textual features are in keeping with Barbara Harlow's suggestion that Third World women's prison narratives typically combine "formal questions of literary convention with the urgent demand for documentation and records," and that this combination is the definitive sign of contemporary Third World literature (506).

Because Sikakane's narrative is not entirely devoted to her prison experience, she can provide documented social and economic data on Soweto even as she describes her family and childhood. Like Wole Soyinka's *Aké* (a more conventional autobiography), *A Window on Soweto* is the story of a place, not just a person. But while Aké was a place where people were able to maintain their traditions and dignity with little interference from European colonizers, such is not the case in Soweto.

Sikakane's grandfather considered himself a "detribalised African" (18) and bought land and property in a South African township. These achievements were nullified when the Afrikaner Nationalist Party came to power in 1948 and implemented apartheid. The Party declared that no permanent urbanized African population existed and forbade African home or land ownership in urban areas. Sikakane's grandfather, along with many other Africans, lost his property.

Shantytowns like Soweto were constructed to house the African work force; here Africans could live as tenants in overcrowded, poorly constructed four-room houses, which Sikakane illustrates with sketches and photographs, another form of documentation. Living beneath the poverty line, Africans in Soweto were not allowed on the streets without a work pass and were subjected to frequent searches, harassment, and arrests.

Sikakane, trained as a journalist, was the first African woman to be employed by the *Rand Daily Mail,* a liberal Johannesburg newspaper whose workers showed no liberal traits regarding apartheid. Sikakane tells of an incident when an emergency forced her to use the white women's restroom in the newspaper office. Immediately, a group of angry white women pulled her off the toilet. Sikakane can present this incident humorously, but her humor pales as she continues with accounts of the threats, physical dangers, and lack of recourse experienced by South African blacks.

Although Sikakane had lived a lifetime under apartheid and was intimately acquainted with its injustices, she never realized her vulnerability until incarceration. Then, asked to become a state witness, to give evidence against others like her friend Winnie Mandela, Sikakane confronted the same dilemma that had been posed for Ginzburg by her interrogators:

> From what they know one has to judge what to admit and what to hide . . . because it flashes into your mind what risk to others is involved, and also the possibility of being tortured yourself and whether the type of information you have is worth dying for. (62)

Sikakane reasoned that her "crime"—trying to arrange for families of prisoners to visit the incarcerated—would not be considered "terroristic" by any rational person, so she admitted what she had done. However, she refused to implicate others, which resulted in her being kept in prison for seven additional months and then put on trial.

In two crucial paragraphs, Sikakane describes the epiphany of her prison experience, which occurred the day before her trial. For some reason, the security police brought the five women who were to stand trial (and who had been placed in solitary) together in one room. Sikakane lists the names of the other four women as if to give them and this experience concrete textual substance. Then she describes the women's feelings of joy and victory as they realized that no one in this group had agreed to give evidence.

From this point on, during the trial and retrial of the five female and seventeen male defendants, Sikakane uses the pronouns "we" and "our" to describe the collective nature of the experience. Like American black prisoners, whose narratives H. Bruce Franklin describes, the South Africans realized that their prison experience was part of a society's attempt to control an entire group, not any one individual. Such awareness creates what Franklin calls a "collective aesthetic," which is expressed by a writer who speaks as a representative of others. Ironically, imprisonment made possible the very bonding and unity among Africans that the white South African government had tried for twenty years to prevent. Under apartheid, it would be difficult for an individual like Sikakane to stage an effective political protest, but, again ironically, imprisonment provided her with an opportunity to resist and be heard. Saying "no" to her interrogators was empowering for Sikakane; not even the newspaper articles she had published were as effective as this monosyllable. And although the prison experience itself is narrated in only a few short chapters of *A Window on Soweto,* it seems to have been the catalyst for the entire book.

Being in prison didn't raise Sikakane's consciousness as it did Ginzburg's nor provide opportunity for reflections like Deming's. The prison experience truly changed Sikakane's life. In spite of, or perhaps because of, her acquittal, Sikakane was served with banning orders, which virtually prohibited her from finding work in South Africa. After numerous attempts to support herself and her child had failed, Sikakane eventually arranged her own escape from a homeland that was never really a home. Her narrative, then, was written from the relative security of the West, where she, unlike her twenty-one codefendants, faced no threats of reimprisonment and retrial.

Sikakane's prison experience and post-prison life illustrate one woman's rebellion against a dehumanizing system. Just as she refused to assume the political role of state witness that the interrogators pressed upon her, Sikakane also refused to accept the cultural and social roles that apartheid prescribed. After escaping from South Africa, she was reunited with her Scottish fiancé, whom she eventually married. (This reunion was unplanned and coincidental, like so many of the reunions narrated by Ginzburg.) In her life, as in her narrative, then, Sikakane remained defiant, refusing to accept restrictions imposed by the color line.

A defiant, subversive woman who rejects societal expectations might also become a subversive writer, challenging literary paradigms and conventions. But in *Let Me Speak!*, Domitila Barrios de Chungara goes even further and calls into question the act of writing itself. Her narrative exists as a written text only because a collaborator has transcribed her spoken words from taped interviews, conversations, and speeches. As its subtitle and the subheading on its first page proclaim, this work exists to provide "testimony," a word connoting oral as well as written statements.

Like Sikakane, Barrios de Chungara's purpose is to describe and denounce exploitation, which in Bolivia was directed against a class rather than a race. Invited to participate in the 1975 International Women's Tribunal sponsored by the United Nations, Barrios de Chungara attended but rejected its premise of gendered solidarity. Instead, she reiterated that class differences made it impossible for women to share goals. Her only purpose in attending the conference, she insisted, was to speak in behalf of the Bolivian mineworkers.

Interestingly, it is because Barrios de Chungara did not behave according to Latin American cultural codes of feminine behavior that she was treated so harshly. Even her husband did not approve of her activist role, which caused him to lose his job. His boss at the mines explained:

> It's your wife's fault we're firing you from the company, because you're a sissy. You know who's wearing the pants in your family.

> Now you'll learn to control your wife. . . . What do you want with a political wife? . . . A woman like that isn't any good for anything. . . . She doesn't even seem like a woman. (137)

It is this tension between the roles of political activist and traditional wife and mother that underlies the narrative. Barrios de Chungara acknowledges its presence but believes that ultimately most compañeros accept women as part of "the people." However, the military regime does not look favorably upon an upstart woman, as one brutal incident illustrates. Unlike the civil rights protesters in the United States, Barrios de Chungara and most Third World prisoners are not able to exercise "control over the body" while in prison. At the time of her second incarceration, Barrios de Chungara was pregnant but was nevertheless accosted sexually and then physically beaten when she resisted. The narrative depicts a defiant and violent woman who bites a large piece of flesh from the hand of her persecutor. This image, like many others in *Let Me Speak!,* accords with the imagery of violence, rebellion, and rejection of society said to characterize male prison narratives. As Harlow has observed, it is difficult to apply gender criticism to many Third World narratives because they reflect an experience "not based on bonds of gender, race, or ethnicity" (503).

However, the most graphic imagery in Barrios de Chungara's account could occur only in a woman's writing. Since the man whose hand she had bitten was a colonel's son, the colonel himself intervened to ensure that no woman as "unnatural" as this one would bear a child. Barrios de Chungara lapsed into unconsciousness as a result of the beating the colonel inflicted upon her and the labor that followed. When she recovered, she located her baby in the dark cell by tracing the umbilical cord. The narration then climaxes with the nightmare vision of all mothers: the baby is dead.

During her first imprisonment, Barrios de Chungara had almost believed her incarcerators' lies when they claimed to have imprisoned her children. Unlike Ginzburg and Sikakane, she was ready to sign papers, to betray others, if it would save her children. One of her fellow prisoners forced her to reconsider, however, by reminding her that she must think as a leader, not as a mother (125). Barrios de Chungara followed the advice. Even the painful loss of her baby during her second imprisonment led to reaffirmation of a political identity: "With everything I'd suffered in the arrests, in jail, and in Los Yungas, I'd acquired a political consciousness. In other words, I'd found myself" (160).

That self, as the "testimony" of her narrative demonstrates, is a spokesperson for the marginalized—the workers and even the peasants of Bolivia. Like Sikakane, Barrios de Chungara invokes the pronoun "we," but in this narrative, it appears in political statements on behalf of groups like the Housewives' Committee: "We think our liberation consists primarily in our country being freed forever from the yoke of imperialism" (41). The plurality suggested by this statement seems strictly rhetorical, however; it does not convey the communal or collective sense of shared experience that Sikakane creates.

Barrios de Chungara would probably not mind having her speech labeled "rhetorical"; she emphasizes that her narrative is didactic and clearly expresses its purpose in the book's concluding paragraph:

> ... this testimony now returns to the working class so that ... [it] can learn from the experiences, analyze and also learn from the mistakes we've committed in the past, so that through correcting these errors we'll be able to do better things in the future ... see the reality of our country and create our own instruments to improve our struggle.... (235)

Unlike the other writers in this study, Barrios de Chungara has constructed her narrative for one specific audience, and she has deliberately had her story transcribed into writing so that it can serve as a permanent blueprint for her audience. Speaking to and for others, Barrios de Chungara comes to authorship and voice in a unique way. Nonetheless, her opening words in *Let Me Speak!* could apply equally well to the other writers discussed in this paper: "I don't want anyone at any moment to interpret the story I'm about to tell as something that is only personal" (15).

All of these women authors of contemporary prison narratives have developed voices that in some way incorporate those of others. The resulting concept of self projected by the narrative participates in a group as well as an individual identity. No longer do such women write confessionally, acknowledging a transgression against their society's laws or mores. Instead, as a result of the political awareness they develop or deepen through the prison experience, each is able to identify the injustices in her society that have resulted in incarceration. Coming to voice in her writing, each author counters the stereotype of the silent, passive, conforming woman, the role prescribed for her as prisoner and citizen, whether in the capitalist, communist, or Third World. Refusal and subversion are both strategies employed by women in prison, and articulating them in a narrative allows women to counter the male prison voice that has spoken so dominantly, with images of destruction and transcendence.

The four women in this study have drawn on numerous genres to construct their narratives, including oral history, testimony, traditional autobiography, letter, diary, and textbook. Not satisfied with the spoken and written word alone, they have used photographs, maps, sketches, and statistics to communicate their stories. Most significantly, in addition to contributing new voices and new literary constructs within their narratives, these writers reflect triumphs external to narrative: release, escape, acquittal, social change. In such a way, the individual, communal, and political truly merge.

Works Cited

Abramowitz, Isidore, ed. *The Great Prisoners: The First Anthology of Literature Written in Prison.* New York: Dutton, 1946.

Akhmatova, Anna. *The Complete Poems of Anna Akhmatova.* Vol. 2. Trans. Judith Hemschemeyer. Somerville, MA: Zephyr, 1990.

Barrios de Chungara, Domitila, and Moema Viezzer. *Let Me Speak! Testimony of Domitila, A Woman of the Bolivian Mines.* Trans. Victoria Ortiz. New York: Monthly Review Press, 1978. Trans. of *"Si me permiten hablar..."* *testimonio de Domitila, una mujer de las minas de Bolivia.*

Camus, Albert. *The Rebel: An Essay on Man in Revolt.* Trans. Anthony Bower. New York: Knopf, 1957. Trans. of *L'Homme révolté.* 1951.

Deming, Barbara. *Prison Notes.* New York: Grossman Publishers, 1966.

Foucault, Michel. *Discipline and Punish: The Birth of the Prison.* Trans. Alan Sheridan. New York: Pantheon, 1977. Trans. of *Surveiller et punir: Naissance de la prison.* 1975.

Franklin, H. Bruce. *The Victim as Criminal and Artist: Literature from the American Prison.* New York: Oxford UP, 1978.

Gelfand, Elissa. *Imagination in Confinement: Women's Writings from French Prisons.* Ithaca, New York: Cornell UP, 1983.

Ginzburg, Eugenia Semyonovna. *Journey into the Whirlwind.* Trans. Paul Stevenson and Max Hayward. New York: Harcourt Brace and World, 1967. Trans. of *Krutoj Marsrut.*

———. *Within the Whirlwind.* Trans. Ian Boland. New York: Harcourt Brace Jovanovich, 1979.

Harlow, Barbara. "From the Women's Prison: Third World Women's Narratives of Prison." *Feminist Studies* 12.3 (1986): 501–24.

Salisbury, Harrison. "Loyalty Was the Error." Rev. of *Journey into the Whirlwind,* by Eugenia Ginzburg. *New York Times Book Review* 19 November 1967: 4.

Scheffler, Judith. *Wall Tappings: An Anthology of Writings by Women Prisoners.* Boston: Northwestern Press, 1986.

Sikakane, Joyce. *A Window on Soweto.* London: International Defence and Aid Fund, 1977.

6 Sacriture: The Sacred as a Literary Genre

Mackie J. V. Blanton
University of New Orleans

Of all the questions we might confront ourselves with, one of the most puzzling, notes Isaac Bashevis Singer, is "Why must we die?" (qtd. in Farrell 200). This question, of course, remains unanswered—but this does not necessarily mean that it is unanswerable. Indeed, the fact that it is unanswered and yet continually asked suggests that perhaps it is answerable, and thus various cultures and civilizations take their turn in formulating an answer—or rather, a response. The more we look through the history of our species, the more we realize that the interesting questions in life are not so much those with answers as those that elicit responses, for such questions challenge the species and its cultures to evolve, both morally and intellectually. The responses become stories, narrative moments for us, about each brief stay of a life on earth. Because these narratives attempt to explain or solve the riddle of human existence, they become, over time, sacred reckonings. They are what I call (borrowing from Lacan's "stécriture," the discourse of the state) *sacriture*—the discourse of the sacred. Sacriture constitutes our stories.

Hence, the most puzzling of questions leads, in our attempt to respond, to yet another question—"Why do we tell stories?" Perhaps we do so simply because we must die; perhaps we die so that some of us may tell stories for all of us before each of us does individually die. Our stories, therefore, are ways we work out narrative explanations of human nature; they are ways of leaving a record behind; for these reasons, they are sacred to us. And so, perhaps the purpose of undecipherable death is that it leads to the question about death, for without death perhaps we would not turn toward ourselves and toward one another with narrative explanations. If we did not die, we perhaps would not pay attention to life. Perhaps the purpose of the bewildering question about our death is that, to respond to it, we must all see ourselves as open texts where the real answer—the real story—might lurk.

The differences that separate the world's religions may seem so overwhelming as to deny one another's existence. It is, however, their like-mindedness, their shared traits, that must become evident to students of sacred discourse. And in order to recognize these commonalities, the student of sacriture must recognize an alternative, sacred concept of time, one put forth by Steinsaltz in *The Essential Talmud*: "Time is not an ever-flowing stream in which the present always obliterates the past; it is understood organically as a living and developing essence, present and future being founded on the living past" (8). Because the present is where we experience change and flexibility, it is apparently the present that is mutable while the past is immutable. But the work of creation is self-renewing, ongoing into the present, and therefore what is immutable is always part of our own essence— which originated in the past—and of the essence of the sacred, which is unoriginate. This is the essential living past on which we raise the present and the future.

We query the living past, not because we doubt, but as if we doubted. Expressing a sense of doubt, questioning the original sacred books, is not only expected in the practice of sacred language, but it is also indispensable to sacred study. Indeed, this questioning, which is essential to the practice of sacred language, is how the present and the future speak to us in the organic, living past. It is as if the sacred (or the divine) through us is continually saying at the moment of creation, "What shall I do next?" And we are the ones who have the opportunity to respond. But we respond by asking further questions—of ourselves. We also query. Our querying is a response to the divine question.

One who studies sacred language is not able to act like an editor who refuses to publish your thoughts on a topic because of the contradictions or the incompleteness in the work submitted. These contradictions must be encountered, and therefore released, by others, who also find release in the process. The submission—the offer—of a work, like the work of creation, is a never-ending, self-renewing process. "After absorbing the basic material," Steinsaltz explains, students are expected to pose questions to themselves and to others and to "voice doubts and reservations.... True knowledge can only be attained through spiritual communion, and the student must participate intellectually and emotionally... becoming, to a certain degree, a creator" (9).

At some beginning point, a single individual or a small group within a community initiates "the basic material" of an ever-evolving sacriture. One of these individuals will develop some explanation regarding creation, or the environment, or some phenomenon in nature not yet perceived as natural and taken, therefore, as a miracle or as supernatural; and feeling inspired, even divinely inspired, this seer will talk about his or her hunches with others. At subsequent times, the rest of us open up those canons, thereby creating commentaries on the basic material. We do this by becoming interpreters, by finding ourselves in the very basic conversations. The commentaries are responses and, as responses inducing further responses, become part of an endless chain. And thus we see that it is the manner rather than the content that becomes the praxis of texts of sacred conversation. We listen in order to respond, in order to interpret.

Eventually, the content of sacred conversations become recorded on stone and, over time, scribbled on papyrus or parchment, or keystroked across a computer screen. This sacred discourse may assume any one of a number of possible forms when it is written: it may appear as different editions of a text or as translations of an original edition or as commentaries on an edition or as commentaries on commentaries. The sacred text may also take the form of prophecies, proverbs, songs and hymns, news announcements (i.e., gospels), letters, enactments, laws, and commandments. Wisdom literature as a form or structure may also be received into a culture as illustrations, glossaries, bibliographies, or indices. And so, a thought or hunch has become a conversation and discussion; the conversation and discussion eventually become stories. The oral stories eventually become oral traditions. Oral traditions become written traditions. Traditions generate commentaries and glossaries. So a hunch or thought about the sacred eventually generates forms that converse with us in ongoing, textualized sacred conversations.

All sacred texts, then, start from a posed question—and the rest is commentary on that question. At times "the rest" becomes basic scripture or evolving, spiritual, canonical commentary on what emerges as the basic canon. To a certain extent, all exegetical commentary is framed by questions and responses. In sacred study, scripture is a statement, a declaration. When we read a literature of this sort as a context for making potentially universal statements, we reconstruct the question that we assume must have been posed in the first place, that engendered the declarations that became sacred scripture. In other words, all thoughts originating as questions are themselves responses to prior questions. A truly sacred text is one that encourages others to question it.

Sacriture offers the study of *the sacred* as a literary genre, focusing on selections from the exoteric and esoteric writings of believing communities, perhaps thereby also providing a close examination of the history, demographics, and linguistics of the mystical experiences of the peoples under discussion. But the course of study I am suggesting here would not be a focus on religions (religions do not occupy the living past: they carve out blocks of time into present and future in order to justify a personal historicism or to guarantee a not-yet-here future existence). Nor would our course be a mere accounting of the sacred in secular literature; that too would be an altogether different course. I am more interested in how a sense of the sacred arises in the first place; in an examination of the presence of the sacred as a literary and linguistic experience; in how the genre of the sacred is constituted by language, by experience, and by interpretation.

Literary genres do not exist because categories exist. Literary genres exist because the language of categories exists. "Poetry," "drama," and "the novel" are categories, not genres, just as the poem, the dramatic piece, or the novel is not a genre. The genre is poetic or dramatic or prosodic language. Language is genre. It is the language of the text, not the text itself, nor the category that the text fits into, that is the genre. There is no better evidence to help us understand this concept than the impulse of sacred texts, that is, than the language of sacred texts.

It is through the act of interpretation that we engage the practice of sacred language, not the holy books—such as the Jew's *Tanakh,* or the Christian's *Evangelion,* or the Hindu's *Vedas,* or the Muslim's *Qur'aan*—that contain sacred language. The sacred dwells in these holy books, as it does in human nature; but these books, like human beings, become open canons when, through interpretation, we open them, releasing the sacred through the furthering practice of language.

Sacred texts are a presentation of the intuited presence of the sacred. Sacred language is a theory about human spiritual intuition. As linguists, critical analysts, teachers, rabbis, or priests, we may choose any number of ways to objectify sacred language, in order to instruct it, for example, or simply to describe it for others. Furthermore, in some way, as we converse about sacred language, we need to demonstrate a belief in the suspected presence of the sacred intuited in language assumed to be sacred. For such a conversation, because of its reverence for the student's intuition and for human intuition in general, can itself become a sacred text. These conversations in the classroom can become inspired responses to the sacred in our midst and act as sources of revelation. It might very well turn out one day that how we revere even seemingly secular subject matter, such as that of the sciences or the liberal arts, can transform these texts into texts of sacred language.

The set of texts that one might select for such a course should range effectively over the rich and varied tradition of teachings and practices of spiritual communities (see the Supplemental Bibliography). The instructor should, to the extent possible, select texts that make all such communities accessible, thereby inspiring the student to further reading and discussion. The major focus in the course will be those primary texts selected for study, interpretation, and analysis, supplemented by critical studies.A primary text is a more direct source to the sacred. But again: we must bear in mind that any text referring to the sacred may become, just because of the way that it is studied, a source leading to the sacred. Inspiration, of course, may very well lead to revelation.

The inevitable outcome of courses in sacriture will be the possibility for a post-postmodern mysticism, for such courses will be examining, and experiencing by examining, the persistent yearnings of human nature for transcendent experience.

Works Consulted

Blanton, Mackie. "Many Sentences and Difficult Texts." In *Language Topics: Essays in Honour of Michael Halliday.* Ed. Ross Steele and Terry Threadgold. Amsterdam: John Benjamins, 1987. 401–11.

———. "Places of the Self: The Good Analytic Hour in Robert Penn Warren." *Arkansas Quarterly* 2.1 (1993): 42–57.

Camphausen, Rufus C. *The Divine Library: A Comprehensive Reference Guide to the Sacred Texts and Spiritual Literature of the World.* Rochester, VT: Inner Traditions International, 1992.

Eliade, Mircea. *The Sacred and the Profane: The Nature of Religion.* 1959. New York: Harcourt Brace Jovanovich, 1987.

Farrell, Grace, ed. *Isaac Bashevis Singer: Conversations.* Jackson: UP of Mississippi, 1992.

Steinsaltz, Adin. *The Essential Talmud.* Trans. Chaya Galai. New York: Basic Books, 1976.

Supplemental Bibliography: Toward a Study of Sacriture

Ariel, David S. *The Mystic Quest: An Introduction to Jewish Mysticism.* New York: Schocken, 1988.

Armstrong, Karen. *A History of God: The Four-Thousand-Year Quest of Judaism, Christianity, and Islam.* New York: Knopf, 1993.

ben haKana, Rabbi Nehunia. *The Bahir.* Translation and commentary by Aryeh Kaplan. York Beach, ME: Samuel Weiser, 1979.

Blofeld, John. *Taoism: The Road to Immortality.* Boston: Shambhala, 1978.

Bloom, Harold. *Kabbalah and Criticism.* New York: Seabury Press, 1975.

————. *Ruin the Sacred Truths: Poetry and Belief from the Bible to the Present.* Cambridge: Harvard UP, 1989.

Climacus, John. *The Ladder of Divine Ascent.* New York: Paulist Press, 1982.

Epstein, Isidore. *Judaism.* New York: Penguin, 1975.

Green, Arthur. *Devotion and Commandment: The Faith of Abraham in the Hasidic Imagination.* Cincinnati: Hebrew Union College P, 1989.

Green, Arthur, and Barry W. Holtz, eds. *Your Word Is Fire: The Hasidic Masters on Contemplative Prayer.* New York: Schocken, 1987.

Giller, Pinchas. *The Enlightened Will Shine: Symbolization and Theory in the Later Strata of the Zohar.* Albany: State U of New York P, 1994.

Helminski, Kabir Edmund. *Living Presence: A Sufi Way to Mindfulness and the Essential Self.* Los Angeles: Jeremy P. Tarcher, 1992.

Ibn, Muhyiddin 'Arabi. *The Wisdom of the Prophets.* Aldsworth, Gloucestershire: Beshara, 1975.

Kaplan, Aryeh. *Sefer Yetzirah: The Book of Creation.* York Beach, ME: Samuel Weiser, 1990.

Kristeva, Julia. *Language—The Unknown: An Initiation into Linguistics.* Trans. Anne M. Menke. New York: Columbia UP, 1989.

Le Gai Eaton, Charles. *Islam and the Destiny of Man.* Albany: The Islamic Texts Society, State U of New York P, 1985.

Mann, John, and Lar Short. *The Body of Light: History and Practical Techniques for Awakening Your Subtle Body.* New York: Globe Press, 1990.

M'Bow, Amadou-Mahtar. *Islam, Philosophy, and Science: Four Public Lectures Organized by UNESCO, June 1980.* Paris: UNESCO, 1981.

Meyendorff, John, ed. and collector. *Gregory Palamas: The Triads.* Trans. Nicholas Gendle. Classics of Western Spirituality Series. New York: Paulist Press, 1983.

Mendes-Flohr, Paul. *Ecstatic Confessions: Collected and Introduced by Martin Buber.* Trans. Esther Cameron. San Francisco: Harper and Row, 1985. From the 1909 German edition.

Mitchell, Stephen. *The Enlightened Heart: An Anthology of Sacred Poetry.* New York: Harper and Row, 1989.

Murata, Sachiko. *The Tao of Islam: A Sourcebook on Gender Relationships in Islamic Thought.* Albany: State U of New York P, 1992.

Nasr, Seyyed Hossein. *Knowledge and the Sacred.* Albany: State U of New York P, 1989.

Neusner, Jacob. *Midrash in Context: Exegesis in Formative Judaism.* Philadelphia: Fortress Press, 1983.

Palmer, G. E. H., Philip Sherrard, and Kallistos Ware. *The Philokalia.* 5 vols. London: Faber and Faber, 1984.

Schmemann, Alexander. *The Eucharist: Sacrament of the Kingdom.* Crestwood, NY: St. Vladimir's Seminary P, 1988.

Schimmel, Annemarie. *Deciphering the Signs of God: A Phenomenological Approach to Islam.* Albany: State U of New York P, 1994.

————. *And Muhammad Is His Messenger: The Veneration of the Prophet in Islamic Piety.* Chapel Hill: U of North Carolina P, 1985.

Scupoli, Lorenzo. *Unseen Warfare: The Spiritual Combat and Path to Paradise of Lorenzo Scupoli.* Crestwood, NY: St. Vladimir's Seminary P, 1987.

Steiner, George. *Real Presences.* U of Chicago P, 1989.

Steinsaltz, Adin. *The Thirteen Petalled Rose.* New York: Basic Books, 1980.

Tigunait, Pandit Rajmani. *Seven Systems of Indian Philosophy.* Honesdale, PA: Himalayan International, 1983.

Tresmontant, Claude. *The Hebrew Christ: Language in the Age of the Gospels.* Chicago: Franciscan Herald P, 1989.

Ware, Kallistos. *The Orthodox Church.* New York: Penguin, 1964.

Weiner, Herbert. *9 1/2 Mystics: The Kabbalah Today.* New York: Collier Books, 1969.

Williams, Benjamin D., and Harold B. Anstall. *Orthodox Worship: A Living Continuity with the Temple, the Synagogue, and the Early Church.* Minneapolis: Light and Life, 1990.

Zalman, Rabbi Schneur (of Liadi). *Likutei Amarim Tanya.* Brooklyn: Kehot Publishing Society, 1984.

Zizioulas, Jean D. *Being as Communion: Studies in Personhood and the Church.* Crestwood, NY: St. Vladimir's Seminary P, 1985.

III Pedagogical and Curricular Concerns

7 Nonnative English Literature and the World Literature Syllabus

Ismail S. Talib
National University of Singapore

Some of the townsmen said Okolo's eyes were not right, his head was not correct. This they said was the result of his knowing too much book, walking too much in the bush, and others said it was due to his staying too long by the river.

So the town of Amatu talked and whispered; so the world talked and whispered. Okolo had no chest, they said. His chest was not strong and he had no shadow. Everything in this world that spoiled a man's name they said of him, all because he dared to search for it. He was in search of *it* with all his inside and with all his shadow.

Okolo started his search when he came out of school and returned home to his people. When he returned home to his people, words of the coming thing, rumours of the coming thing, were in the air flying like birds, swimming like fishes in the river. But Okolo did not join them in their joy because what was there was no longer there and things had no more roots. So he started his search for *it*. And this stopped the Elders from slapping their thighs in joy because of the coming thing.

---

ah beng is so smart,
already he can watch tv & know the whole story.
your kim cheong is also quite smart,
what boy is he in the exam?
this playground is not too bad, but i'm always
so worried, car here, car there.

at exam time, it's worse.

because you know why?

kim cheong eats so little.

give him some complan. my ah beng was like that,
now he's different. if you give him anything
he's sure to finish it all up.

sure, sure. cheong's father buys him
vitamins but he keeps it inside his mouth
& later gives it to the cat.
i scold like mad but what for?
if i don't see it, how can i scold?

on saturday, tv showed a new type,
special for children. why don't you call
his father buy some? maybe they are better.

money's no problem. it's not that
we want to save. if we buy it
& he doesn't eat it, throwing money
into the jamban is the same.
ah beng's father spends so much,
takes out the mosaic floor & wants
to make terrazzo or what.

we also got new furniture, bought from diethelm.
the sofa is so soft. i dare not sit. they all
sit like don't want to get up. so expensive.
nearly two thousand dollars, sure must be good.

that you can't say. my toa-soh
bought an expensive sewing machine,
after 6 months, it is already spoilt.
she took it back . . . . beng,
come here, come, don't play the fool.
your tuition teacher is coming.
wah! kim cheong, now you're quite big.

come, cheong, quick go home & bathe.
ah pah wants to take you chya-hong in new motor-car.

The first of these two passages is from *The Voice,* by Nigerian novelist
Gabriel Okara; the second is "2 mothers in a h d b playground," by a
Singaporean poet, Arthur Yap. It is obvious that both passages are in
English; it is just as obvious that this is not the kind of English generally
found in the United States, Great Britain, or other predominantly white
Anglophone countries. More important, these two works are from
different parts of the world, reminding us that there is a *world literature
in English.* While this concept is probably unfamiliar to many literary
scholars and teachers, there is in fact a growing body of works in these
new varieties of English, many of which have been favorably judged
indeed. Some of the authors writing in "world English" include Chinua
Achebe, Bessie Head, Ngũgĩ wa Thiong'o (before his abandonment of
English for Gikuyu), Wole Soyinka, Buchi Emecheta, Wilson Harris,
Olive Senior, George Lamming, Raja Rao, Anita Desai, and R. K.
Narayan. There are also several anthologies devoted to world English
(discussed later in this chapter) as well as a number of academic

journals, such as *World Literature Written in English, Kunapipi,* and *ARIEL (A Review of International English Literature)*.

The existence of this rich new literature creates a unique opportunity for the world literature curriculum, for unlike the traditional world literature course, which is heavily reliant on translation (see Aldridge 10–11, 19–25; Block, "Objectives," 5–6; Freedman; Will), a world English syllabus has the major advantage of foregrounding language. As we know, in the traditional world literature course the only linguistic factor that is usually mentioned, if at all, is the accuracy of translation.

The approach proposed here, however, is not without its own language-related problems, particularly regarding the use of dialect. The fear of letting students read dialects, along with a more orthodox concept of comparative literature (see Aldridge 38), has often led to the avoidance of these texts. There is the belief among some teachers of English (a belief that is not always clearly or honestly put) that literature in English should deal with the "best" English, that works in "nonstandard" English are inherently "substandard," and that therefore nonnative English literature has no legitimate place in the curriculum (see Talib, "Why Not Teach . . ." 51). In spite of these inhibitors, the restriction of literature in English to that produced in the traditional countries is no longer possible after the advent of writers such as V. S. Naipaul and Salman Rushdie, who have had a great impact on contemporary literature generally, and on literature in English in particular. Even if we want to regard Naipaul and Rushdie as British writers (since both reside in Britain), we may not be able to understand their works adequately unless we view them in relation to other works in English by other Caribbean and Indian authors.

While the existence of a world literature in English is a *fait accompli,* the presentation of these works in terms of the educational curriculum is not, and the creation of a syllabus based on this new "world English" literature remains problematic. One solution would be to include translated works and divide the course into two units, translated works and works written in English. A syllabus designed in this way could also be used for a comparative literature course (using non-English texts in their original) in which the focus of study would be the similarities and differences between English and non-English texts. This would be particularly important if the course were further focused on the influence that a literature in a particular language may have had on the English texts, as in the case of the direct or indirect influence of the language and literature of Urdu or Hindi on the novels of Amitav Ghosh or Anita Desai (both of whom write in English). One might also recall the influence that East and West Asian literature has had

on European writers, a prominent example being the founder of world
literature himself, Goethe (Alberson 45; Aldridge 30–31; Jackson; Yu).

But there are other programmatic choices; for example, a world
literature in English syllabus might also be designed in relation to a
program in English linguistics; while literary study is generally avoided
or minimized in such programs, in this case there would be a particular
advantage, for texts could be studied not only for their intrinsic merits
(however defined), but also as illustrations of the use of English around
the world. Furthermore, the intimate connection between, on the one
hand, a world literature in English, and, on the other, English as a
world language, is a much-neglected topic, one that could be fruitfully
explored. In this regard, the use of nonnative literary texts in English,
especially those whose language is markedly different from standard
British or American English, would highlight the variety and range of
world English, which would in turn help students understand both the
extent to which English must indeed be regarded as a world language,
with all the attendant complexities that such "worldness" entails. As
mentioned, there is a tendency in linguistics courses to view only
samples of language from literary texts. Viewing these works holistically,
however, is important, not merely for aesthetic reasons: it may facilitate
language teaching as well, for the exclusive reading of extracts may
result in students regarding them as representative of actual language
use, whereas reading entire texts may enable them to understand how
(and why) writers take creative liberties with language.

One linguistic subtlety that could be fruitfully studied would be the
negotiation between dialect and standard English in this literature. For
example, Okara has pointed out that *The Voice* attempts, not a
representation of an actual dialect of nonnative English, but rather a
literary representation of the Ijaw language in English (Lindfors 137–
38). Much the same may be said of Yap's poem, in which there is
frequent and systematic recourse to certain features of English which
one associates with more standardized usage, such as singular number
concord in the verbs ("buys," "keeps," "gives," "spends," "takes," and
"wants"), the simple past tense ("showed," "bought," and "took"), the
copula, which also conforms to the appropriate tense and number of
the subject ("is," "was," and "are"), contracted forms of the copula,
which again conform to the appropriate number concord (as in the
use of "is" and "am" in "i'm," "it's," "he's," "money's," and "you're"),
and contracted forms of auxiliary verbs of negative polarity (as in
"doesn't" and "can't").

The English of many works differs from standard British or American
English only in relation to their lexicons, and even in this regard, there

are usually only a few words not found in standard British or American English, which can be defined in a short glossary at the end of the work. For instance, the problems in understanding Yap's poem are easily cleared up by pointing out to the reader that "what boy in the exam" refers to the boy's academic standing, "jamban" (a Malay word) means "toilet," the verb "chya-hong" (a Hokkien word) refers to the act of taking a ride or of going for a short break, and "h d b" stands for the Singaporean Housing and Development Board. And in Okara's *The Voice,* some expressions ("knowing too much book," "had a chest," "had no shadow," and "in search of *it* with all his inside and with all his shadow"), although apparently derived from Ijaw idioms, are highly effective metaphorical expressions in English, and, in my view, are not more difficult to understand than, for example, the symbolism employed in Yeats's poetry.

A teacher whose primary focus is linguistics may choose excerpts instead of whole texts, or design a nonnative English literature syllabus consisting of short works and extracts from longer works. The extracts must of course be judiciously chosen by the teacher, who should have a good knowledge of the text's source dialect, and who should point out whether it is faithfully represented in the text. The alternative is to depend on a textbook which does this. Unfortunately, such a textbook—a well-annotated anthology consisting of short works and extracts from longer works collected by a group of co-editors, each of whom is conversant with the language and literature of the works he or she selects—is not presently available (although Ramraj's recently published anthology, *Concert of Voices,* is a step in the right direction). Such an anthology might allow a more extensive exploration of texts with different linguistic varieties, which would otherwise be restricted by the limited expertise of the teacher.

In most instances, however, a world literature in English course would not have a rigorous focus on either comparative literature and translation or on linguistics; it would more likely appear in the general education (or "core") curriculum, in which case the main organizational principle would probably (and most effectively) be that of geographic regions. Although the regional grouping of texts may create some pedagogical problems, such as the difficulty of establishing thematic linkages among texts from various regions, not to use a regional organization might result in the erroneous assumption that there is a unity of the various nonnative literatures. While there may be some merit to a thematic organization, a syllabus arranged in accordance with regional categories places texts in appropriate cultural, sociopolitical, and historical contexts, since there is indeed a strong correlation between region and these other contexts. In any case, the regional approach would ultimately make thematic comparisons easier, for such comparisons would be more sophisticated if the student were to first become more familiar with the cultural context of each region.

Once having decided on a regional schema, one must face some logistical problems. It is of course possible to determine a fixed number of texts per geographical category; this may be inevitable if there are separate lecturers dealing with the literature from each region, and each of them has an equal workload. But if the world literature in English course is taught by one person (as is more likely), she or he may wish to use other criteria, which would entail an unequal regional distribution. One criterion which might be used is that of "literary merit." Such a criterion, however, may be too hazy for some, and hence they may employ thematic criteria, which may also entail an unequal number of texts in each geographical category. In that case one might select some additional texts from underrepresented regions, even if they do not strictly meet the valuative and thematic yardsticks set up at the start of the selection procedure. This would serve the purpose of preserving the course's focus on the phenomenon of a newly emergent monolingual world literature.

Another organizational difficulty arises in regard to genre, a familiar method for presenting texts in a general survey course but one which is somewhat problematic when combined with the concepts of world English and regionalism. One could, without too much difficulty, design subunits on fiction, drama, and poetry for each region covered; however, the possibility of dealing with each of the major genres may depend on the availability of texts. This is less of a problem today than it was two or three decades ago; nonetheless, it is still somewhat difficult to provide an equitable selection of texts from each of the designated regions. For example, drama in English appears to be particularly strong in Africa, with such major writers as Athol Fugard and the Nobel Prize–winning Wole Soyinka, but there are at present few published dramatic works of quality from India, Singapore, or Malaysia. Another problem with generic divisions is the underemphasis they may place on some important cross-generic features or themes, such as the nature of the nonnative English used in poetry, drama, and fiction (especially when its nonnative features are striking), and the colonial theme running through works of different genres.

These problems, however, are truly minor ones, particularly when compared to the major educational advantages to be reaped from the development of these courses, one of which would be a more effective presentation of lyric poetry from around the world. It has often been observed that in the case of lyric poetry, the problem of translation is particularly vexing, for the sound, the idiom, and some of the meta-phorical features of short poems are often language-specific, and are indeed virtually untranslatable (Aldridge 30; Will 24–26, 28–29). (For this reason, it is not far-fetched to suggest that if one is interested in literary quality and wishes to give equal treatment to each of the genres in the general world literature syllabus, one would do well to rely heavily on nonnative English poetry in the poetry section of the syllabus, even if one does not want to concentrate on literature originally written in English elsewhere in the syllabus.) Fortunately, there are a number of readily available anthologies which provide us with a representative selection of poetry in English from particular regions, such as *The Heinemann Book of African Poetry in English, Ten Twentieth-Century Indian Poets,* and *The Penguin Book of Caribbean Verse,* which does a particularly good job of presenting the whole range of Caribbean verse, from Bob Marley to Edward Kamau Brathwaite, and includes a number of poems written in varieties of English strikingly different from standard British or American English.

Having discussed some of the problematics of a world English syllabus as well as some of the more narrow, curricular reasons for the creation of such a course, it is time to discuss some of the broader social reasons for instituting such a curricular reform—reasons that are well-illustrated by the first stanza of "The Song of the Banana Man," by Evan Jones:

> Touris, white man, wipin his face,
> Met me in Golden Grove market place.
> He looked at m'ol' clothes brown wid stain,
> An soaked right through wid de Portlan rain,
> He cas his eye, turn up his nose,
> He says, "You're a beggar man, I suppose?"
> He says, "Boy, get some occupation,
> Be of some value to your nation."
>> I said, "By God and dis big right han
>> You mus recognize a banana man."

> (In Burnett 222–24)

One reason such a poem should be taught has to do with linguistic awareness and tolerance, which may in turn have a connection with other values which teachers may want to instill in their students. Literature that uses a distinct nonnative variety of English can be used to enhance the students' cultural identity and their sense of belonging to the community in which the variety is spoken (Talib "Why Not Teach . . ."). And of course, the study of world literature will enhance the students' awareness or understanding of the world at large; this argument is a familiar one, and was in fact advocated by Goethe, the first significant proponent of the teaching of world literature (Alberson 45–51; Friederich 11, 19–22; Williams 76). In addition to these two reasons, we can also advance a more specific integrative aim in relation to the teaching of nonnative English literature as a world literature, and this has to do with an enhanced integration of the worldwide community of English speakers. Many of these speakers do not use standard American or British English, and, as English is now a world language, perhaps the time has come to dissociate English from any simplistic association with one or two of its varieties (see Hope 165; Aldridge 38–39). As I have said elsewhere, the English language "is no longer a British, American, or Anglo-Saxon preserve," but is "a language which is truly international" (Talib, *Letter* 10). Consequently, the norms of usage, especially among peoples that use it as a second (i.e., not as a *foreign*) language, should no longer be invariably established and perpetuated by Britain and the United States (see Kachru; Melchers; Phillipson).

Although the world is saturated with the English language through pop songs, movies, and television, the varieties of English used in these media are largely American or British. There are of course some notable exceptions to this, such as in the field of popular music, with calypso and reggae music from the Caribbean and the use of Black Vernacular English in rap—nonetheless, songs sung with nonnative accents are still relatively rare. The indirect promotion of American and British varieties of English through popular culture (cultural colonialism through inadvertent means) does not give us a true picture of the English language today. As popular culture, at least in its usual forms, cannot help to expose students to non-American or non-British varieties of English, especially within America or Britain itself, one of the ways students can gain such exposure (quite apart from undergoing a course in "global English" [Melchers]), is through a course in nonnative English literature, with a representative selection of texts such as those quoted earlier. Such a course will put students in a better position to understand the "naturalness" of nonnative varieties of English in countries outside America or Britain, and the anomaly of the attempt to conform to standard American or British English in these countries. This will in turn help them develop not only an awareness of, but also an appreciation for, other varieties of English, which will in turn enhance their awareness of English as a world language. Given the importance of English in the world, such an awareness and appreciation may contribute to international understanding as well.

Works Cited

Alberson, Hazel S. "Non-Western Literature in the World Literature Program." Block, *Teaching* 45–52.

Aldridge, A. Owen. *The Reemergence of World Literature: A Study of Asia and the West.* Newark: U of Delaware P; London: Associated U Presses, 1986.

Block, Haskell M. "The Objectives of the Conference." Block, *Teaching* 1–7.

———, ed. *The Teaching of World Literature.* Proceedings of a Conference at the University of Wisconsin. 24–25, April 1959. Chapel Hill: U of North Carolina P, 1960.

Burnett, Paula, ed. *The Penguin Book of Caribbean Verse in English.* London: Penguin, 1986.

Freedman, Ralph. "Correlating the Teaching of Literature in Translation." Block, *Teaching* 109–19.

Friederich, Werner P. "On the Integrity of Our Planning." Block, *Teaching* 9–22.

Hope, A. D. "Teaching Australian Literature." *The Literary Criterion* 15.3/4 (1980): 157–65.

Jackson, C. T. "Oriental Ideas in American Thought." *Dictionary of the History of Ideas.* Vol. 3. Ed. Philip P. Wiener. New York: Charles Scribner's, 1973. 427–39.

Jones, Evan. "The Song of the Banana Man." Burnett 222–24.

Kachru, Braj B. "Institutionalized Second Language Varieties." In *The English Language Today.* Ed. Sidney Greenbaum. Oxford: Pergamon, 1985. 211–26.

Lindfors, Bernth. Interview with Gabriel Okara. *World Literature Written in English* 12 (1973): 133–41.

Maja-Pearce, Adewale, comp. and ed. *The Heinemann Book of African Poetry in English.* Jordan Hill, Oxford: Heinemann, 1990.

———. Introduction. *The Heinemann Book of African Poetry in English.* xiii–xvi.

Melchers, Gunnel. "Teaching 'Global English.' " In *A Sense of Place: Essays in Post-Colonial Literatures.* Ed. Britta Olinder. Gothenburg: English Dept. of Gothenburg U, 1984. 210–25.

Okara, Gabriel. *The Voice.* London: Heinemann, 1964.

Parthasarathy, R., comp. and ed. *Ten Twentieth-Century Indian Poets.* Delhi: Oxford UP, 1976.

Phillipson, Robert. "ELT: The Native Speaker's Burden?" *The English Language Teaching Journal* 46 (1992): 12–18.

Ramraj, Victor J. *Concert of Voices: An Anthology of World Writing in English.* Petersborough, ON, Canada: Broadview P, 1995.

Rao, Raja. "The Caste of English." *Awakened Conscience: Studies in Commonwealth Literature.* Ed. C. D. Narasimhaiah. New Delhi: Sterling P, 1978. 420–22.

Talib, Ismail S. Letter. *The Council Chronicle* 1.5 (June 1992): 10.

———. "Why Not Teach Non-Native English Literature?" *The English Language Teaching Journal* 46 (1992): 51–55.

Will, Frederic. "The Evaluation and Use of Translations." Block, *Teaching* 23–30.

Williams, Weldon M. "Intensive and Extensive Approaches in the Teaching of World Literature." Block, *Teaching* 73–81.

Yap, Arthur. "2 Mothers in an HDB Playground." *Down the Line*. Singapore: Heinemann, 1980. 54–55.

Yu, Beongcheon. *The Great Circle: American Writers and the Orient*. Detroit: Wayne State UP, 1983.

8 Contemporary Latin American Theater: Theatricality as a Key to Classroom Performance

Howard M. Fraser
College of William and Mary

Teachers have frequently assumed the role of actor on classroom stages before their student audiences; they may, however, find that by replacing this more traditional role with a new one—that of *director*—they will produce more acute and varied stimuli for class discussion. This revision of roles is particularly valuable in courses dedicated to literature in languages other than English, where heightened proficiency in the target language serves, not only as an end in itself, but also as a means for communicating the literary values of foreign cultures. This directorial approach, moreover, is, in general, open-ended, sensitive to students' differing personalities and learning styles, and regards class members as capable of developing and refining their productive and receptive language skills at the same time that they master the content of the literary selections.

Plays such as the Mexican Emilio Carballido's "El censo," the Cuban Antón Arrufat's "La repetición," the Argentinean Sergio Vodanović's "El delantal blanco," and (also Argentinean) Griselda Gámbaro's "El campo" use theatricality as a means to revise the traditional boundaries between actors and their audiences. It seems appropriate, therefore, that in the teaching of these works the traditional roles played by teachers and students might also be revised.

An excellent point of departure for our interactive, theatrically based course is Carballido's "El censo." This one-act play combines several themes associated with the modern era, principally that of a world turned upside down, expressed within a thoroughgoing theatrical framework. In "El censo," the setting is appropriately theatrical: a Mexican seamstresses' shop located in a private home. For obvious reasons, this dual setting is the source of considerable dramatic tension. When a census-taker arrives, the owner of the shop and his workers close ranks to act out a play within a play. Thinking that the census-taker will report their illegal home industry to the government, they pretend that they are the members of a family and not workers in a private enterprise. Their anxiety over being found out is matched by that of the census-taker. In fear of losing his job for falling behind in his daily quota of interviews, he rashly accepts their advice and assistance to falsify census interviews. The end of the play brings the question of deceit and theatricality full circle when the seamstresses expertly combine their wit and instinct for survival as they and the census-taker embroider upon the truth and, in so doing, reveal the fabrication and fiction that are the basis of the government's records.

One way in which the instructor can prepare students for class discussion is with questions referring to the construction of the play, and one reference tool that is exceptionally useful in this regard is *Aproximaciones al estudio de la literatura hispánica.* This is an anthology of literary texts covering four genres (narrative, poetry, drama, essay) and their historical backgrounds and basic structures, as well as a glossary of critical terminology and a reader's guide that prompts students to discover the most salient points of the literary works under study. The "Guida general para el drama" contains questions such as "¿Cuál es el marco escénico de la obra? ¿Se explica en detalle o no?": "¿Quiénes son los personajes y cuáles son las relaciones entre ellos? ¿Cuáles son actores y cuáles son actantes?"; "¿Qué situación dramática se presenta en la obra? ¿Cómo progresa la acción de la obra? ¿Cuáles son las etapas de esa acción?"; "¿Cuál es el tema principal de la obra? ¿Cuáles son los temas secundarios? ¿Tiene la obra un fin didáctico o comprometido?" The list also contains more challenging questions, such as: "En la obra, ¿se pone más énfasis en la creación de una empatía entre actor y espectador (lector) o en una separación sentimental y un acercamiento intelectual a la situación dramática? ¿Hay ejemplos de metateatro?" (229).

Work in small groups (of no more than four students each) should also be one of the principal organizing features of class discussions for this kind of course, for such groups permit students to interact more freely and express themselves at length in the target language. Furthermore, students who would otherwise seem shy and who might feel intimidated by the presence of students in a larger class will typically speak more in a smaller group and will gain self-confidence throughout the semester. The composition of groups should change daily so that students are eventually grouped with all others in the class. Operating independently for ten to twenty minutes during class, each group should have a specific assignment (such as one or two of the above list of study questions) to accomplish.

In "El censo," students should be able to develop these basic questions into fuller commentary upon the dual setting, which mirrors the general sense of confusion and ambiguity evident in this farcical play. In a sense, the world of appearances and deceit staged in the seamstresses' shop is clearly distinguished from the so-called real world as expressed from the point of view of the shop's clientele at the start of the play. Disorder and the chaotic obliteration of this division take hold of the action once the census-taker enters the shop, ultimately infecting the entire world surrounding the play. The deceptive atmosphere of the seamstresses' shop serves as a microcosm of the society out of which it grows because it reflects the sham of a census that is the government's claim to accuracy and truth.

Because the visual impression a theatrical production makes affects the viewer's and reader's understanding of the play, one group might work on proposing a set design to the class that places the actors and props in strategic locations. In this way, students will call attention to objects crucial to the play's development (i.e., a deforming mirror, sewing machines, etc.) and explain how they enhance its meaning.

Another excellent play for our purposes here is Arrufat's "La repetición," which, with its masked characters and symbolic settings, entails to a remarkable degree a theatrical vision of the world. Even the title underscores the notion of the play within a play, for "repetición" suggests that the play's action ends poised to repeat itself, thus producing an infinite series of identically circular plots which reiterate the main action endlessly. As a commentary on the futility and pessimism of modern life (Dauster 9), notions reinforced by the image of circularity, "La repetición" presents the story of two women who live in structurally similar apartments. Despite their similarities, however, the two apartments symbolize the cruel passage of time that has left the dwelling of the downstairs neighbor, an older, married woman, in disarray and disrepair. Her furniture is old and soiled; her household plants, withered. In contrast, in the young woman's upstairs apartment, pots and pans shine in the afternoon sun, and her plants flourish. Her youth and vitality soon attract the attentions of a door-to-door salesman, who asks her out to a Saturday night dance. His interest in her suggests the possibility of change, perhaps progress, in her life, but this bright promise fades as rapidly as it arrived. After the salesman leaves, the young woman descends to her neighbor's apartment, enters and exchanges masks with her, thus closing the circle which opened at the outset of the play.

Students should, first and foremost, be able to visualize the set design, complete with details of the placement of furnishings and significant objects, in order to comment on the similarities and differences in the two apartments. Of particular interest is the stairway which connects the two places. Reinforcing the play's action and themes, this winding stairway ("escalera de caracol") denotes physically what is suggested by the action: repetition, reiteration, and circularity. In another sense, it serves to remind the audience of the futility associated with the women's desire for change and progress. As the play opens, the downstairs neighbor bewails her poverty and the stagnation in her life with the lament: "Te digo que es imposible vivir así. . . . ¿No te parece que ya va siendo hora de que las cosas cambien?" (39). As she contemplates her arid future, she sees the only possibility of change and prosperity in the hope of winning the lottery. In this regard, students should discuss her statement, "La cosa es entrar en el juego" (40), as a statement with a broad and ambiguous set of possible references— as much in praise of the sense of chance in each of the women's lives as an acknowledgment of the absurd nature of life without meaning and substance.

The teacher should propose several areas for class discussion that focuses on characters, their masks as an indication of how people play roles in daily life, the use of time, both in the pacing of the action and in its treatment as a thematic underpinning of the work, and universal themes such as our need for routine, the nature of work, and the possibility of change.

Role-playing and the need for change form the backdrop of Vodanović's "El delantal blanco." Perhaps the most disquieting portrait of modern life turned upside down included in these one-act plays, this piece highlights the characters' sense of frustration brought about by society's inertia and injustice. An article of clothing, the white uniform of the title, becomes the symbol of the gross disparities between social classes in the Latino world, as characterized by a wealthy woman, "La Señora," and her maid, "La Empleada."

While on summer vacation at the beach, "La Señora" discusses her desire to see the world from the maid's perspective, and so they exchange clothes. More than merely to overcome her boredom and loneliness, the wealthy woman chooses this theatrical ploy to prove her hypothesis that "clase," i.e. her innate personal style, social position and status, will still be visible through the maid's attire. Once they change their appearance, however, the Señora's theory of her innate power disintegrates as the Empleada assumes the imperious identity of her employer. The action moves toward a shocking climax when the Señora, now entangled in the dramatic intrigue she herself has written, asks spectators on the beach to restore her to her original role but fails to convince them that the Empleada is an impostor.

I have found that students are often fascinated by the various treatments in this play of the theme of power, which takes the form of domination in marriage, in the family, and in employment. Of course, questions of social injustice are foremost in the piece as well as the general theme of freedom as it applies to these two women who are, both in their own ways, captives within a rigid social system. As evidence of society's semiotic nature, clothing serves to broadcast distinctions such as class, position, and wealth for each of the characters. To the extent that these same distinctions form a part of their own complex system of signs and values, students will be eager to discuss how clothing functions within a theatrical social setting, both as costumes and masks in their own lives.

One of the principal questions groups should address in their class discussions is Vodanović's choice of the beach as the setting of the play. Early on, the Señora criticizes her son for toppling his sister's sand castle. This offstage gesture immediately disarms the spectator by describing one of the innocuous pastimes of life at the seashore. Events and statements occurring later in the piece, however, indicate that the destruction of the sand castle is a central image of the play, which is reflected in the Señora's unsatisfactory marriage to an absent, philandering husband and whose most violent reflection is the symbolic exile of the Señora herself at the end of the play as she is dethroned by her own Empleada. For this reason, the seemingly offhand remark a spectator makes upon witnessing the struggle between the two women is bitterly ironic. When "El caballero distinguido" says, "Es el símbolo de nuestro tiempo. . . . La subversión del orden establecido. Los viejos quieren ser jóvenes; los jóvenes quieren ser viejos; los pobres quieren ser ricos y los ricos quieren ser pobres" (12–13), he unwittingly describes the somewhat bizarre transfer of clothing and roles that the audience has witnessed, although he thinks he is referring to the Señora's unsuccessful attempt to restore herself to power.

But there is another irony here as he adds, "Mi nuera va todas las tardes a tejer con mujeres de poblaciones callampas. ¡Y le gusta hacerlo!" (13). As he scoffs at the attempts his daughter-in-law makes to work joyfully side by side with women in the slums of the city, he draws a very sharp distinction between the situation in his family and the spectacle we have just witnessed on stage. He seems to say that the sharing of life's meager meal is possible, as in his daughter-in-law's case, but this kind of demonstration of sisterly love should not become an everyday occurrence.

Since "El delantal blanco" directly comments on the act of role-playing, it is a particularly good choice for one of the most compelling directorial methods, one which allows the students a more dramatic involvement in the action of the play through a dramatic reading or role-playing. Depending on the interests and talents of the students, the reading of a portion of a play can be a valuable first step in their comprehension of the language as well as of the psychological dynamism of the characters. If the students demonstrate fascination with the characters, or sense an affinity with them, the teacher may wish to organize a panel or roundtable discussion in which the dramatic characters themselves appear to exchange ideas. Students may volunteer to assume the roles of the characters and express opinions as these characters. The teacher or other class members should feel free to ask the student role-players questions about their actions and attitudes relevant to the action of the play. Or students speaking through their characters may speculate on their responses to contemporary issues and individuals.

An excellent companion piece to "El delantal blanco" is a full-length play by Griselda Gámbaro, "El campo," whose central theme is society's injustice toward women. While referring to the horrors of the Holocaust by setting the main action in a concentration camp, Gámbaro's drama simultaneously focuses upon the systematic use of torture and repression in Nazi Germany, Vietnam (Cypess 103), and Argentina during the "Dirty War" (1976–82) (Albuquerque 141; Taylor 10). The play contains an exhaustive inventory of violent acts, including physical and verbal abuse directed principally toward Emma, a woman prisoner, as well as toward Martín, an accountant who arrives to organize the camp's finances but who finally discovers that chaos and irration-ality rule in such a place.

As dramatic spectacle, "El campo" projects a series of stimuli which assault the audience's senses. References to the odor of burning flesh, the sounds of dogs barking, and the images of acts of torture present the full range of techniques of repression that shock yet edify the audience.

As a reflection of the human deformity cultivated in this camp, the systematic distortion and subversion of language by the camp's director, appropriately named "Franco," might stimulate class discussion. Students should be sensitive to the use of euphemisms and other forms of verbal deception as weapons used to control victims of a complex and inhuman institution such as the Holocaust. For example, when Emma states, "El trabajo engendra libertad" (Work brings freedom) she utters a sentence which contains various half-truths. Of course, this statement translates the phrase emblazoned over Auschwitz ("Arbeit macht Frei") and thus parrots the Nazi's deception of camp prisoners regarding their role in the Wehrmacht. But Emma also underlines how the concept of "freedom" has been redefined in this camp to justify suffering and death as the reward for her labor and that of other victims. Other deceptions, such as the roles characters play within the play, serve as Brechtian distancing techniques in "El campo" that further underscore the importance of fraud as an underpinning of the theatricality of the Holocaust.

To focus class discussion on Gámbaro's use of theatricality, the teacher might have students pay special attention to the staged movements and gestures of the characters. Emma's seemingly uncontrollable scratching, for example, suggests the presence of insect infestations or of a paranoid obsessive-compulsive disorder, and is thus symptomatic of the infectious dehumanization fostered by the camp. Such gestures as Emma exhibits reinforce the sense of corruption that saturates the camp, especially in the person of Franco, himself a Kafkaesque insectoid.

Since "El campo" provides a sustained examination of the use and abuse of language, it is an excellent opportunity to employ an activity that combines all receptive and productive language skills. This method requires that class members first write critical comments about one or more aspects of the play they have read and then form groups to collect all of their comments about a single aspect. After groups discuss these comments, the reporters summarize each group's observations, which are then "published"—i.e., distributed to the class and the teacher for further comment. For best results, the teacher should schedule this activity several times, most effectively late in the semester when the students have refined their oral and written expression to such a extent that they feel comfortable writing for an audience of their peers as well as receiving and transmitting the opinions of others. Students should feel free to write whatever they think about the subject the teacher poses for their response and to write anonymously; and group members will collect, react to, and summarize their peers' comments and will not criticize them judgmentally.

In addition to the directorial teaching techniques presented herein, the teacher should, as in other courses devoted to literature, make basic reference tools available to students. Whether these be histories of theater or articles relating to individual authors and works, critical sources will aid teachers and students in shaping a vocabulary they will use in the course as well as in providing a body of critical judgments that are essential to supporting the students' own research and written work. In addition to the material in *Aproximaciones,* useful critical discussions of contemporary Latin American drama may be found in Leon F. Lyday and George W. Woodyard's *Dramatists in Revolt: The New Latin American Theater,* William I. Oliver's *Voices of Change in the Spanish American Theater,* and George E. Wellwarth's *The New Wave Spanish Drama: An Anthology.* And recent books by Diana Taylor (*Theatre of Crisis: Drama and Politics in Latin America*) and Severino João Albuquerque (*Violent Acts: A Study of Contemporary Latin American Theatre*) highlight the context of violence, political and social, which forms a strong undercurrent of contemporary Latin American drama.

From these sources as well as other recent essays (Stephen M. Hart's "Some Examples of the *Topos* of the World Upside-Down in Modern Hispanic Literature and Art"; Evelyn Picon Garfield and Ivan A. Schulman's *Las entrañas del vacío: Ensayos sobre la modernidad hispanoamericana*), several themes emerge which characterize contemporary Latin American literature in general and the theater in particular. The instructor might discuss the vision of life in the Latin American world as depicted in specific plays. Furthermore, while the subject of theatricality as an organizing principle for a course in literature has received limited attention in scholarly literature, two relatively recent studies of this topic should be considered essential focal points for future discussions: David Gies's *Performance Guides to Spanish Texts* (1987, 1989), and M. Clare Mather's article, "Getting Off the Page and Making a Scene: Teaching Drama in the Classroom" (1989). Both of these works comment upon the energy teachers are able to instill in their students through the use of theater in the classroom, whether this activity be the adaptation to the stage of a work of fiction or poetry (Gies) or the theatrical performance of a text included in a drama course (Mather).

The expansion of the instructor's repertoire of teaching functions to include directing alongside acting permits greater flexibility in organizing and managing stimulating class discussions. Students appreciate the variety of activities used in the class as a means to discuss the works in depth. Because they are expected to generate much of the class discussion, students feel responsible for the success of the course, and they take advantage of the instructor's invitation to participate more effectively than they might under other circumstances. It is hoped that these approaches and practical suggestions for a new theatrical approach to a course on Latin American drama may be adapted to a variety of courses in literature in which all participants will enjoy taking an active role in developing their ideas while refining their language skills. Given that the dramatic works discussed here present characters who feel victimized by the profound changes running rife in modern society, and who ultimately discover that the world defies empirical analysis because of the deceptive appearances, illusions, and general disorientation of the modern age, it seems particularly appropriate that in teaching these works we employ methods that underscore the theatricality of their construction as well as the humanity of their vision.

Works Consulted

Albuquerque, Severino João. *Violent Acts: A Study of Contemporary Latin American Theatre*. Detroit: Wayne State UP, 1991.

Arrufat, Antón. "La repetición." Dauster and Lyday, 39–50.

Buero Vallejo, Antonio. *En la ardiente oscuridad*. New York: Scribner's, 1969.

———. *Historia de una escalera*. Madrid: Escelicer, 1972.

Carballido, Emilio. "El censo." Dauster and Lyday, 55–65.

Chang-Rodríguez, Raquel, and Malva E. Filer. *Voces de Hispanoamérica*. Boston: Heinle and Heinle, 1988.

Cypess, Sandra Messinger. "The Plays of Griselda Gámbaro." In *Dramatists in Revolt: The New Latin American Theater*. Ed. Leon F. Lyday and George W. Woodyard. Austin: U of Texas P, 1976. 95–109.

Dauster, Frank. "The Theater of Antón Arrufat." Lyday and Woodyard 3–18.

Dauster, Frank, and Leon F. Lyday. *En un acto: Diez piezas hispanoamericanas*. 2d ed. Boston: Heinle and Heinle, 1983.

Dauster, Frank, Leon Lyday, and George Woodyard, eds. *Nueve dramaturgos hispanoamericanos*. 3 vols. Ottawa: Girol Books, 1979.

Gámbaro, Griselda. "El campo." Oliver, 47–103.

Garfield, Evelyn Picon, and Ivan A. Schulman. *Las entrañas del vacío: Ensayos sobre la modernidad hispanoamericana*. Mexico City: Ediciones Cuadernos Americanos, 1984.

Gies, David. *Performance Guides to Spanish Texts* [including Jorge Luis Borges, *Ficciones*; Miguel de Cervantes Saavedra, *Don Quijote de la Mancha*; Federico García Lorca, *Romancero gitano* y *Bodas de sangre*; Gabriel García Márquez, *El coronel no tiene quien le escriba*; Ana María Matute, *Historias de la Artámila*; Pablo Neruda, *Veinte poemas de amor* y *Canto general*; Miguel de Unamuno, *San Manual Bueno, Mártir*]. Charlottesville: U of Virginia P, 1987, 1989.

Hart, Stephen M. "Some Examples of the *Topos* of the World Upside-Down in Modern Hispanic Literature and Art." *Revista Canadiense de Estudios Hispánicos* 12 (1988): 459–72.

Lyday, Leon F., and George W. Woodyard, eds. *Dramatists in Revolt: The New Latin American Theater*. Austin: U of Texas P, 1976.

Marqués, René. "Los soles truncos." Dauster, Lyday, and Woodyard 3:7–58.

Mather, M. Clare. "Getting Off the Page and Making a Scene: Teaching Drama in the Classroom." *ADFL Bulletin* 20.2 (Jan. 1989): 58–63.

Oliver, William I., ed. *Voices of Change in the Spanish American Theater: An Anthology.* Austin: U of Texas P, 1971.

Taylor, Diana. *Theatre of Crisis: Drama and Politics in Latin America.* Lexington: UP of Kentucky, 1991.

Virgillo, Carmelo, L. Teresa Valdivieso, and Edward H. Friedman, eds. *Aproximaciones al estudio de la literatura hispánica.* New York: Random House, 1989.

Vodanović, Sergio. "El delantal blanco." Dauster and Lyday, 3–14.

Wellwarth, George E., ed. *The New Wave Spanish Drama: An Anthology.* New York: New York UP, 1970.

9 Mass, Multi, and High: Aeneas, Rambo, and the Pedagogy of "World Lit."

Michael Thomas Carroll
New Mexico Highlands University

One of the most important new college texts is the *Heath Anthology of American Literature* (1990), edited by Paul Lauter, a proponent of canon reform in American literary studies. In this work we witness the attempt of institutionalized literary studies to "correct" itself. There are, for example, excerpts from the literature of Spanish exploration and colonization as a supplement to already familiar works of the English colonial period. Also included are fugitive slave narratives other than that of Frederick Douglass, and more works by contemporary women and minority writers. And so, it would seem, the *Heath* text presents a peaceable kingdom in anthologized form; but before academia begins to congratulate itself for its ability to reformulate around a more inclusive cultural vision, we might want to take a closer look.

In the contemporary section, we find a selection of poetry by Sonia Sanchez. The introduction tells us that if Sanchez's poems are to be appreciated at all, then the reader must "forget all conceptions of what a 'poem' is, and listen attentively to Sanchez's attacks on the Euro-American political, social, and aesthetic establishments." We are furthermore told that the unorthodoxies of Sanchez's poetry must be understood in the social and aesthetic context of African American culture; and that her poetry "echoes the style of popular artists like Aretha Franklin and James Brown" (Joyce 2440). My question is this: if these popular artists are so influential on Sanchez's practice—as indeed they are—then why has *their* work been excluded from this revolutionary anthology, whose overt aim is nothing less than to bring the literary canon into alignment with the diversity of American cultural practice? Why are figures from contemporary music (both black and white) who are, after all, the popular poets of this era, excluded? The answer, of course, is that they are not, in the sense promoted by the academy, "poets." Thus, the editorial stance of the *Heath* doubles back on itself: we are asked to abandon our conceptual baggage regarding what constitutes poetry, and yet in its composition the anthology covertly draws a very clear line between what may be regarded as poetry and what may not. Similar examples include the exclusion from the anthologies of, on the one hand, Charles Bukowski, a poet and fiction writer with a kind of cult status, a sizable international audience, and a penchant for raunch, and on the other hand, the objectivist poets, most notably George Oppen, a "poet's poet" who is perhaps too difficult to "market" in the classroom (see Young, in this anthology).

Another recent anthology whose apparatus suggests similar ideological underpinnings is Donna Rosenberg's *World Mythology,* which likewise, and I think admirably, seeks to correct the academy's Eurocentric predispositions. In addition to the familiar mythology of the Greco-Roman and Norse worlds, Rosenberg has wisely included stories from ancient Babylon, Egypt, India, China, the Americas, and Nigeria. However, the exclusion of anything from the cornucopia of mythological materials to be found in contemporary popular culture encourages the student to view myth as a dead thing. One wishes that the editor had remembered the words of Joseph Campbell, who was well aware of the mythic structure of much of popular culture. "The latest incarnation of Oedipus," says Campbell, stands today at the corner this very afternoon "waiting for the traffic light to change" (4).

In both of these recently published anthologies we witness an expansion of the canon of official culture through the inclusion of non-Western material, and yet an apparent reluctance to deal with materials from popular culture. And just as the *Heath,* in spite of disclaimers to the contrary, endorses an elitist definition of "poetry," so does the Rosenberg anthology endorse a similar concept of "myth." There are numerous examples of this kind of thing; but more to the point, while it is true that the North American academy has opened its arms, perhaps somewhat narrowly, to the productions of other cultures, the culture most familiar and accessible to students, contemporary popular culture, remains, for the most part, excluded. Why?

That we as human beings are "socially constructed" is a truism of contemporary critical theory; this, however, is a rather monolithic rendering of the cultural superstructure, and I think it would be more productive to look at how we are *institutionally constructed.* A methodological point of departure to this end may be found in the "charter theory" of institutional function. According to Bronislaw Malinowski, a myth is a story which serves to provide "charter"— that is, it performs the function of justifying an institution in the present and thus sustaining and ensuring its continuance. To provide some examples: in Max Gluckmann's study of Zulu culture, he concludes that the feud, far from threatening the stability of the culture, actually works to maintain order by providing a "safety valve." More obviously, the "myth" of British royalty serves to strengthen the moral consensus of British society—or so conclude historians Shils and Young in their study of the coronation of Elizabeth II. Institutions, in other words, are, above all, self-perpetuating, and the notion of charter helps explain *how* institutional structures persist while the individuals who constitute them continually change.

However, as the functionalist model has been critiqued for valorizing social stability, it needs to be said that in all cultures (and particularly in dynamic and institutionally diverse ones) much of social change may be understood as the antagonistic interactions of institutions, and that in such an atmosphere of institutional diversity, one institution might gain dominance, cause systemic instability, and thus cause other institutions to fall in line by characterizing themselves in terms of the dominant. Thus, institutions can survive not only by resisting change, but by embracing it, if not in essence then in terms of charter.

Consider, for instance, paradigmatically, the institutional changes that occurred in the eighteenth century. At that time, the scientific and philosophic institutions, which in the preceding centuries had been dominated by the church, now rose to dominance themselves. Advances in the natural sciences occurred at a nearly exponential rate, outstripping philosophy; and philosophy perforce became obsessed with the problems of epistemology, for epistemology is concerned with the grounds and limits of knowledge of the natural world. The arts, too, characterized themselves in terms of rationalism in order to maintain their charter, and thus Samuel Johnson claimed that it is "justly considered as the greatest excellency of art, to imitate nature." There are of course complications and subtleties: Johnson combined this focus on the imitation of nature with the new Protestant, middle-class morality based on self-interest and common sense. The fictional narrative, says Johnson, should "help us avoid the snares which are laid for us by treachery for innocence" and give us "the power of counteracting fraud, without the temptation to practice it" (326)—an ethos best expressed not in Johnson, but in the novels of Samuel Richardson. To know vice from virtue, Johnson would assert, the faculty of reason must be consulted. The institutional strategy implied here—that of an institution characterizing itself in the guise of a more dominant one— is only one of many. The Roman Catholic Church, with Rubens as a kind of ad campaign manager, took the tack of selling what Protestant Rationalism could not—mystery and beauty. In this regard one must also consider Immanuel Kant, whose phenomenological aesthetic, one which valorized complexity over all other considerations, is, in the final essence, the aesthetic of a philosopher and perhaps more important, a mathematician.

There are still other, more radical approaches to shifts in interinstitutional structure. There is the example of Laurence Sterne, who, in *Tristram Shandy,* propounded an aesthetic practice that lionized an unbounded, eccentric creative vision over that of philosophic reason, as seen in his critique of Locke. For example, his preface, which, with typical Shandean wit, appears in the middle of the text, claims that philosophic efforts to separate wit and judgment are unwise, for they "never go together; inasmuch as they are two operations differing from each other as wide as east is from west.—So says Locke;—so are farting and hiccupping, say I" (140). In Sterne, then, we have that segment of the literary establishment that chooses not to characterize itself in terms of the dominant, but rather to challenge the dominant on the basis of art's unique characteristics. As Helene Moglen notes, Sterne's novel is an attempt to supersede philosophy: much more than a "naive disciple of Locke," the hypotheses of the novel "demand that Sterne be taken seriously as a perceptive and creative critic of philosophy" (10).

This kind of complex interinstitutional dynamic has played itself out within the academy, and more specifically in literary studies, in more recent times, and again we witness a number of institutional strategies. Most notable among them are what I regard as the retreat strategy, informed by linguistics, versus the "adjust to the dominant" strategy, characterized by narratology.

The linguistic orientation of much of contemporary literary studies has its roots in Saussurian structuralism, the rudiments of which are familiar but worth reviewing. Saussure describes languages in terms of differential relationships, sign systems which are only (with the exceptions of onomatopoeic words) arbitrarily related to the nonlinguistic objects they name. In other words, language functions not so much because of any relationship between signifier and signified, but because we recognize differences between words—we know "bat" because of its difference from "hat" and "cat," for example (Shumway 161). In the second phase of structuralism—poststructuralism—the connotative power of this system of linguistic difference is deemphasized in favor of the notion that there is always a slippage between signifier and signified, that meanings are always unstable. This view is associated with the philosophy of Jacques Derrida and the Yale School of deconstructive literary criticism (Geoffrey Hartman and Paul De Man)— critical moves which are now somewhat dated yet which have left a firm and admittedly valuable impress on critical thought and methodology. Nonetheless, the linguistic orientation of poststructuralist literary criticism is, in institutional terms, like the New Criticism that preceded it, a centrifugal move, one which attempts (in spite of its own overt declarations) to find safety in some "essence" of literature and language; in short, a secure and isolated base of authority.

Conversely, the movement toward narratology is, in institutional terms, centripetal rather than centrifugal. In *Recent Theories of Narrative,* Wallace Martin notes the shift in critical discourse from "the novel" to "narrative" during the course of the 1960s, but as his purposes lie elsewhere, he does not investigate the institutional causes of this shift. This period saw the rise of communications as an academic discipline, the European "art" film, *auteur* criticism, and, in general, the MacLuhanite assault on the print medium. Given this, it is not surprising that the literary establishment shifted the terms of discussion in order to characterize itself in terms of the dominant and broaden its area of claimed authority to include other narrative forms. In this regard, it is interesting to note the slightly nervous conclusion to Scholes and Kellogg's *Nature of Narrative,* in which the MGM lion, once a bit of kitschy amusement, lies down with the lamb of literature—perhaps with devilish intent. A more recent phenomenon is the movement, in many college philosophy departments, toward the new field of cognitive science, a kind of interdisciplinary phenomenology with the computer as an informing model and metaphor. The institutional strategy, the structural intent, is obvious: as the universities shift their orientation from arts to technologies, the philosophy department attempts to change its now-deadly liberal arts coloration.

Institutional history and the charters or myths that justify the existence of a given institution must be understood in order to grasp the conflict between traditional academic culture and popular culture. The institutional structure of the literary academy has its clearest origins in the rise of the middle-class in (to return there once again) the eighteenth century, an economic event that entailed a new superstructural phenomenon which Jürgen Habermas has termed the liberal bourgeois "public sphere"—the world of coffee houses, discussion groups, and, perhaps most important, journals such as Addison and Steele's *Spectator* with its "gentlemanly" and urbane discourse. As we have looked briefly at religion, aesthetics, and morality during this period, we now need to turn to a detail of the economic/technical superstructure. Starting in the 1730s, the public sphere faced the challenge of increased "bookseller power" and by midcentury the establishment of "the profession of letters" as the obsolete system of literary patronage gave its slow death rattle (Eagleton 30–31). These events, Terry Eagleton notes, signaled the rise of Grub Street power and the first inklings of mass culture as we know it—driven by capital, technology, population growth, and a dynamic class structure—in short, commodified literary production. As Kathy MacDermott (drawing on Raymond Williams) notes, it is at this time that the term *literary,* which up until then was synonymous with *literate,* began to take on the connotations of "elegance," "refinement," "polite learning"—markers that could be used to deepen the furrow between the public-sphere intelligentsia and the Grub Street hacks and their ever-growing audience. This cultural separation remains with us to this day, and it is one of the reasons the eighteenth is the first century which has a distinctly modern character. And of course it is no accident that this is also the period in which many of our modern institutions—medical, legal, educational—come into being; for in fact, what I am arguing is that the highbrow/lowbrow dichotomy could *only* take place in an institutionalized atmosphere. It was in the mid–nineteenth century, however, that academic culture as we now know it took firm root. As Eagleton notes, it is in the Victorian era that the man of letters learns the "unpalatable truth that the public taste he seeks to form is now decisively determined by the market. The sage, partly in reaction to this dismal condition, removes himself from the social arena to the less contaminated heights, but in so doing merely lapses into ineffectual idealism." This turn in institutional history, exemplified by Matthew Arnold, completes the withdrawal of the academic from the public life and into a hermetically sealed academic sphere, encircled as it is by what was regarded as a "society incapable of fine discrimination" (60–63). It is from within the Arnoldian academy that our notions of high culture, and of world literature and the canon of great works, emanates. In short, Arnold formulated *the charter* of the literary academy, and it is one which still functions. After all, it was only a few years ago that Allan Bloom's *The Closing of the American Mind,* an Arnoldian text if ever there was one, achieved its momentary notoriety.

Once upon a time, an aristocrat was trying to impress upon his servant that he, the aristocrat, was to be revered because he came from a very old family; the servant, either innocently or with ironic intent, said that he did not understand, for certainly any given family is as old as any other family. Although we don't normally think of it in such terms, popular culture is also institutionally structured and historically rooted.

The electronic forms of media we now have, which are generally understood only ahistorically, have their antecedents in the popular culture of the Old World. Henry Louis Gates, for example, pointed out at the 2 Live Crew obscenity trial in Florida in 1990 that rap dates back at least to the confrontation between West Africans and the Portuguese in the sixteenth century. And as historian Peter Burke notes in *Popular Culture in Early Modern Europe,* between 1500 and 1800 a great many traveling performers enjoyed a kind of fame as they promulgated a lively popular culture throughout Europe. As Burke notes, these performers included "ballad-singers, bear-wards, buffoons, charlatans, clowns, comedians, fencers, fools, hocus-pocus men, jugglers, merry-andrews, minstrels, mountebanks, players, puppet-masters, quacks, rope-dancers, showmen, tooth-drawers, and tumblers" (94).

It has been the practice to regard the culture of the people before the industrial revolution as *folk* rather than *popular* culture, the basis of the distinction being that in folk culture there is a unity of audience and performer (the exemplar being the Appalachian family that entertains itself by making its own music) and in popular culture the product is passively consumed; Burke's study of the *popular* entertainment of the latter Middle Ages establishes the historicity of popular culture. And so, just as academic poets and artists can claim an Eliotic lineage with a Great Tradition, popular culture figures can do the same. (Perhaps the best single study of this is found in Roland Barthes's essay on professional wrestling, which suggests a homology between this pseudo-sport and the commedia dell'arte.) And just as popular culture is historically determined, so is it, for better or worse, institutionally manifested; if high literary culture has its universities and museums, so too does popular culture have its Warner Brothers Corporation and its multiplex malls. And if the Arnoldian academic charter may be understood by the phrase, "the best which has been thought and said," then the charter of the popular culture establishment is likewise crystallized in phrases like "entertainment value" and "nonstop action."

We have, then, in the conflict between high and popular culture, an institutional standoff. This at least partly explains—to return to the beginning of this paper—the resistance, on the part of the editors of college literature anthologies, to popular culture—and anthologies are, after all, the attempt, in textual form, to institutionalize culture, to package it, to make it coherent and consumable according to one or another "official" concept of culture. And so while change is taking place in the academic world, a good deal of traditionalism is preserved by importing only materials which are easily converted into the commodities of official culture. My hunch is that popular culture, as

opposed to "foreign import" or "multi" culture, is problematic for the
academy precisely because its "non-foreignness," its omnipresent familiarity (everyone has knowledge of it), and the vast financial power
of its institutions present an explicit challenge to the academy's claims
of cultural monopoly and thus to the academy's charter, a charter
which is based on a myth—the myth of the authority of knowledge.

It was one of those moments which one knows to be significant before
the significance is grasped. I was late to class; I set my lecture notes
atop the wooden lectern and set some books and papers into the
lectern's enclosure. It was then that my pencil rolled into the depths
of the enclosure. I tilted the lectern in order to thrust my arm inside
more fully, and then I saw the label on the underside. It read as follows:
MANUFACTURED BY NEW MEXICO CORRECTIONAL INDUSTRIES. I was
stunned, first by the image of prisoners on an assembly line turning
out one lectern after another (just as I was turning out one lecture
after another). How many of these things did they make? Did they
enjoy the work? What crimes had they committed, or, what crimes
were they accused of? Who, in short, were they? In addition to serving
as an unsettling reminder of just what kind of world we live in, this
ominous label, to my way of thinking, serves as a metaphor for what
we as teachers can do with popular culture and the institutional
structures that inform cultural hierarchy. The university is an institution,
existing in a web with other institutions—in this case, prisons (as
Malinowski says, "a culture functions . . . by a means of a system of
related institutions" [*Freedom* 35]). And there may be more parallels
than initially meet the eye. Both prisons and universities, after all, are
ways of warehousing people, and both attempt to somehow improve
people. Universities cannot be understood without an inquiry into their
relationships with other institutions, and of course I do not mean
simply in the form of material culture, as my anecdote might suggest.

Perhaps, then, to return to the main argument, we should reject the
prevailing ghettoization—in our critical discourse—of popular culture,
for its separateness from high culture is an illusion, a kind of mirror-
trick rigged by institutions and their charter/myths (as Gerald Graff
notes, "we too are part of the culture industry" [28]). The nature of
this illusion is well-illustrated by the fact that the distinction between
high and low cultures, though institutionally clear (as with universities
and prisons), is not always so clear when manifested in texts and
artifacts. The touchstone questions of such a pedagogy, then, would

be: how is culture mediated? What kinds of instructions do we receive as to the status of cultural artifacts, and why? What kinds of institutional charters are embodied in given cultural/textual objects? The contextual webbing (social, institutional, and historical) in which texts exist is precisely what we should seek to expose, analyze, and discuss. We can work with the concept of aesthetic hierarchy, endeavoring to show where it comes from and how it operates.

In my "World Literature to 1700" class, I have a section dealing with various culturally specific definitions of national heroism. One of our assignments is Virgil's *Aeneid,* after which we view the most successful of the rash of early 1980s war films (part of a movement Greenberg calls "the new Decaturism"), namely, *Rambo: First Blood, Part Two.* What is first of all curious is the way in which these artifacts are, before the student has given them any serious consideration at all, already commodified, already institutionally identified by the highbrow/ lowbrow dichotomy. A good place to get a fix on the preconceived notions regarding *The Aeneid* can be found in *Cliff's Notes,* odd artifacts in themselves, attached to the academic institution in an underground way, resented by college teachers (yet written by them), and popular with students (perhaps *because* they are resented by teachers); and thus providing a fairly good indicator of how students are preconditioned. *Cliff's Notes,* then, gets into Virgil with a rather astonishing opener: "*The Aeneid* of Virgil," we are told matter-of-factly, "is probably the single most important poem to have been written in the history of Western Civilization" (Milch 5). The undeniable greatness of Virgil's poem (which the student must, apparently, passively and uncritically imbibe), however, rests upon an evaluative fissure: *The Aeneid,* as we know, was never completed by Virgil, and thus it lacks, in the Latin, the poetic polish of the *Georgics*; and in any case, our students in the world literature survey will not be reading Virgil in the Latin. Scholars have often bemoaned the fact that much is lost in translation.

Certainly, I should not want to "level" all aesthetic artifacts and practices, all difference; on the other hand, there may be some advantages to translation, and we may term this advantage *the law of narrative reduction.* That is, in the absence of competence in the original language and culture of a given text, the reader will rightly defer all judgments to a work's mythic and/or narrative virtues. Similarly, in the relative absence of aesthetic value in the text itself, the reader often proceeds similarly, and thus aesthetically questionable works such as Stoker's *Dracula* and Cooper's *Last of the Mohicans* often succeed, particularly in terms of cultural mythos, in spite of themselves. In like terms, our students experience Virgil primarily through the grid of narrativity, and thus plot, characterization, and scene will perforce be the focus of their attention. This is far from a bad thing; in fact, perhaps this is precisely how it should be, for narrative more fully exposes the workings of ideology than does poetics. And so, we find that our students respond most fully to the characterization of Aeneas—laconic, quietly suffering, a higher goal always in mind. In this narrative reduction, we quickly come to expose the propagandistic qualities of the text, and it is of course well known that Virgil was greatly influenced by his patron and protector, the instigator of fascistic rule in Rome, Caesar Augustus: both Virgil and Augustus were preoccupied with Rome's mission in the world.

Virgil and Stallone: one would have to look long and hard for a greater cultural antipathy. On the one hand, we have Homer's poetic son, Dante's poetic father, the "virtuous pagan" of Roman letters; on the other hand, we have a contemporary popular icon who has been rejected by the reactionary intellectual right (who regard all popular culture as degenerate) as well as by the intellectual left (who see a complicity between the *Rambo* series and Reagan-era militarism). Given this cultural frame, one might find it difficult to get students to leave their ideological baggage outside the classroom door. Nonetheless, students quickly perceive a parallel between Virgil's suffering hero of Roman patriarchy and Stallone's martyr for the cause of the American failure in Vietnam: as Charles Molesworth points out, *Rambo* is "about power, the power of nations and the power of individuals" (109), and much the same may be said of *The Aeneid*.

Like Aeneas, Rambo is pagan (he claims American Indian blood and prefers primitive weapons), and yet he oddly conforms to the sacrificial model of Virgil's hero (as well as to Campbell's monomyth and Slotkin's "cultural archetype"). And like Aeneas, Rambo goes through a hellish underworld; more important, just as Aeneas must forsake the loving arms of Queen Dido, Rambo's newfound love, Co Bao, a beautiful and virtuous Vietnamese confederate who wants to go with Rambo to America, is cut down by enemy gunfire. A similar ideological imperative is at work here: according to the almost gynophobic model of patriarchal heroism, the true national hero, as evidence of his pure masculinity, must proceed *sans* female: as William Warner observes, Co Bao must die after receiving Rambo's fatal kiss, "because any special entanglement with another, especially a woman, would imperil his isolation." (681). My students even saw a similarity between certain devices. Aeneas' and Achates' tour of Carthage under the "cloudy mantle" provided by Venus struck students, and for that matter me, as being uncannily similar to Rambo's ability to disappear, as in the scene in which he emerges from a bank of mud to slay one of his enemies. Furthermore, the well-known "pre-Christianity" of Virgil (both in *The Aeneid* and in the fourth *Eclogue*) is likewise echoed in Stallone's fable of national heroism, for at least twice in the film Rambo assumes the crucifixion posture—once on an actual cross and once on an electrified box spring (the brainchild of a now anachronistically evil Soviet officer).

I would imagine that, traditionally, teachers of world literature have discouraged these kind of discussions. However, I feel that such parallels should not be suppressed: they should be encouraged and used. To return to the case at hand, more interesting than the question, "Which is 'better'—*The Aeneid* or *Rambo?*" are questions pertaining to our cultural preconceptions. How are we influenced by these preconceptions, by institutional structures and their charters? Why is one high and the other low?

And how is a university like a prison?

Although space does not permit me to multiply examples of how the ideological and institutional framework of cultural hierarchy can become part of the pedagogical imperative of "World Lit.," I can briefly catalog a few examples from my own practice. Some literary works already contain within them opportunities for doing so. Flaubert's *Madame Bovary,* for example, specifically addresses the problems of mass-mediated consciousness. In part 2, chapter 15—the well-known opera scene—we find an example of how critical consciousness may be brought to bear on all forms of culture, for it is here that Emma momentarily penetrates the illusion of sentimental romance and concludes that the happiness presented in such entertainments are "a lie invented to cause the despair of all desire." Soon thereafter, when, with her newly acquired critical consciousness, she glimpses the prop man, in spite of his black camouflage "she smiled to herself with disdainful pity" (217). In this scene Emma thus has a moment not unlike that in which I found the insidious label on my lectern. She has glimpsed the otherwise invisible hand of institutional power and ideology, and her moment is a good model for what it is that we can do in the teaching of culture and cultural hierarchy. The tragedy of course is that Emma's moment is a brief one, and she soon surrenders to a passive and uncritical reception of the dictates of romantic ideology.

Similarly, Kafka's "The Hunger Artist" is a work that addresses the question of mediated culture, with the suffering protagonist representing

the "artiste" of high culture drowning in a sea of commercial entertainment, handled, as he is, by an impresario who limits his fasting to
forty days in order to manipulate the public interest in much the same
way that Colonel Tom Parker controlled Elvis Presley's public exposure
over the years (thus ensuring Presley's godlike status while other teen
stars from the 1950s faded, due to overexposure, into obscurity). It is
furthermore interesting to note that Kafka does not, in this story, glorify
the "artiste"; in fact, the story may easily be read as an argument in
favor of mass culture, for the panther who replaces the hunger artist
is a symbol of health and vitality: "Even the most insensitive felt it
refreshing to see this wild creature leaping around the cage that had
so long been dreary. . . . they braced themselves, crowded round the
cage, and did not want ever to move away" (462). Indeed, the hunger
artist and the panther embody, on the one hand, the charter of high
culture (the patience of the artist, the need for understanding and
patience on the part of the audience, suffering, monastic dedication)
and on the other, the charter of popular culture (action, excitement,
danger).

In closing, perhaps I should acknowledge that I may be accused of
presenting an all-too-rosy picture of popular culture pedagogy. Indeed,
there is a problem, perhaps unavoidable, in teaching about popular
culture. Popular culture, already and by definition a commodity within
the general economy, can only be *recommodified* for the academic
subeconomy if it can be defamiliarized, thus allowing institutional
"agents" (professors) to present themselves as possessing the power-
knowledge which alone confers their status within the institution. This
double bind is accurately described and analyzed by Lawrence Grossberg
in his discussion of a "rock and roll pedagogy" which led to resistance
on the part of his students, who "jealously guarded their music, claiming
that, in the very attempt to dismantle and interpret its significance, I
not only demonstrated my lack of understanding but also betrayed the
music by contributing to rock and roll's unwanted legitimation" (179).
In other words, Grossberg's students bemoaned the fact that since
popular culture is not an area of scholarly interest, now you need
academics, so the academics say, to explain and perhaps ruin your
entertainment for you. While in all candor it must be admitted that
this problem is a persistent one—perhaps an inevitable one given the
institutional structure of higher education—it need not be a debilitating
one if we focus our gaze unflinchingly on those very institutional
structures which inform the cultural worlds we and our students
endeavor to inhabit, enjoy, and understand.

Works Consulted

Abrahamson, Mark. *Functionalism.* Englewood Cliffs, NJ: Prentice-Hall, 1978.

Barthes, Roland. *Mythologies.* 1957. Trans. Richard Howard. New York: Peter Smith, 1983.

Bloom, Allan. *The Closing of the American Mind.* New York: Simon and Schuster, 1988.

Burke, Peter. *Popular Culture in Early Modern Europe.* New York: New York UP, 1978.

———. *Sociology and History.* London: Allen and Unwin, 1980.

Campbell, Joseph. *The Hero with a Thousand Faces.* New York: Meridian, 1956.

Cawelti, John G. *Adventure, Mystery, and Romance.* Chicago: U of Chicago P, 1976.

Colomy, Paul. *Neofunctionalist Sociology.* Brookfield, VT: Ashgate, 1990.

Eagleton, Terry. *The Function of Criticism: From* The Spectator *to Post-Structuralism.* London: Verso, 1984.

Flaubert, Gustave. *Madame Bovary.* 1857. Trans. Mildred Marmur. New York: Signet, 1964.

Gluckman, Max. *Custom and Conflict in Africa.* Cambridge, MA: Blackwell, 1965.

Graff, Gerald. "The University *Is* Popular Culture." *Democratic Culture.* 3.1 (Spring 1994): 28–30.

Greenberg, Harvey. "Dangerous Recuperations: *Red Dawn, Rambo,* and the New Decaturism." *Journal of Popular Film and Television.* 15.2 (Summer 1987): 60–70.

Grossberg, Lawrence. "Teaching the Popular." In *Theory in the Classroom.* Ed. Cary Nelson. Urbana: U of Illinois P, 1986.

Jewett, Robert, and John Shelton Lawrence. *The American Monomyth.* New York: Anchor, 1977.

Johnson, Samuel. "On Fiction." *The Rambler* #4. In *Critical Theory since Plato.* Ed. Hazard Adams. New York: Harcourt Brace Jovanovich, 1971. 324–27.

Joyce, Joyce. "Sonia Sanchez." *The Heath Anthology of American Literature.* Vol 2. Ed. Paul Lauter et al. Lexington, MA: Heath, 1990. 2440–41.

Kafka, Franz. "A Hunger Artist." Trans. Wila Muir and Edwin Muir. In *The Norton Introduction to Fiction.* Ed. Jerome Beaty. New York: Norton, 1985. 456–62.

Malinowski, Bronislaw. *Freedom and Civilization.* New York: Roy, 1944.

———. *Dynamics of Culture Change.* Glenwood, IL: Greenwood, 1946.

———. *Magic, Science, and Religion.* Glenwood, IL: Greenwood, 1954.

Martin, Wallace. *Recent Theories of Narrative.* Ithaca, NY: Cornell UP, 1986.

MacDermott, Kathy. "Literature and the Grub Street Myth." In *Popular Fictions: Essays in Literature and History.* Ed. Peter Humm, Paul Stigant, and Peter Widdowson. London: Methuen, 1986. 16–28.

Merton, Robert. *Social Theory and Social Structure.* New York: Free Press, 1968.

Milch, Robert. *Cliff's Notes on Virgil's* Aeneid. Lincoln, NE: Cliff's Notes, 1963.

Moglen, Helene. *The Philosophical Irony of Laurence Sterne.* Gainesville, FL: U of Florida P, 1975.

Molesworth, Charles. "Rambo, Passion, and Power." *Dissent* 88 (Winter 1986): 109–11.

Rollin, Roger B. "Beowulf to Batman: The Epic Hero and Pop Culture." *College English* 31 (1970): 431–49.

Rosenberg, Donna. *World Mythology: An Anthology of the Great Myths and Epics.* Lincolnwood, IL: National Textbook Company, 1989.

Scholes, Robert, and Robert Kellogg. *The Nature of Narrative.* New York: Oxford UP, 1966.

Sen, Abhijit. "Global Culture: American Pop Culture and the Third World." *Proteus.* 11.1 (Spring 1994): 21–28.

Shils, E., and M. Young. "The Meaning of the Coronation." *Sociological Review* 1.2 (1953): 63–80.

Shumway, David R. "Post-Structuralism and Popular Culture." In *Symbiosis: Popular Culture and Other Fields.* Ed. Ray B. Browne and Marshall Fishwick. Bowling Green, OH: Popular Press, 1988. 160–69.

Slotkin, Richard. *Regeneration through Violence.* Middletown, CT: Wesleyan UP, 1973.

Sterne, Laurence. *Tristram Shandy.* New York: Airmont, 1967.

Warner, William. "Spectacular Action: Rambo and the Popular Pleasures of Pain." In *Cultural Studies.* Ed. Lawrence Grossberg, Cary Nelson, and Paula A. Treichler. New York: Routledge, 1992.

Webster, Grant. *The Republic of Letters: A History of Postwar American Literary Opinion.* Baltimore: Johns Hopkins UP, 1979.

Young, Dennis. "Anthologies, Canonicity, and the Objectivist Imagination: The Case of George Oppen." Chapter 12, this volume.

10 The Intellectual and Pedagogical Value of Traditional African Literature in the Western Classroom

Erskine Peters
University of Notre Dame

The central concern of this essay is with the intellectual function of knowledge and, specifically, with the pedagogical value and specific use of traditional African values and concepts in the Western classroom. Students who are descendants of the African continental dispersion certainly stand in profound ontological need of information about precolonial African thought. But while providing African descendants with the legacy of African thought, one would need to take advantage of the opportunity to introduce *all* students in classes to the origins of much of Western thought, particularly the modern Western worldview. Few students know enough about the specific intellectual origins and currents of Europe and America from which they draw their highly valued modern Western identities. Indeed, so intellectually naive are general American students that they, like the general society, make little discrimination or see no distinction, for example, between democracy and capitalist enterprise, particularly since freedom is seen as the common denominator of both. Because the traditional African worldview often stands in contrast to the modern Western worldview, it can be intellectually stimulating, challenging, and rewarding to use the African cultural view to introduce and discuss the Western.

Much has already been said over the recent two decades about the spiritual, social, political, emotional, and intellectual processes and patterns with which black Americans have become engaged and entangled over the last several centuries due to the establishment and execution by Europeans of the West African slave trade. Black historians, social scientists, theologians, and artists have sought to articulate, often in similar terms, the deep nature of the dilemma as it reveals itself. Carter G. Woodson and Charles Wesley's early study of the African in

This essay appeared in *The Western Journal of Black Studies* 13.1 (1989): 28–35, and is used here with their permission.

American history opens with the statement that "most historians know practically nothing about the Negroes in Africa prior to their enslavement, and there has been little systematic effort to study them" (Woodson and Wesley 1).

This unenlightened state is certainly the effect of the calculation of the slavemaster. Until the enslaved found themselves gradually able to remove the dust from their own eyes the crucial bridge leading from the past for clarification of the present was often tragically nonexistent.

The Trinidadian Lennox Brown states "You give the human being a link in the continuum, a link to the human past when you approach him mythologically" (qtd. in Harrison 28)—and mythology is actually no more than the parables of history, personal or social, which the African American needed to reassemble. Theologian Albert Cleage perceives it to be of critical importance that human beings need to know what they believe about themselves and also the nature of the deity in whom they believe. Thus, he has written that "the existence of Black people in America depends entirely upon whether or not it is possible to change the Black man's theology" (Cleage xvii).

To a great degree, then, knowledge, when it is allowed to do its work, heals the wounds of a peculiar psychological condition. For as we know rather fully now, most historical-cultural problems create binds in the thoughts of the people which cannot be loosened by government mandate alone. The government mandate is only a signal of what needs to be done on a psychological level.

"The culture of slavery was never undone for either master or slave," write William Grier and Price Cobbs in their erstwhile controversial *Black Rage*. "The civilization that tolerated slavery," they continue, "dropped its slaveholding cloak but the inner feelings remained. The 'peculiar institution' continues to exert its evil influence over the nation. The practice of slavery stopped over a hundred years ago, but the minds of our citizens have never been freed" (26). Even as late as 1975, the Nigerian Chinweizu could write most fervently in the opening paragraph of his commanding study, *The West and the Rest of Us*: "For nearly six centuries now western Europe and its diaspora have been disturbing the peace of the world. . . . And even now, the fury of their expansionist assault upon the rest of us has not abated" (26).

In its best sense, classroom teaching surely is not a setting in which information packets are given out, but is rather the setting for a process in which students and teachers are led out of various levels of ignorance. Thus, in its highest sense teaching is a ritual through which life can be created or restored. This process of restoration or creation is the essence of what was proclaimed with such fervor in the sixties when African

Americans said that they needed to move into a state of black awareness, indicating, too, that without the awareness there could be no true coming of black power.

Needless to say, black Americans still need to be involved in this birthing and regenerative process until the essentials seep so pervasively into the black community that the total school culture becomes seriously affected. The school culture would need to be so affected that when the students come to the college classroom they can be taken far beyond those primary stages of the awakening process. But now, much introductory work still has to be done on the college level in terms of breaking the ground to initiate the student into the profound resources residing in the traditional African background through which contemporary life can be illuminated.

It is rather common knowledge that for most Americans, history, which tends to be defined more as a past deemed worthy of recording by the power holders, than as a record of the general human past, still has its beginning very much in one or two places, that is, in Europe or the Bible or a confusion of both. Because of these very parochial but influential and dominant connotations which have gathered around the word *history* in the West, many who continue to teach courses related to any aspect of the history of black Americans find that a great percentage of black American students are still inclined to attempt to trace their past, quite exclusively, by way of Europe or the Bible. The culture of the heart of black Africa still has to be given its long-overdue attention if the black student coming of age in America or any Western culture is to arrive at and maintain an adequate mental balance. Black American students must think very critically and conscientiously about what they are imbibing as history.

What is it then that seems to happen in the black American mind when it comes into possession of a greater degree of knowledge of what has happened during and before the course of its historical American existence? What, one asks, do black American students, in general, yet recall of what existed in their African past back beyond 1619 or so? For the most part, beyond 1619 their minds become hazy or, more often than not, blank except for a few images of Egypt or other imperialistic African kingdoms. The general black American mind encounters after this point something of a psychological gulf, a void, a space of emptiness. This is a state of consciousness which can be, and has been, very debilitating, because in light of this absence of historical knowledge Western history maintains its dominance in having one believe that this African void, over which one finds oneself dangling, is yet, fundamentally, a void of degradation and nothingness.

Materials on the traditional African background such as John S. Mbiti's *African Religions and Philosophy*[1] can play a crucial role in quelling the intellectual turbulence in the minds of those who begin to entertain the foregoing questions and who undertake this spiritual and epistemological quest. With the use of Mbiti's work, for instance, the students' whole notion of existence is challenged. The first fifty pages alone of Mbiti's work would be seminal. Essential concepts regarding time, space, and religion are presented from another angle from that to which the American is accustomed. These essential differences cannot but shake the foundations of students' acquired thought patterns, while at the same time providing them with the opportunity to retrieve an intellectual and spiritual heritage.

As with any general study (e.g., de Tocqueville's *Democracy in America,* Fanon's *The Wretched of the Earth*), one certainly cannot expect Mbiti to present *the* African worldview, yet Mbiti does provide an opening to the comprehension of Africa's general thought system and structure. The problem with the average college student in the West is that he or she has no concrete perception of African traditional life as a *developed* and *coherent* system. Mbiti's book seeks mainly to depict African societies as self-created and self-authenticating organizations and systems based upon African *thought.* Mbiti has been criticized for his obvious monotheistic Christian bias, but he never actually denies the existence of the indigenous spiritual hierarchy. In fact, he gives impressive primacy to the omnipresence of a life filled with spirits in the African's everyday existence.

Many African American students are only distinguishable from their European American counterparts in the same classroom to the extent that the African American student *feels* and *hopes* African society was not savage, i.e., disorganized, incoherent, unreasoned. The black student generally does not have enough specific knowledge to prove that it was not, however. The psychological and intellectual boost for the African American student is in having come to *know* this specific knowledge rather than having to feel and hope it. Mbiti's work surely can help provide an opportunity and the specifics can then be pursued through the study of his bibliography and through investigation of studies published subsequent to Mbiti's.

In Mbiti's work one reads, for example, that religion permeates so deeply all aspects of life that it is difficult for one to isolate it simply as a segment of the culture, as is so often done in Western society. Writes Mbiti:

> Because traditional religions permeate all the departments of life,
> there is no formal distinction between the sacred and the secular,

between the religious and non-religious, between the spiritual and the material areas of life. Wherever the African is, there is his religion: he carries it to the fields where he is sowing seeds or harvesting a new crop; he takes it with him to the beer party or to attend a funeral ceremony; and if he is educated, he takes religion with him to the examination room at school or in the university; if he is a politician he takes it to the house of parliament. (2)

Religion has this great an impact, asserts Mbiti, even though a large number of African languages have no word in their vocabularies which specifically means religion. In the same line, and this may be even more revealing to the Western student, concepts such as time and space, which Westerners take so much for granted as separate entities, are often denoted by the same words in African languages. The power of the revelations stimulated by this African view cannot be underestimated once the students begin not only to perceive how they are affected by these new ways of thinking and being, but the revelations may be even more powerful in helping students understand their historical circumstances once they are able to place themselves in the position of their enslaved African ancestors who encountered the shock of the Western concepts. Students are then better able to trace and reconstruct the evolution of African American jokes, tales, jazz, sorrow songs, etc. They come to see through an enriched perspective that the slave trade meant that mental states, not simply men and women, were at war.

In more specific terms, once the students have opened themselves up to dealing with this new frame of reference, they usually find themselves on a new intellectual horizon. The increased openness and subsequent intellectual potency may enable the students to be stimulated to the point that they not only want to know what all of the old African reality was about and was like, but, ideally, they may be stimulated into rigorous inquiry about the nature of that essential and still so very obscured experience of transition from being African to being confronted with a major attempt to transform one into something else, slave, wretch, nigger, or what have you. Students begin to know more of the nature of what the bondmen must have experienced in feeling and thought when they became aware that in this new world, because of the greater separation of the sacred and the secular, not even conversion to the European's interpretation of the Christian religion would make them a part of what was considered the society of man. For as it was decreed by the Bishop of London, Dr. Gibson, who urged that spiritual attention be given to the African in slavery:

Christianity and the embracing of the Gospel does not make the
least alteration in civil property, or in any of the duties which
belong to civil relations; but in these respects, it continues persons
just as in the same state as it found them. (qtd. in Jones 21)

Beyond the aforementioned, there is a series of other concepts offered
by Mbiti which will prove to be just as provocative. If the students
have had difficulty in grasping the idea that religion permeates all
aspects of life and that there is no great distinction between the sacred
and the secular, chances are that the students will have more or at
least as great difficulty with the concept that relates to the traditional
African view of the person to his or her society. This is mainly because
of the high emotional investments that the Westerner places upon the
concept of individualism. Since individualism is a phenomenon that
Western students assume they have inherited by birthright rather than
by culture, something crucial happens when the students encounter a
different concept of the person presented through the African worldview.
Students begin to see even more clearly that if they are to comprehend
the world of their African ancestors they will have to give up something
very great: their Western conceptualization of the self.

For nearly all of their lives, Western students' greatest ambition has
been to live long enough to lay claim to their *individuality*. Their
raison d'être may very well have been the fact that they wanted to
grow up and live as they pleased, to do what they wanted to do when
they wanted to do it. Thus they may become quite disarmed to hear
Mbiti's assertion that in traditional African society, "To be human is
to belong to the whole community, and to do so involves participating
in the beliefs, ceremonies, rituals and festivals of that community.
Persons cannot detach themselves from the religion of their group, for
to do so is to be severed from their roots, their foundation, their context
of security, their kinships and the entire group of those who make
them aware of their existence" (3).

This realization can be a difficult and excruciating challenge to the
Westerner but, nevertheless, in coming to grasp the distinction between
what one may call African personhood, as opposed to individualism,
the students find it easier to know the meaning of African traditional
life when they are challenged about the origin of their own values and
their presumptions. If the students have been disarmed by Mbiti's
assertions, when they are led back to the origins of modern Western
thought they may even become more astonished to learn that this
individualism which they seem so certain stems from their blood is
not really older than the Protestant Reformation itself. Students come
to realize that their Western sense of individuality has much of its basic

source in Luther's arguments that each person should be directly responsible to God, not to the Pope or his priests, for the state of his or her conscience; that each person should be able to interpret the scriptures for him- or herself under the authority of his own conscience through God; and that these factors, coupled with the rise of mercantilism and, then, industrialism and capitalism, are what have bequeathed to Westerners that to which they cling with great pride and know best as their individuality.

The learning experience is therefore compounded when African and European concepts are explored historically. In learning more about their African history the students are almost compelled to do more research into their European heritage. The ramifications are, of course, extensive. Nevertheless, when the students have had time to recompose themselves from their new astonishment, they very often reenter the world with a much more magnificent intellectual charge. In a sense, they have been made naked, and their intellectual sense has been magnified to a degree rather similar to that of an awestruck child.

Certain ideas and forces, like individuality, while they do exist in various forms outside America nevertheless often coalesce on the American scene with a peculiar intensity, producing what is called the American personality. Most students do not know that this acceptable American personality type is not common to all cultures, ancient or contemporary, nor that it was formed by certain historical forces, key among which are Protestantism, capitalism and industrialism, and the experience of the American frontier. But by being introduced to another worldview students can become enlightened not simply about an African concept of the world but also about their own peculiar historical selves.

When the students begin to acquire a new body of concepts and information, Africa becomes not only new, but actual. Among the numerous creations that have been handed down through the centuries from the African past are two works which seem to function exceptionally well in bringing about this new mental ordering through classroom discussion. One is the well-known epic *Sundiata,* and the other is the relatively less-known but stupendous work from the region of the Republic of Zaire called *The Mwindo Epic.* Most of the attention here will be given to the latter.

The prefatory remarks to *Sundiata: An Epic of Old Mali* made by a griot to the recorder D. T. Niane are especially stimulating for the minds of the students. From these cogent remarks the students not only acquire historical knowledge itself, but also some very special knowledge about the sacred place given to history in the culture of the ancient African empire of Mali and of the great sense of reverence shown to the knowledge-holders by the society. Students learn that the ancient griot, the authority of history, perceives himself as "the memory of mankind." He is thought of as the vessel of speech, a repository which harbors "secrets many centuries old." He is not part of some random oral tradition, but is a part of a sophisticated oral tradition and belongs to a group of orators who have trained for long years in the highly skilled "art of eloquence" (1). Indeed the students learn that the knowledge and the art through which knowledge is transmitted are held in so much reverence in traditional African societies that before one could attain to the degree of master in the area, the vow of secrecy often had to be taken concerning what could be revealed and how it was to be revealed. In essence, the students learn that the griot is entrusted with preserving the keys to his people's cosmos and existence. They learn that the traditional griot would be grossly underrated if he were called simply a historian.

The value of a people's cosmos and their interrelation with and obligation to it are the major themes of the centuries-old *Mwindo Epic*. This work serves as a supreme example for presenting the students with a coherent African value system. In studying and examining this work the students observe an African system functioning for itself, articulating itself, and conserving and regenerating itself, thereby sustaining its people. It is precisely traditional African materials of this nature that can play a particularly significant role in bringing about the rebirth of the African American mind.

Once the students are familiar with the world of *The Mwindo Epic,* they do not have to imagine, fantasize, or wish what was. As they begin to abstract the values and value system from such a world as is presented here, they come to *know* what was. They begin to see more clearly that after all is said and done, the root of all the facets of oppression that the black American has had to deal with historically— whether economic, political, or cultural—is actually related to values and nothing else. They begin to understand how it is that when one attempts to strip human beings of their values one is actually attempting to strip away their identity.

Frantz Fanon wrote in *The Wretched of the Earth* that "in order to assimilate and to experience the oppressor's culture, the native has to leave certain of his intellectual possessions in pawn" (49). Thus, when the students encounter materials such as *The Mwindo Epic,* which is so vast in its richness, they understand that to a large degree they have made a journey down the road of time back to the pawnshop to reclaim their original African identity.

The general story of *The Mwindo Epic* is that in a time long ago, that is, far back into the mythic-historical past, Chief Shemwindo, father of an unwanted child, Mwindo, builds a village called Tubondo. Chief Shemwindo marries seven women, and, after calling them together before an assembly of the entire community, forbids any of these wives ever to bear him a son. Chief Shemwindo has one royal sister, Iyangura, and during the impregnation of all the seven wives, this royal sister marries Mutitti the Water Spirit and moves away to a distant village. This royal sister is important because by custom she is supposed to have some sway over the chief's actions.

It is Chief Shemwindo's mandate to his seven wives never to bear a male child that activates the plot of the story. In the telling of the story the value system of the culture, violated by Chief Shemwindo with the complicity of the village elders, is laid out for us. Such a mandate that none of his wives should bear him male children leads us directly to wonder about the chief's personal values and motivations. As soon as we hear the chief's decree, a series of questions is immediately generated in our minds. We want to know what it is that drives this chief: Is it vanity? Is it greed? Is it jealousy? Or all? Then we want to know what forces and values he as chief is going against. How and to whom will he be held accountable? And probably most of all, what will be his sentence? In posing such questions, then, we as students of the African past have not simply expressed interest in the outcome of the story but have simultaneously expressed an interest in this particular culture's values, the morals and the ethics of the people, and their judicial system; in short, its cosmology. For it is the chief who is expected to be the representative and caretaker of the community's sacred values and therefore of its life. But the way we pose these questions as Westerners also says a lot about our own values and expectations.

As fate would have it, it is Chief Shemwindo's royal wife or preferred wife, the one from whom the line of succession would naturally proceed, who is the longest in delivering her child and who is alone among the seven wives to bear a male child. So forcefully has the chief made clear that his decree should be upheld, that when the male child is born the midwives are terrified to reveal it. It is an agent in the form of a cricket, who is present in the hut at the time of the boy's birth, who informs Chief Shemwindo of the event. In his outrage, the chief first attempts to kill his son by throwing his spear into the hut while the mother and the midwives are still there. But this unusual son, named Mwindo because he is the first male child to follow all the female births, out of compassion asks the gods for protection for his mother and the midwives, which the gods do grant.

In time the midwives are able to flee from the danger. The chief is exhausted from his useless attempts to destroy his son and proceeds to carry out an alternative solution by calling in his elders and asking them to take the child out to bury it, which they do. But, as stated, this is an unusual child, who, guided by higher spirits, is not only able to understand what is going on soon after his birth, but who was doing a great deal of meditating and ruminating while still in his mother's womb. He is such a precocious and maturely developed child that he even decides how or from what part of his mother's body he wishes to be born. He chooses to be born from her medius, that is, her middle finger, because he feels that to come naturally from her womb is degrading to one of his foreordained greatness or prowess. All of this is because he views women as weaker than men and, therefore, does not want it thought that he emanates from a weaker form than himself.

Not unexpectedly, then, this unusual child, when carried out and buried by the village counselors and elders, howls from beneath the grave and calls out a curse upon his father, saying in essence that his father will be brought to judgment. Because the child Mwindo has the protection of the good spirits, and is, in a sense, their agent of retribution or justice, at the time of his birth he was given four emblems or instruments which he can always call upon to aid in his deliverance or salvation. They are (1) a *conga*-scepter, a sacred emblem and instrument of the hero's physical and mental force; (2) an adze, a small cutting instrument, often associated with those who have the authority to perform masked dances or to organize the traditional ceremonies of circumcision; (3) a small utility bag, also symbolic of the spirit of good fortune; and (4) a rope or cord, a kind of magical line which Mwindo is able to use to communicate with his paternal aunt Iyangura. Thus, making use of these instruments, Mwindo arises from the grave in the night and returns to his mother's hut.

From this point onward the chief engages members of the village in a number of acts of desperation. Two swimmers are ordered to take the child Mwindo, who has been sealed in a drum, to the bottom of the river and leave him, and when Nyamwindo his mother is found weeping for her son, the chief turns her into his most despised wife and threatens to throw her into the river also. The earth and the heavens revolt at all the chief's actions and send rains for seven days and seven nights, bringing much hardship to the village. The appropriate spiritual course for Mwindo to take now is to make his way to the village of his aunt to call upon her to exert her counsel and sacred influence over her brother. Mwindo's path to this aunt is beset with many obstructions, but he finally arrives there and explains the circumstances. What becomes apparent now is that Chief Shemwindo's steadfastness in his violation of the sanctity of human life and of the natural order will be tested.

In due course, one finds that more than to seek out his aunt's influence, Mwindo, in all of his prowess and pride, has also gone to his aunt's village to organize forces to move against his father. In ignoring his aunt's appeals to him to relent, he also ignores the risks to his own moral growth as he stands ready to proceed. Since the aunt understands that Mwindo will not give in, she decides to accompany him with her maidens, horrified that in the outcome the father will destroy or vanquish the son. By this time, we notice that a complication has also arisen in the character of the son Mwindo. Although born with the blessings of the gods, he becomes presumptuous about his own strengths and powers, and is haughty and boastful, overflowing with pride. Thus he, too, begins to some degree to stand in violation of the values of the community in which the individual should think first about the preservation of the community and not himself, and in which youth is expected to heed the counsel of the chosen and experienced elders, such as his aunt. For in the end, after all of his virtuous triumphs, Mwindo, like his father, will himself be called to give account before the gods for his own unrestrained passions, which lead him to think individualistically and therefore faultily according to Tubondo culture.

In seeing his son approaching with the intention of entering into combat, the father, in all his boasting and arrogance, can only perceive the son as a swaggering fool. The father's pride and arrogance blind him to his son's strength, and the father soon finds that it is best for him to flee. From this point onward, through the many ordeals and trials through which Mwindo will have to pass in order to capture his father, the suspense seems to be focused upon to what indeed will the son subject his father once he seizes him. But Mwindo's search or quest for the father turns out to be as much a quest or adventure during which Mwindo himself, the heir apparent to the throne, has to prove himself worthy of that position and demonstrate that he has attained the appropriate level of wisdom to assume the responsibility of the position, which belongs not to an individual but to the society.

Consequently, before he is allowed by the gods to take his father captive, among other things Mwindo has to learn about the true nature of pride, respect, self-esteem, dignity, compassion, and true prowess. The overall lesson of all of these values appears to be to teach the would-be ruler Mwindo that even the man of heroic proportions cannot make it totally on his own. For in the thinking of Mwindo's Aunt Iyangura, "The lonely path is not nice; it never fails to find something that could kill a man" (79). All of this had to be well learned before the guiding spirits reveal to Mwindo that the major objective for seeking out his father is not revenge, as he might have been inclined to think, but instead to bring his father to the bench of justice. Thus, when all the lessons are learned, Mwindo is given a mandate that when he and his forces are about to seize Chief Shemwindo, the son is not to lay his hands upon him. It will be the son's duty to direct his assistants in bringing their captive back to the community. Here, in Chief Shemwindo's being brought to stand in shame for the crime he has attempted against his son, nature, and the community—because of his greed for the dowries of marriage which daughters could bring, and out of jealousy of a son as a rival force to his power—the misfortunes that the chief has brought upon the community can begin to be reversed.

But in the shaming of the chief also comes the admission of guilt by the community. The shame has to be shared in order for the redemptive ritual to be completed; for it was after all the community elders themselves who permitted the chief to go as far in his extremes as he did. There is a reciprocal responsibility and relationship connected with a system of values which exists between the ruler and the people and between the people and the ruler if the community is to prosper and live on. The pursuit and expression of individual passions put the future of the society at great risk.

Misfortune is thus turned into fortune and the past can be made to be an agent or tool for rebirth and regeneration once those responsible admit their errors. Such was the lesson Mwindo learned, and when he did become chief of Tubondo he was able to create a set of nine great laws or commandments that expressed what he had learned:

> (1) May you grow many foods and many crops. (2) May you live in good houses; may you moreover live in a beautiful village. (3) Don't quarrel with one another. (4) Don't pursue another's spouse. (5) Don't mock the invalid passing in the village. (6) And he who seduces another's wife will be killed! (7) Accept the chief; fear him; may he also fear you. (8) May you agree with one another, all together; no enmity in the land nor too much hate. (9) May you bring forth tall and short children; in so doing you will bring them forth for the chief. (144)

It is not necessary to go on at length about the great moral worth of such a work as *The Mwindo Epic,* except to say that everyone should experience that greatness through reading the text and by reflecting upon its meaning and how that meaning is artistically achieved. Teachers and students may all come away from a work like *The Mwindo Epic* with more than knowledge as information—some stuff to fill the void— but with knowledge which leads to insight. One learns not only of an actual African value system, but also something about the rationale upon which the value system is grounded. Therefore, one becomes acquainted with a traditional African concept of living. The void of the African heritage, then, is not only being filled, but in its being filled it begins to serve a regenerative function of building psychological security for those black students who need something to stand on as they walk into the past beyond 1619. This new knowledge sheds an essential light upon the seeds of hidden aspects of African American existence and provides for the stimulation of new growth in understanding also the European heritage if undertaken for study through historical comparison.

After having learned from the experience of the village of Tubondo, all that one has ever read, heard, or witnessed about the African American past and the European past comes under a new scrutiny. Every African American tale may have a new possibility and all of those tones and moods and phrasings in the folk ballads and the spirituals take on even deeper meanings and other degrees of interpretation. On a much higher level, one may sense the intellectual and emotional potency of what Mbiti means when he says that in traditional African society

> space and time are closely linked, and often the same word is used for both. As with time, it is the content which defines space. . . . The land provides (the people) with the roots of existence, as well as binding them mystically to their departed. People walk on the graves of their forefathers, and it is feared that anything separating them from these ties will bring disaster to family and community life. To remove Africans by force from their land is an act of such great injustice that no foreigner can fathom it. (34–35)

This entire approach of walking into the past, discovering and illuminating the unknown about black American life could be extended, no doubt, to include the use of traditional African concepts of art, music, or dance. In music, there are endless revelations which may be derived from having more precise knowledge of the meanings associated with various African beats, rhythms, or instruments; or in art with the significance of the unique use of proportion. Needless to say, a knowledge of the significance of all of these many factors combined offers the utmost challenge to the enlightenment, rebirth, and revitalization of the African American life-force. The new or alternative way of seeing the past strengthens African Americans' intellectual force, expands their minds, and brings a new sense of value to what may have been a rather uncertain regard for their cultural and racial identity.

Note

1. Some scholars are skeptical of Mbiti's work owing to his Christian biases. However, Mbiti's introduction to *African Religions and Philosophy* serves as a fine avenue into traditional African cosmology. Anozie (52–61), for example, finds Mbiti's book useful for his own discussion of the poetics of synchronic and diachronic time but is critical of Mbiti's explanation concerning expression of the future tense in African languages. He is particularly perturbed that Mbiti's concept of the future in the general African sense of time "should be limited to two years and no more, no less" and that Mbiti states quite "categorically, that in Africa, 'people have little or no active interest in events that lie in the future beyond, at most, two years from now'" (52–61). I think, however, that Professor Anozie, like numerous other critics, misses the tone of caution which Mbiti attempts to inject in his book from the outset.

Works Consulted

Anozie, Sunday O. *Structural Models and African Poetics.* London: Routledge and Kegan Paul, 1981.

Beibuyck, Daniel P., and Kahombo C. Mateene, eds., trans. *The Mwindo Epic.* Berkeley and Los Angeles: U of California P, 1971.

Chinweizu. *The West and the Rest of Us.* New York: Vintage, 1975.

Cleage, Albert B., Jr. *Black Christian Nationalism: New Directions for the Black Church.* New York: William Morrow, 1972.

Fanon, Frantz. *The Wretched of the Earth.* New York: Grove, 1968.

Grier, William H., and Price M. Cobbs. *Black Rage.* New York: Basic Books, 1968.

Harrison, Paul Carter. *Kuntu Drama.* New York: Grove, 1974.

Jones, Charles Colcock. *The Religious Instruction of the Negroes in the United States.* Savannah: Thomas Purse, 1842. Freeport, NY: Books for Libraries Press, 1971.

Mbiti, John S. *African Religions and Philosophy.* New York: Doubleday Anchor Books, 1970.

Niane, D. T., ed. *Sundiata: An Epic of Old Mali.* London: Longman, 1965.

Woodson, Carter G., and Charles Wesley. *The Negro in Our History.* 12th ed. Washington, DC: Associated Pubs., 1972.

IV "New" Texts

11 Haroun's Mystic Journey: Salman Rushdie's *Haroun and the Sea of Stories*

Aron Aji and Katrina Runge
Butler University

In "Is Nothing Sacred?" Salman Rushdie asks if art might not have the power to mediate "between the material and spiritual worlds; might it, by 'swallowing' both worlds, offer us something new—something that might even be called a secular definition of transcendence?" His answer: "I believe it can. I believe it must. And I believe that, at its best, it does" (*Imaginary Homelands* 420). For Rushdie, then, art, like religion, ought to satisfy our need to know "exaltation," "awe," and "wonder," and to experience "transcendence": that "flight of the human spirit outside the confines of its material, physical existence. . . . The sense of being more than oneself, of being in some way joined to the whole of life" (421).

As a number of critics have observed, Rushdie's *Haroun and the Sea of Stories,* published in the same year, affirms faith in creativity and the power of narrative and evidences Rushdie's fondness for magical realism and the fantastic. David Appelbaum points to the "fabulous creations" in *Haroun* (132), while for Alison Lurie *Haroun* "is a lively, wonderfully inventive comic tale with an updated Arabian Nights background" from which it also derives its "supernatural" elements (1). Jean-Pierre Durix describes various aspects of *Haroun* as being "miraculous" (114), "magical" (115), "science-fiction" (121), or "metafictional" (117). While these observations are both valid and valuable, they fail to account for Rushdie's notion of art as "secular transcendence"—a notion that informs not only his theoretical position, but his creative practice as well. The only allusions to transcendence or mysticism are made in passing by Durix and Carlo Coppola, both of whom observe an affinity between *Haroun* and Rushdie's first novel *Grimus,* since both texts draw from the Sufi classic *The Conference of the Birds* (Durix 121; Coppola 234). And yet, neither critic explores the mystical possibilities of Haroun's journey.

131

The progression of Haroun's fairy-tale journey from a state of uncertainty and doubt to one of intense commitment and transcendent attainment runs parallel to that of the mystic quest as described by Sufi esoterism and as articulated in the teachings of Jalal al-Din Rumi (1207–73). This parallelism holds true except for the fact that the ultimate object of the young hero's attainment is the source of all stories, rather than the Sufi's Divine Beloved, the Source of Creation. Yet, this variation proves necessary since the fairy tale advocates the idea that stories can offer the kind of transcendent experience usually associated with religious mysticism, as Rushdie claims in "Is Nothing Sacred?"

Our reading of *Haroun* from the perspective of Sufi mysticism involves a parallel examination of, first, the hero's transformation as he attempts to find the source of all stories (which entails a fantastic trip to the moon Kahani and its Ocean of Stories), and, second, the mystic path, described in the teachings of Rumi, that brings the Sufi initiate to a union with God. In attempting such an examination, it is useful to outline first the main tenets of Sufi mysticism and its path of attainment.

To a large extent, classical Sufi doctrine is derived from literary works and inspirational writings, such as Farid ud-Din Attar's *The Conference of the Birds* and *Book of Secrets,* or Rumi's recorded teachings and poetry in his *Masnavi*. At the core of Sufi mysticism is the longing for God that must culminate in the transcendent union with Him. Such a union is the confirmation of *Wahdad al-Wujud* (the oneness of body/being), the concept that defines the universe as the single and comprehensive creation of God, in which everything transient and relative, including the Sufi seeker, is part of His all-permanent and absolute Being. The mystic quest consists of three stages, all entailing arduous learning and discovery about the self, the world, and God as the source and all-encompassing essence of creation. While an enlightened Sufi teacher provides the seeker with inspiration and guidance during the early part of the quest, the ultimate union with God is an intensely personal experience and therefore remains the seeker's responsibility. In the first stage, the Sufi initiates move from *uncertainty* to the *realization* that there is an all-encompassing whole to which they belong. This realization, initially empirical in nature, has to be internalized and rendered sincere (*ihsan*). To this end, the seekers must undermine their egos and understand their identities in terms of this belonging. The seekers then enter the second stage of *surrender* or *absorption,* in which they strive to abandon conventional and relativistic truths, and to cultivate an inward purification in preparation for the experience of the divine presence within and all around them. Only through intense absorption in the pursuit can the seekers ultimately reach the supreme stage—the transcendent *attainment* or *union* with the divine that is *Wahdad al-Wujud.* Inevitably, what follows the "moment" of attainment is separation—the seekers' return to the mundane. Since every worldly thing now recalls the divine, the Sufis experience sorrow and nostalgia, and they desire the quest, this time even with more intensity because of having once tasted the incomparable joy of attainment.

Haroun's search for the source of stories is initiated when his mother, Soraya, leaves him and his father, Rashid Khalifa, because Rashid has too much imagination for his own good. As her new suitor, Mr. Sengupta, tells Soraya: "That husband of yours. . . . [h]e's got his head stuck in the air and his feet off the ground. . . . What's the use of stories that aren't even true?" (20). Rashid is devastated; he loses his ability to tell stories. As for Haroun, he cannot "get [Sengupta's] terrible question out of his head" (20). His uncertainty, however, does not signify a loss of his faith in stories so much as his need to confirm it, a condition similar to the Sufi's desire concerning attainment. Rumi states, "So long as you have an appetite and exhibit utter desire, [divine blessing] comes toward you and becomes your food. But when appetite and inclination fail . . . [i]t hides its face in the veil and does not show you its face" (129; unless otherwise specified, Rumi citations are from *Discourses*).

An important feature of the mystic quest is that its motivation and its object of attainment are closely linked since the "food" that sustains the Sufi's "appetite and inclination" comes in the form of worldly phenomena that manifest the divine. In order to recognize and benefit from this nourishment, the Sufi initiate receives the guidance of an enlightened teacher. For Haroun, Rashid and his stories provide similar guidance and motivation. What Rumi says about "words" applies to Rashid's stories: "They set you searching and excite you, not that the object of the quest should be attained through words" (202). For the Sufi, words are linked to meaning as "branches" to "root," or as "forms" to "reality" (55), offering guidance and direction toward their source. As Rumi explains, "God revealed this present world in order that you may acknowledge the other stages which yet lie ahead" (32). Likewise, the reason Haroun constantly asks his father to tell him where "all these stories come from" (16) is that they compel him to imagine a source beyond themselves. Rashid's answer—that his stories come from "the great Story Sea" (17)—sounds like yet another story to Haroun and therefore excites him even more to pursue the source of stories.

Rashid's stories also offer Haroun mental training similar to that offered by the Sufi teacher, who uses poems, stories, and anecdotes in order to prepare the initiate for the quest. One particular effect of Rashid's stories has distinct mystical possibilities: "His stories were really lots of different tales juggled together, and Rashid kept them going in a sort of dizzy whirl and never made a mistake" (16). The dizzying imagery suggests the kind of entrancement induced through music, chanting, poetry, and whirling by the Sufis. Moreover, Rashid's juggling causes the stories to blur into one circling entity, preventing even the loyal listener (Haroun) from recognizing them as single, separate forms. In a mystical sense, this blurring can lead the mind to free itself from attachment to outward forms and differences so that it becomes ready to bear witness to *Wahdad al-Wujud*. The more Rashid juggles his stories, the more Haroun is capable of going past the individual tales—the branches—in order to contemplate where they come from—their root. In this regard, his progress mirrors Rumi's advice to the initiate: "Though to outward form they are of various kinds and differ widely in their states and acts and words, from the standpoint of the object it is one thing only, namely the quest of God" (34).

Thus having been raised with his father's stories, Haroun turns out to have already begun acquiring the knowledge necessary to move from a state of uncertainty to the realization that stories do matter. His education continues when he travels to Dull Lake, where he witnesses firsthand the power of imagination and "the use of stories that aren't even true." Haroun takes the trip with his father, who is invited by the politician Mr. Buttoo to tell stories at a campaign rally. This trip proves important, for everything Haroun learns prepares him for his mystic quest to the fantastic moon, Kahani. On the way to Dull Lake, he is able to persuade Butt the Mail Coach Driver to speed up so that they can view the Valley of K before sunset and be filled with its legendary magnificence. Because Haroun initially learns about the Valley of K from his father, he believes that the view will uplift Rashid's soul and perhaps inspire him to conjure his lost stories. What Haroun hopes will happen to his father is akin to the experience of the Sufi initiate, who is inspired to pursue God through the objects that reflect His essence—objects in which the initiate can witness shining "the light of the Majesty of God" (48). Rashid needs to see the magnificent lake so that he can find the inspiration to imagine magnificence once again.

Rashid thanks Haroun for bringing him to view the valley, yet he admits, "I thought we were all fixed good and proper, I mean done for, finito, *khattam-shud*" (39). Responding to Haroun's curiosity about the last expression, the father explains: "Khattam-Shud . . . is the Arch-Enemy of all Stories, even of Language itself. He is the Prince of Silence and the Foe of Speech. And because everything ends, because dreams end, stories end, life ends, at the finish of everything we use his name. 'It's finished,' we tell one another, 'it's over. Khattam-Shud: The End' " (39). Rashid's explanation introduces Haroun to the villain he will encounter in Kahani and to the fundamental truth that opposition and negation are integral to any human venture. In Kahani, Haroun will discover that Khattam-Shud is the enemy within: he belongs in the very tradition of stories that he is intent on destroying. His condition of belonging, however, is also what gives stories the ability to contain and, by containing, to transcend his destructive power. This is indeed the fate assigned to Khattam-Shud: he is forever contained in the story entitled "Haroun and the Sea of Stories" that Rashid tells about his little boy toward the end of the fairy tale. The wisdom about Khattam-Shud that Haroun will come to grasp fully by the end of his journey to Kahani recalls the Sufi creed on the containment of opposites and the nature of God, who is both manifest in and transcends things good and evil. Just as evil is in the world to promulgate belief in God, Khattam-Shud is a constant presence in stories in order to promulgate belief in stories.

When the group enters the Valley of K, Haroun notices its welcome sign, altered to read, "WELCOME TO KOSH-MAR," which occasions for him another invaluable lesson with mystical implications. Rashid tells his son that the valley now known as K has had several names in its past, i.e., "Kache-mer," the "Franj" word for "the place that hides a Sea," and "Kosh-Mar," which means "nightmare" (40). Rashid also instructs Haroun that "all names mean something" (40). In other words, one can uncover the valley's forgotten origin by charting out a path back through its names. The meaning-origin linkage again recalls Rumi's figurative "branch-root" metaphor representing the relationship between all things created and their divine source. For Haroun, Rashid's wisdom about the names has to do with how the little boy can rescue his father's stories: by tracing them, as he will, all the way back to their wellspring.

Throughout the tale, Haroun becomes less dependent on his father just as he becomes more confident in his ability to find his own answers. In turn, his developing sense of confidence leads to discoveries of increasing significance, as though the world around him reveals its

riches according to his ability. "There is no end to words [wisdom],"
Rumi asserts, "but they are imparted according to the capacity of the
seeker"; this is why "one man comes along whom oceans do not satisfy
[while] another man finds a few drops enough, and more than that
would be harmful to him" (41).

Haroun makes his most important discovery yet when the travelers
reach the Dull Lake, which, to Haroun's amazement, mirrors "the Tale
of the Moody Land . . . one of Rashid Khalifa's best-loved stories" (47).
He notices that the land surrounding the lake is as "temperamental"
as the Moody Land in his father's story. In both places, "the sun would
shine all night if there were enough joyful people around . . . and when
people got angry the ground would shake" (48). Facing a dense "Mist
of Misery" hovering over the Dull Lake that he attributes to his father's
sadness, Haroun asks Rashid whether the lake is the place in the story.
The father replies, "The Moody Land was only a story, Haroun. . . . Here
we're somewhere real" (48). Contrary to his father's claim, however,
Haroun chooses to conduct an experiment, and with "a new note of
authority [that] had come into his voice" (49), he tells the people
around him: "Think of the happiest times you can remember. Think
of the view of the Valley of K we saw when we came through the
Tunnel of I. Think of your wedding day" (50). Sure enough, the mist
"tore apart like the shreds of an old shirt and drifted away on a cool
night breeze" (50). This incident marks a crucial turning point in
Haroun's development, on four counts. First, *he* makes the connection
between stories and reality. Second, he trusts his own judgment despite
that of his father. Third, he effects a change, driven by inner conviction
and inspired by Rashid's story. Fourth, all by himself, he tests and
confirms the transformative power of imagination. "He knew what he
knew: that the real world was full of magic, so magical worlds could
easily be real" (50).

Haroun's turning point is also meaningful in light of the mystic
path he is traveling. His movement from ignorance to realization is
almost complete since he has not only witnessed firsthand the power
of stories but also become capable of exercising that power. At this
point, however, Haroun's knowledge about stories is, in Sufi terminology, an "intellectual" knowledge, based as it is on empirical evidence
and deductive reasoning—i.e., if the real world is magical, then stories
can be real. He can achieve the full realization necessary for entering
the next stage of the mystic path only when his intellectual knowledge
gives way to faith.

It is also important to note the change in the father-son relationship
resulting from the changes in Haroun. Haroun's dismissal of Rashid's

claim that stories are not real signals a critical shift of control and authority from the father to the son, who, of course, thanks to his father's teachings, is now able to heed the wisdom of stories without outside guidance. The fairy tale accentuates this critical shift in a scene during the restless night the father and son spend aboard Mr. Buttoo's houseboat, "Arabian Nights Plus One." Haroun and Rashid are given separate sleeping quarters in which neither is able to sleep. Haroun finds the oversized turtle-shell-shaped bed too strange and Rashid is equally disturbed by his enormous peacock-shaped bed. Father and son switch places. The belly of the fanciful peacock seems appropriate for Haroun, who will lead the pursuit, while the shell of the aged and experienced turtle befits Rashid, who no longer leads but lets Haroun guide his own endeavors.

The same night, Haroun encounters the flamboyant Iff, the Water Genie, who will guide him on the journey to Kahani. It is likely that Haroun conjures Iff in a dream, given that the boy "had just dozed off when he was woken by a creaking and a rumbling and a groaning and a mumbling" (54). This likelihood is further reinforced by the fact that Haroun's adventure in Kahani takes place "in a single night" (204) and he finds himself back in Mr. Buttoo's houseboat the morning after. In this light, Iff can be viewed as a materialization of Haroun's imagination, his inner yearning to travel to where magic worlds are real so that he can restore his father's talent. In fact, much of what Iff tells Haroun about Kahani and its Ocean of the Streams of Story consists of variations on details that the boy has previously learned from his father's stories, indicating that Haroun's imagination plays a vital role throughout his entire quest in Kahani. True action on the mystic path, says Rumi, "is an inward meaning" (86). By the same token, Iff the Water Genie, born as he is out of Haroun, is the affirmation of the boy's "inward meaning." Iff is especially instrumental in enabling Haroun to proceed from his intellectual knowledge about stories to faith in them, thereby taking the crucial step that concludes his stage of realization. As though pointing out the limitations of intellectual knowledge, the Genie first asks Haroun to use his Disconnecting Tool and tap a seemingly empty space where Rashid's Story Tap is presumably fixed. "Ding went the Disconnecting Tool as it struck something extremely solid and extremely invisible" (59), leading Haroun to wonder if it is possible to believe in what is not visible. Iff then tells Haroun, "Believe in your own eyes and you'll get into a lot of trouble," and says that he would do better to "choose what he cannot see," that is, to act on faith. In this instance, Iff's wisdom echoes that in Rumi's words: "You must labor to acquire [and trust] an inward light, that you may escape and be secure from this mire of confusion" (102). Thus willing to act on faith, Haroun is ready to move to the next stage of the mystic path, to be absorbed wholly by the pursuit of stories and ultimately of their wellspring.

In order to get to Kahani, Iff suggests that Haroun choose from among the miniature birds in the palm of his hand. Iff is especially pleased when Haroun picks the Hoopoe, the "crested bird that was giving him a sidelong look through one highly intelligent eye" (64). Iff explains that in the old stories, the Hoopoe guides other birds to their destination. The best-known of these old stories is, of course, the Sufi classic, *The Conference of the Birds* by Attar, which describes the birds' journey to mystical attainment. Haroun's choice, therefore, is very telling. Just as Attar's Hoopoe guides thirty birds to Simorgh, literally meaning thirty birds (Attar 16), so will Butt, Haroun's Hoopoe, guide the little boy on his journey to Kahani whose end will be none other than *Haroun and the Sea of Stories*. That Haroun and Butt the Hoopoe communicate telepathically also points to the mystical possibilities of their association. Though two separate beings, they are bound by the same purpose and can mirror each other's inner meanings.

On the second stage of the mystic path, the Sufi seekers strive to surrender their being completely to the call of the quest. This surrender involves a sincere devotion to understanding—no longer intellectually but spiritually—the nature of what Rumi calls the "unseen world" of God (102), and to serving Him. All the seekers' efforts at this stage are aimed at preparing them for the utmost stage of attainment, when their wills become one with the will of God. This preparation requires a slow and diligent process of self-emptying, in which the seekers struggle to divorce themselves from earthly preoccupations, their desire for self-control, and all of their selfish interests. The emptier of such attachments become the seekers, the more room they make in themselves for the all-subsuming union with the divine.

Haroun's journey on Kahani's ocean clearly echoes many of the features of this second stage of the mystic path. After his affirmation of faith, Haroun's customary skepticism decreases significantly. He is willing to take Iff, and later, Butt, on their word, letting them lead the way to Kahani. The boy finds it easy to trust his companions, perhaps because the two belong to and seem intimately familiar with the magical worlds in which Haroun chooses to invest his faith. Once in Kahani, Haroun soon realizes that he is a part of the world of stories, having acquired a great deal of intellectual knowledge about them and their power through his previous experiences. However, especially in the earlier part of the journey, Haroun's faith is rivaled by the worldly concerns that still linger in his mind and inhibit his concentration on his quest. The boy is still worried about his father's lost talent and his mother's desertion. He must also deal with his short, eleven-minute attention span, which he acquired when his mother left them and his father, angry and forlorn, crushed all the clocks in the house at exactly eleven o'clock.

The little boy's mental unrest becomes most evident when Iff gives him a vial of Wishwater to ingest and tells him to make a wish. He takes a gulp, and finds that a "golden glow was all around him, and inside him, too; and everything was very, very still, as if the entire cosmos were waiting upon his command" (70). Yet he is confused as to what wish to make, whether to ask for his mother's return or for the recovery of his father's talent, and when eleven minutes pass and he loses his concentration, the Wishwater's power wears out. This early on his journey, it seems, Haroun has not yet escaped from what Rumi calls "the mire of confusion" that inhibits the seeker's resolve. Since the boy is still thinking in terms of outward distinctions, he is unable to realize that what he sees as conflicting wishes are actually one and the same. Moreover, Haroun is still attached to ideas of control; his wishes cannot come true unless he ceases to think that "the entire universe [was] waiting upon his command." Just as the speaker in one of Rumi's verses asks, "Pour [the wine] in my mouth / I've lost the way to my mouth" (*Unseen Rain* 69), Haroun too must let Kahani and its ocean work their magic on him. Such surrender is very important because the less he thinks of his father's talent and his mother's return, the more he can become one with Kahani's magic (and, paradoxically, the closer he gets to fulfilling his wishes concerning his parents). "When a man has acquired such an inward light [of the unseen world of the divine]," says Rumi, "all mundane circumstances appertaining to this world such as rank, command, vizierate, shining upon his inward heart pass like a lightning-flash" (102).

With as much concentration as he can muster after the incident with the Wishwater, Haroun begins to take in all the wonders of the Ocean that are revealed to him. This is how he learns about the nature of the story streams that spring from the Wellspring in the Old Zone of Kahani, and that mix with one another to create new stories from the old. Already, Haroun is so amazed by the Ocean that when Iff offers him "water from a single, pure Stream of Story... so that the magic of the story can restore his spirits," the boy drinks it "without saying a word" (72). Haroun also discovers conflict in Kahani: the pollution spreading throughout the Ocean, threatening to destroy the stories. Butt the Hoopoe attributes the occurrence to Khattam-Shud—

whom Haroun readily remembers, of course, from his father's stories. As the travelers reach Gup City, the nature of the conflict becomes clearer to Haroun, who finds out about the two lands of Kahani, Gup and Chup, and the Twilight Strip between the two that was formed when the Gup scientists, the Eggheads, halted the rotation of the moon to keep Gup in perpetual light and Chup in darkness. The peoples of Kahani are in bitter rivalry: the Guppees, who revel in disagreements and long arguments, are the defenders of stories and speech, while the Chupwalas, the subjects of the censorious Khattam-Shud, are intent on plugging the Wellspring, eradicating stories, and drowning the moon in complete silence. A lesser calamity perhaps is the kidnapping of the Gup Prince Bolo's beloved, Princess Batcheat, by the Chupwalas. By the time Haroun finds himself amidst the Guppees, who are getting ready for war and shouting their battle cries, "Save the Ocean" and "For Batcheat and the Ocean" (91), the little boy is almost completely absorbed in the reality of Kahani, so much so that when his father suddenly appears in Gup City, he is utterly astonished (98).

The strife in Kahani shows Haroun that saving the Ocean and its Wellspring ought to be the greater mission at hand than that of recuperating his father's talent and having his mother back. His discovery goes a long way toward alleviating the internal discord that had previously frustrated his wishes about his parents. In fact, his father's unexpected appearance in Kahani is the material evidence for the gradual coalescence of Haroun's goals, albeit unbeknownst to him at this point.

Furthermore, what happened to Haroun in the Valley of K happens to him again in Kahani. As with the true mystic, the more he learns about the story moon, the more capable he is of witnessing its subtler truths so he can save the Wellspring. Accompanying the Gup scouting party and his father to the Twilight Strip, Haroun meets the Chupwala warrior Mudra engaged in a silent "martial dance" with his shadow, whose "movements don't match the man's" (124). Mudra's divided being is common to all the Chupwalas, and it is the doing of Khattam-Shud, who ensures the obedience of his subjects by fomenting inner discord in each, thus preventing them from uniting against him. While watching Mudra's dance, Haroun makes three critical and related observations about Kahani. First, he notes all the "opposites . . . at war in the battle between Gup and Chup." While Gup is "bright . . . warm" and "all chattering and noise," Chup is "dark . . . freezing cold" and "silent as a shadow." And while Guppees "love Stories and Speech," Chupwalas "hate these things just as strongly." At first, Haroun concludes that what he is witnessing is a war between "Love (of the Ocean, or the Princess) and Death (which was what Cultmaster Khattam-Shud had in mind for the Ocean, and for the Princess, too)." However, the Shadow Warrior's dance soon compels him to modify his insight as he realizes that "silence had its own grace and beauty (just as speech could be graceless and ugly)" and that "Action could be as noble as Words; and that creatures of darkness could be as lovely as the children of the light" (125). Thus realizing an essential sameness in opposites on the grounds of positive virtues—beauty, grace, nobility, love—Haroun makes his most significant observation yet: that opposites attract, and therefore Kahani can be brought together in peace and harmony (125).

Haroun's chain of insights bears significance in light of the mystic quest. To begin with, he is able to penetrate the outward opposites and see their essence, which, according to Rumi, "is truly seeing and knowing" (50). "Beauty," "grace," "nobility," and "love" are also the binding verities that the Sufi sees in the harmony and design of the universe. Next, what Haroun notes as a potential in the story moon echoes attributes of *Wahdad al-Wujud* which, according to Rumi, simultaneously contains and transcends opposites. Rumi states: "It is a true saying, that all [opposite] things in relation to God are good and perfect. . . . Fornication and purity, not praying and prayer, unbelief and Islam, polytheism and unitarianism—with God all these are good . . ." (42). "Things are made clear by their opposites," the great teacher says. "It is impossible to make anything known without its opposite" (92), and this is why God contains opposites. Indeed, Kahani's opposites are useful in relation to a greater good: it is on account of them that the imperative to save the Wellspring is made known to Haroun and the Guppees. When the Eggheads halt the rotation of the moon, the Old Zone where the Wellspring is located remains on the dark side and the oldest stories are left to decay by the Guppees. Looking at the Ocean of ruined stories, Iff the Water Genie admits his guilt: "We let them rot, we abandoned them, long before this poisoning. We lost touch with our beginnings, with our roots, our Wellspring, our Source" (146). Therefore, had it not been for Khattam-Shud and the ensuing rivalry between the lands of Gup and Chup, the Wellspring might have continued to deteriorate, perhaps to its end. The seemingly destructive oppositions ultimately serve a recuperative purpose.

Haroun's insights duly align him in the path of attainment, singular in purpose, clear in motivation. That he contemplates the reunification of Kahani's peoples signals his intense absorption in his mission to save the Wellspring. At this stage, what the boy is after, the source of all stories, is analogous to what the mystic is after, the source of all creation. Rumi says, "The people of God have become wholly God's and their faces are turned on God; they are preoccupied with and absorbed in God" (100). When Haroun volunteers to travel to Chup in order to spy on Khattam-Shud's dark machinations, his resolve is so apparent that even the Gup Prince Bolo, who is not known for intelligence and discernment, can acknowledge that "this boy's destiny is to rescue what he loves: that is, the Ocean of Stories" (138).

In the last stage of his quest, joining Haroun are Iff and Butt, and later, Mali the Floating Gardener. Before the group can travel far on the murky waters of Chup, it is captured by the Chupwalas, and Haroun finally gets to encounter Khattam-Shud, who functions as the perfect foil for the little boy. Their opposing attitudes and goals concerning stories and the Wellspring make all the more clear Haroun's fitness for his attainment. The tyrant displays an insatiable hunger for power and control, telling Haroun, "Your world, my world, all worlds. . . . They are all there to be ruled." He is determined to destroy the Wellspring of stories, for inside every story is, he says, "a storyworld, that I cannot Rule at all" (161). Unlike Khattam-Shud, Haroun has no interest in ruling stories. His whole adventure—from the time he was in the Valley of K to the moment of encountering the Prince of Darkness—has been possible because of his willingness to surrender to the power of stories. When they first meet, the Cultmaster scolds Haroun, "What brought you up here, eh? . . . *Stories,* I suppose" (155). Khattam-Shud does not know how close to the truth he is, for his zeal for control prevents him from seeing any wisdom in such surrender. "We are like a bowl on the surface of the water," Rumi says. "The movement of the bowl . . . is controlled not by the bowl but by the water" (160).

True to the nature of the mystic quest, Haroun must leave behind his companions and alone witness the Wellspring. His ensuing attainment marks a genuine state of Oneness (*Wahdad al-Wujud*) as the peoples of the story moon Kahani are unified and the Ocean of the Stream of Stories is restored. Haroun has succeeded in escaping from Khattam-Shud when Mali the Floating Gardener causes a major power outage. When the little boy dives heedlessly into the poisoned waters, "wonder of wonders, he caught sight of the Source itself":

> The Source of Stories was a hole or a chasm or crater in the sea-bed, and through that hole . . . the flow of pure, unpolluted stories came bubbling up from the very heart of Kahani. There were so many Streams of Story, of so many different colors, all pouring out of the Source at once, that it looked like a huge underwater fountain of shining white light. (167–68)

Literally "enlightening" him, Haroun's act of witnessing the Wellspring also signals his state of utter selflessness and perfect consort with the destiny of Kahani's universe. When he remembers the vial of Wishwater in his pocket and drinks from it, the golden glow again enables Haroun to transcend his physical form and become one with the Ocean. The wish he makes this time is not about his father or his mother; rather, he wishes "this Moon, Kahani, to turn, so that it's no longer half in light and half in darkness . . ." (170). And this time, his wish comes true. The resumption of the moon's rotation brings to end Khattam-Shud's tyranny by causing the unrelenting darkness in Chup, and the Cultmaster's shadow soldiers, to dissolve. Kahani's natural harmony is restored. Now the Guppees and the Chupwalas, light and dark, warm and cold, love and hate, speech and silence, the imagination of the storytellers and the dull factuality of the Eggheads, and, yes, good and bad stories, can once again coexist in necessary oppositions, ensuring "variety, possibility, . . . the uncertainties and surprises of a shared, public freedom, in its slow and irregular tendency toward good" (Park 463).

The harmony and unity resulting from Haroun's transcendent attainment is not only outward but also inward, evident in his final request to the Gup Comptroller General: " . . . I come from a sad city, a city so sad that it has forgotten its name. I want you to provide a happy ending, not just for my adventure, but for the whole sad city as well" (202). His request implies his sense of belonging to a whole larger than himself and of shared destiny with others. Haroun seems to understand that his journey imparted to him a wisdom that he must share with others, just as a Sufi mystic does upon returning to mundane existence after experiencing divine union. "My work is to carry this love," says Rumi, "as comfort for those who long for you, / to go everywhere you've walked . . ." (*Unseen Rain* 83). Back in Mr. Buttoo's houseboat, Haroun finds a golden envelope containing a note from his friends in Kahani and the miniature Hoopoe "cocking its head up at him" (204). Yet Haroun has not merely brought back with him the wisdom of Kahani. Because his entire journey was conjured in one night's dream, he embodies at once the source and manifestation of this wisdom. His father, having regained his talent, the next day narrates *Haroun and the Sea of Stories,* thus linking forever the fate of stories to his son's heroism. Rumi urges his disciples to be a mirror to one another (36), each finding in the others the inspiration to walk on the mystic path. Through Rashid's story, Haroun becomes this mirror for others who believe in imagination and stories.

The mystic quest, whether for God or for the Wellspring of Stories, must always end with the seeker returning to worldly existence and resuming the quest because the state of attainment cannot be sustained.

Both the Sufi's God and Kahani's Wellspring must, by their infinite nature, forever surpass the confines of any single attainment. "If He is present in form," Rumi says, "He will flee by way of the spirit" (*Poems* 100), but he also advises against losing hope: " . . . come, do not give up hope: seek and seek forever! Fixing the heart on the goal ensures its attainment" (*Masnavi* 240). The antidote for the Sufi's disillusionment is found in the myriad worldly manifestations of the divine that beckon the seeker to seek again. Similar antidotes are made available to Haroun also.

On returning to his hometown, Haroun shows signs of frustration, of being disheartened by the ordinary surroundings after having experienced the imaginary. He asks his father, "Nothing's really changed, has it?" (207), for he doubts that the "happy ending" he requested before leaving Kahani will ever come true in the real world. Yet it does. First, a wonderful rain starts pouring over the sad city, bringing happiness to all. Then, Haroun learns that the people have remembered their town's name which, much to his amazement, is Kahani. Haroun apparently needs one more sign, however, and his mood finally breaks only when his mother returns. That night, after the family reunion, Haroun goes to bed with his faith in Kahani restored. He tells his Hoopoe: "It's really good to know you'll be here when I need you" (210). What happened once can happen again to him—and to us—as it does every time we read *Haroun and the Sea of Stories*.

In Islam, Haroun is the name of the brother of Moses who is privy to the esoteric truths of God, while Moses is His lawgiver. For this reason, Haroun is a favored prophet among the Sufis. Rushdie's young hero seems no less able to witness and realize the transcendental possibility of stories and imagination. In this light, Haroun Khalifa seems very much a fictional study in Rushdie's lifelong question: whether or not literature can be, "for a secular, material culture, some sort of replacement for what the love of god offers in the world of faith," namely "a repository for our awestruck wonderment at life and an answer to the great questions of existence, and a rule book, too" ("Is Nothing Sacred?" 421). This may be, after all, the use of stories that aren't even true.

Works Consulted

Appelbaum, David. *"Haroun and the Sea of Stories." Parabola* 16.2 (1991): 126–32.

Attar, Farid ud-Din. *The Conference of the Birds.* Trans. Afkham Darbandi and Dick Davis. New York: Penguin, 1984.

Coppola, Carlo. "Salman Rushdie's *Haroun and the Sea of Stories*: Fighting the Good Fight or Knuckling Under." *Journal of South Asian Literature* 26.1–2 (1991): 229–37.

Durix, Jean-Pierre. "'The Gardener of Stories': Salman Rushdie's *Haroun and the Sea of Stories.*" *The Journal of Commonwealth Literature* (1993): 114–22.

Lurie, Alison. "Another Dangerous Story by Salman Rushdie." *The New York Times Book Review* 11 Nov. 1990: 1.

Park, Clara Clairborne. "Horse and Sea Horse: Areopagitica and the Sea of Stories." *The Hudson Review* 46 (1993): 451–70.

Rumi, Mevlana Jelaluddin [Jalal al-Din]. *Discourses.* Trans. and ed. A. J. Arberry. Surrey, UK: Curzon Press, 1993.

———. *Mystical Poems of Rumi.* Trans. A. J. Arberry. Chicago: U of Chicago P, 1968.

———. *Tales from the Masnavi.* Trans. and ed. by A. J. Arberry. Surrey, UK: Curzon Press, 1993.

———. *Unseen Rain.* Trans. John Moyne and Coleman Barks. Putney, VT: Threshold Books, 1986.

Rushdie, Salman. *Haroun and the Sea of Stories.* London: Granta, 1990.

———. *Imaginary Homelands: Essays and Criticism, 1981–1991.* London: Granta, 1991.

12 Anthologies, Canonicity, and the Objectivist Imagination: The Case of George Oppen

Dennis Young
George Mason University

"We begin to suspect that literary judgments are projections of social ones" (qtd. in Scholes 138). Thus, in 1957, Northrop Frye may have sounded the first of many contemporary critiques of the literary canon. Since Frye, several literary critics have continued to criticize canons, largely in social/political terms of exclusion, inclusion, and priorities based on class, gender, or race. On the other side of the debate, most conservative criticisms of canon revision decry the subversive nature of leftist, feminist, deconstructionist, minority, and other apparently discontented literary criticisms. For example, in *The Chronicle of Higher Education* Peter Shaw offers a rebuttal to the 1991 MLA Survey regarding the canon and what English teachers are really teaching; he says that the "chief concern" of supporters of the traditional canon "has been not the number of titles replaced but the principle of assigning literary value according to gender or race" (B3). Instead of reiterating the canon debate on these grounds, however, I wish to suggest that the bias implicit in canon formation—especially the canon of American poetry—is closer to home than the "social group" theory of the canon: it is as close as the syllabus we follow daily. Certain poets are excluded from the classroom and therefore from the canon because of the way we define and teach poetry, which I believe is still largely New Critical in aim and emphasis. To put it another way, authors are included or excluded from the canon largely because they do not conform to a tenacious New Critical mindset that dictates a limited, limiting way of seeing, defining, and teaching poetry.

The institutional-historical context of the teaching of literature and the reproduction of works (exemplified primarily in anthologies), has complex implications: *How* we teach poetry and *what* we teach are closely related and equally significant in the gradual formation of canons. The regulation of what we teach is sustained by the texts produced and reproduced in poetry anthologies, which nearly always—

with a few bold exceptions—privilege poetry in the nineteenth-century romantic-symbolist tradition as opposed to poetry in what Charles Altieri calls "the Objectivist tradition."[1]

After having worked for several years closely and appreciatively with the objectivist poets, I am left to wonder why such poets as Louis Zukofsky, Charles Reznikoff, and, in particular, George Oppen never make it to the major poetry anthologies. I was also led to more general questions: Why do certain significant poets almost never appear in anthologies? What is the basis for selecting (and omitting) anthology poems? Can the omission of the objectivists tell us anything about the assumptions behind the way we perceive, define, and teach poetry?

By looking closely at the kinds of poetry typically included and those excluded from anthologies, we may identify the basis for the canon of American poetry. Current editions of Poulin's *Contemporary American Poetry*, Ellmann and O'Clair's *Norton Anthology of Modern Poetry*, Carruth's *Voice That Is Great within Us*, and Vendler's *Harvard Book of Contemporary American Poetry* include nothing at all from Zukofsky, Reznikoff, or Oppen. These anthologies, because of their popularity and widespread classroom use, may be taken as canonical assessments of recent poetry. It seems as though these three poets—one of the most significant groupings in the field of twentieth-century poetry—never existed. And not to be represented by such standard anthologies means virtual nonexistence for a poet. Oppen's absence in the standard anthologies is especially curious given that, in the past decade, his poetry has received increasing critical attention[2] and many of his poems are quite suited to the anthology format. How do we account for this omission?

Perhaps the objectivist poets are overlooked because of the very nature of their poetics. Objectivist poetics is a counter-poetics that resists certain romantic-idealistic notions of poetry and language. To take on the hegemonic romantic aesthetic and philosophical bias is no easy task; to do so requires a new poetic form and a new consciousness about poetry's function. Given the difficulty of creating a new poetics, poets have grappled with objectivism since the early 1930s. That the term itself is elusive is made evident by the various attempts to define it. Zukofsky, the first to use the term "objectivist," describes the objectivist mode of seeing: "It is the detail, not mirage, of seeing, of thinking with the things as they exist. . . . Shapes suggest themselves, and the mind senses and receives awareness" (273). The uncertainty of his language betrays the complexity of the insight. Reznikoff more simply says that the term objectivist refers to "a writer who does not write directly about his feelings but about what he sees and hears; who is restricted almost to the testimony of a witness in a court of law; and who expresses his feelings indirectly by the selection of his subject-matter and, if he writes in verse, by its music" (194). William Carlos Williams, looking back on his associations with the objectivists, says: "The poem, like every other form of art, is an object, an object that in itself formally presents its case and its meaning by the very form it assumes. . . . [T]o invent an object consonant with his day. This was what we wished to imply by Objectivist" (265). Oppen, a cabinetmaker by trade, points to another possibility of the term by emphasizing the poet's relation to the poem: "If it's perfect you're not in it at all" ("George and Mary Oppen" 12). Charles Olson emphasizes the philosophical dimension of the term: the objectivist attempts to

> get rid of the lyrical interference of the individual as ego, of the "subject" and his soul, that peculiar presumption by which western man has interposed himself between what he is as a creature of nature . . . and those other creations of nature which we may, with no derogation, call objects. . . . For man is himself an object. . . . (24)

Hugh Kenner suggests that an appropriate motto for the objectivists might be "no myths." He goes on to say that "myths stand between facts and words. They are like 'plots' and 'statements' and even . . . messages: units of perception detachable from the language" (187). One detects in each of these definitions an attempt to revise traditional, romantic notions of the poet's stance and relation to things.

––––––––––

Oppen's "Psalm,"[3] one of his most celebrated lyric responses to the world, offers an exemplary model of the objectivist emphasis on poetry not as symbolic, romantic, or expressive, but as building. In the poem Oppen reveals what might be called a "moment of awe," a moment when he moves, through meticulous observation, from sight to insight.

Psalm
Veritas sequitur . . .

In the small beauty of the forest
The wild deer bedding down—
That they are there!

       Their eyes
Effortless, the soft lips
Nuzzle and the alien small teeth
Tear at the grass

       The roots of it
Dangle from their mouths

Scattering earth in the strange woods.
They who are there.

         Their paths
Nibbled thru the fields, the leaves that shade them
Hang in the distances
Of sun

         The small nouns
Crying faith
In this in which the wild deer
Startle, and stare out.
         (1–19)

The poem's form is quite suited to the anthology format; its title, an attenuated echo of the Old Testament, suggests the possibility of an ongoing tradition, a feature that an anthologist might find useful and instructive. The poem sets forth the "lyric valuables," the sense of awe, in its acknowledgment of the otherness of the deer in a forest. The cry of the occasion calls not for self-questioning or self-confession, but praise of the actuality of the visual presence of the deer in the "small forest," and of the "small nouns" by which one names the actuality. The speaker returns to the fundamental, the elemental relation of words to their referent. His praise involves an awareness of the way words refer to objects, and the way in which truth may follow from the careful use of language. Language, the small nouns, shape perception and wield power in the interpretation of phenomena.

Consisting of a series of discrete perceptions of the deer in the forest, the poem moves from a long-distance view of "the small beauty of the forest" to "their eyes," "soft lips," and "small teeth," and then to the "roots" dangling from their mouths and back again to "their paths" and the leaves hanging in the "distances / Of sun." The "small beauty," and the deer's "small teeth," are associated with the "small nouns" in the last stanza, which is a victorious moment of faith in the ability of language to imaginatively grasp the alien and distant materiality of the deer in their natural habitat.

The poem describes a "small" cosmos and contains a cosmos. Such a forest is distant and remote, therefore enchanted, foreign to human eyes. The woods are "strange" to the poet, but not to the deer. The deer are far from human reality, but at the same time the poet realizes "that they are there!" In these lines he is "pointing" at the deer, straining in the imagination after them. The space and indentation between stanzas reinforces that distance, but at the same time the very image of the poem on the page recalls the carpentry technique of joinery.[4] The identical sounds of "there" and "their" bind stanzas one and two, and stanzas three and four. "There" is the place in which the deer enact "their" being. The indented stanzas fit together like pieces of wood or a sculpture, a forged monument to the deer and their surroundings. The poem is an act of meditation and perception, a "gathering" of contiguous perceptions.

The speaker's emphasis on the "small" points to the austere compression in Oppen's work (especially in the earlier poems). The tensions created by the relations of these small nouns to one another (and to the blank page) are explicit in the small poem as Oppen attempts to get at the fundamental relationship of the word to its referent, focusing most sharply on the word itself, as if the word itself were a poem. In an interview Oppen says that he is "really concerned with the substantive, with the subject of the sentence, with what we are talking about, and not rushing over the subject-matter in order to make a comment about it." Each "and," "the," "but," each bit of punctuation in the often sparse poems, is made even more significant by the conscious refusal to elucidate, develop, or explain—all means of asserting the poetic ego.

The "small nouns" are the potent building blocks of language, the essential "naming" instrument. In an interview Oppen reveals the objectivist's deceptively simple, yet fundamental view of language:

> The important thing is that if we are talking about the nature of reality, then we are not really talking about our comment about it; we are talking about the apprehension of some thing, whether it is or not, whether one can make a thing of it or not.... I'm trying to describe how the test of images can be a test of whether one's thought is valid.... ("The 'Objectivist' Poet" 162)

And later, in the same interview, Oppen speaks of the nature of words and their relation to consciousness:

> All the little nouns are the ones that I like the most: the deer, the sun, and so on. You say these perfectly little words and you're asserting that the sun is ninety-three million miles away, and that there is shade because of shadows, and more.... It's a tremendous structure to have built out of a few small nouns. I do think they exist and ... it's certainly an act of faith. (162–63)

Oppen's poems are written out of the faith that things can be seen with clarity, and that words can refer to and name an extant reality without trying to mediate it with transcendental or symbolic overlays. The objectivist seeks to see the thing itself not as a comment on an imagined spiritual life nor as an occasion to compose an anecdotal, first-person lyric, but as it is on its own terms. Seeing, however, is not the same as understanding.

> Impossible to doubt the world: it can be seen
> And because it is irrevocable
>
> It cannot be understood, and I believe that fact is lethal
>
> ("Parousia" 1–3)

In order to de-symbolize an "irrevocable" world, the poet presents rather than represents his perception of it; but to speak of it is not necessarily to understand the world. Our misunderstanding is "lethal." Oppen seeks "clarity / in the sense of transparency," yet he realizes the " 'heartlessness' " of words because they "cannot be wholly transparent" ("Route" 4:1–2); in other words, they cannot disclose "the thing itself."

Yet the objectivist stance, involving a radical shift in perspective, means that the poet's experience of things is transformed from the ground up. Experience becomes the appearance of how things are ontologically constituted, how they stand relationally. "Things" are viewed relationally and the poet's experience is constituted as a thing itself. The poet opens himself, makes himself available to the world so that things stand as one with his consciousness in a verbal place that encompasses both the poet and the object. The landscape, animals, cities, and things in the poems are not divided from the poet's consciousness, but are that consciousness as gathered by means of a sequence of perceptive events. Seeing, itself, is the processional display of things. And so Oppen (as well as Reznikoff and Zukofsky) often employs the poetic sequence in his work as a primary mode of poetic development and process. Whereas the epic poem asks, "How do we know the world and history?" the serial poem asks, "How is being and experience constituted, how does it happen?" The goal of this poetic method is to elide the gap between what seems to be and what is known. Oppen announces this crucial premise in the opening sequence of "Of Being Numerous," his longest serial poem.

> There are things
> We live among 'and to see them
> Is to know ourselves'.
>
> Occurrence, a part
> Of an infinite series,
>
> . . . .
>
> (1:1–5)

At the risk of parodying Heidegger, what is seen can be anything; nothing the poet encounters is "unpoetic."

The poetry moves us to reexamine, to rethink the relation of language to things, of things to things, of poet to language and to things. From the concrete "nouns," the "substantial language," we are thus compelled to move toward a philosophical questioning of our relationship to language, to things, and to reality itself. Such a technique illustrates what Zukofsky means when he speaks of "thinking with things as they exist," a mode of being that allows perception to validate experience.

The aim of Oppen's poetic technique, then, is to establish the material otherness of the visual situation. It involves a close relationship, through the words themselves, to the sheer physicality of the world. In language the reality of the event intensifies for the poet, "for," as Heidegger says in *An Introduction to Metaphysics,* "words and language are not wrappings in which things are packed for commerce of those who write and speak. It is in words and language that things first come into being and are" (11). In order to gain an authentic relation to things, the poet must begin by seeking a precise language, by going beyond (or against) the use of historical, conventional, or metaphorical associations in language. Thinking with things as they exist requires a new sense of relatedness, another way to construct meaning, and a repudiation of "principles of dramatic order" and "theatricalizing the poet's self-conscious stances in quest of sublimity" (Altieri 13).

Yet the visual is for Oppen only one element in a dialectical process in which poetic truth resides neither in the thing itself nor in the poet but in the interaction between the two, in the language itself. In "The Little Hole" (one of "Five Poems about Poetry"), Oppen examines the nature of poetic seeing/encountering.

> The little hole in the eye
> Williams called it, the little hole
>
> Has exposed us naked
> To the world
>
> And will not close.
>
> Blankly the world
> Looks in
>
> And we compose
> Colors
>
> And the sense
> Of home
>
> . . . .

(1–11)

World and self meet in the perceptive eye, and a "home" is created by what we compose (as both Heidegger and Bachelard suggest in quite different ways). Poetry attempts to come into living contact with the world, to enact "worlding." Richard Pevear points out that "Oppen understands the nature of alienation as 'worldlessness'" (318). And "to be a work," Heidegger suggests, "means to set up a world" (*Poetry* 178). Creating a work/world means finding a place for the word, restoring language by bringing it close to things. If, as Oppen would insist, the poet's ultimate aim is truth (*veritas sequitur*), through an open response to the world of appearance, that which is seen has the possibility of being a measure of reality. The creative process of the poet "brings forth" the reality, the truth (Greek *alethia*, disclosure to dis-cover) of the object. By saying "that it is" the poet "grasps" and points to the extraordinary awesomeness of truth.

> Clarity, clarity, surely clarity is the most beautiful
>   thing in the world,
> A limited, limiting clarity
>
> I have not and never did have any motive of poetry
> But to achieve clarity
>
> . . . .
>
> ("Route" 1:19–23)

Clarity can be achieved by first avoiding what Nietzsche called the outmoded "mobile army of metaphors." The deer of "Psalm" are not metaphorical semblances that stand for something else, but "they who are there."[5] Adopting an unmediated relation to things is possible, Heidegger suggests, by avoiding a willful "assault" on the thing, by granting the thing, as it were, a free field to

> display its thingly character directly. Everything that might inter-
> pose itself between the thing and us in apprehending and talking
> about it must first be set aside. Only then do we yield ourselves
> to the undisguised presence of the thing. (*Poetry* 25)

It is the clarity of the first, primitive, eyes that the true poet seeks in order to return to the thing itself, for "the more clearly a thing is defined the more clearly it becomes part of all other things" ("Oppen on Literature" 134), things that have become "the meaning and the color of our lives" ("The Mind's Own Place" 2).

How might Oppen fit into a popular anthology? Where would we find his poetry exhibited? This examination of Oppen's poetry is intended to reveal how the complexity of his technique and the radical nature of his poetics distinguish his work from the typical anthology piece and from the usual introductory poetry classroom. His philosophical sophistication (particularly in a philosophical tradition with which many undergraduates are unfamiliar) might make him seem forbidding for most college literature classrooms. Further, instead of proposing an ego-perceiving world he puts humans in their place—not at the center but in between the phenomenal world and consciousness, in language itself. The anthologies, on the other hand, exhibit a bias toward the vivid presentation of a personality leading them to writers whose public personae are already well established.

We are all familiar with the usual lineup of contemporary anthology poets—especially the so-called "confessional poets" (i.e., Berryman, Roethke, Bishop, Lowell, etc.), all of whom wrote some excellent poems and all of whom were academic poets. They inevitably focus their creative talents on discovering and confessing self, in weaving in their poetry the drama of loneliness, breakdown, lack of fulfillment, and the usual hope of a transcendental salvation. The poets look at themselves in mirrors, in family photographs, in their own manuscripts, and transcribe with a kind of penitent intensity the distortions perceived. The confessionalist-symbolist poets (who descend from the romantics), in sharp contrast with the objectivists, reveal not the presence of the world but the presence of the poet. Evidence of the author's suffering becomes a verification of sincerity. Subject matter narrows ever more tightly around the subjective "I." As Altieri says, "Where a symbolist poet would concentrate on relations that dramatize meanings beyond the event . . . the primary relations [for an objectivist] are denotative (in an imaginary world) rather than connotative or metaphoric" (36).

The objectivist refusal to engage in literary role playing is evident in their lack of concern with fiction making or persona creation and in their denial of a supreme poetic ego. A poetry not wedded to a drama of self, a poetry in which the poet may disappear to give freer play to pattern or melody or the selfless steady state of meditation, offers little to the poetry anthologists. The personality, the intrusive "I," is seen as a constraint by the objectivists, who sought to revive the fundamental Imagistic aesthetic revolt against what Pound saw as the vagueness and softness of Symbolist poetry. A particular kind of literary role playing, not the more eccentric or self-effacing talents or subversives of the prevailing canon, seems to attract the editors of anthologies.

It is curious—and instructive—to note that in Helen Vendler's comprehensive study of twentieth-century American poetry, *The Music of What Happens,* not one word is mentioned about Zukofsky, Reznikoff, or Oppen. She suggests that "the canon . . . is composed of the writers that other writers admire. . . . The evolving canon is not the creation of critics, but of poets" (37–38). I am reminded of the old cliché that the only people nowadays who read poetry are other (aspiring) poets. And to be a poet today almost always means to be an academic poet. This raises another crucial issue: The objectivists were by and large *not* academic poets.

Compare Oppen's poetry, for example, to some of the plainspoken, largely academic workshop poetry that has appeared over the past two or three decades. These poems tend to be self-confessional, extremely self-conscious; intent on displaying the stamp of the poet's personality, they privilege the suffering ego. Issues of *American Poetry Review* are filled with such poems. Since writing (or reading) poetry in this mode demands little in the way of previous literary, philosophical, or cultural knowledge or poetic context, it offers a "basic style" for students in creative writing programs. Even today, the small literary magazines are packed with poems about washing the car, drinking a beer on the street, taking the dog for a walk. Arguably, the audience for this work is largely confined to poets in other creative writing programs.

In contrast, one must read Oppen's poetry with full awareness of the context of other poems and other collections, not to mention the larger cultural, political, and philosophical contexts. The active thought in process, as opposed to the rhetorical finish of most anthology verse, may also account for Oppen's nonexistence in the anthologies. His objectivist poetics speaks for a desire to break out of the reified boundaries of the poem as art object, and in so doing to embark on a more uncertain but also more exciting engagement with the poem as medium of contact with the world. His technique, marked by austere compression and restraint, runs counter to much of the conversational (and often rambling) poetry so popular in university writing workshops.

For Oppen (as for the objectivists in general) books of poetry are less collections of individual poems than developments of a thought or position. One poem is amplified and lit up in the course of the poetic sequence, "playing off" other poems in a relational stance. Poems are thoughts and experiences tracking themselves in order to get to clarity of sight and insight. They are not overly revised or polished but stand as naked thought, to be revised in the thought of a subsequent poem. The dialogism of the poetic series aims at discovering connections and a coherence of its own, initiating a radical change in perspective. Oppen's poetic sequences participate in the fragmentation of experience, signaling not merely a literary crisis but an ontological one, a breakdown of a formalist rigidity of mind that seeks finality and closure in experience. The poems are often fragmentary and incomplete, suggesting, like the cubist or montagist painter, that perception itself is fragmentary and multiple. Paradoxically, Oppen's phenomenological aim is "to see more clearly, to see past the subject matter and the art attitudes of the academy" ("The Mind's Own Place" 2). There is a radical desire to see for the first time "what the first eye saw," to see the "primitive" (that is, first, fundamental, ground). Such poems do not often fit the generic classifications conveniently displayed in anthologies. What Oppen calls a ballad or historical poem intentionally upsets our notions of these poetic forms to make us see them more critically, to engage us in the process of recognizing the values and aesthetic biases which govern our view and teaching of poetry.

The anthology poem, by contrast, has to stand alone, self-reflexive, self-enclosed, usually requiring no reading context beyond what a footnote or two can provide. Collections of what are known as "anthology pieces" give little sense of origins or context or ultimate direction, often offering no clue as to what soil the poems spring from. In a discussion of Oppen and objectivist poetry, John Taggart points out that "the poem which at every point radiates process, often in a jagged hesitating manner, frustrates expectations fed on 'finished' verse. Such a poem reminds us that the anthology piece, by itself, may not be enough, that much more reading may be required, that there are compositions which will not fit neatly on a page or two and that, even if their lines will fit, their thought won't" (256). Poetry emphasizing the very process of thought and perception resists easy classification and reading and is not usually prime anthology material because it challenges our typical smorgasbord mode of teaching poetry piecemeal and out of proper context.

If, as many critics say, a canon is governed by a given set of aesthetic criteria, a new aesthetic is perhaps needed to accommodate diverse, often dissonant voices. Objectivist poetry throws into question aesthetic assumptions and biases about the *finished* verse so highly prized by the closed field of New Criticism. And despite competing deconstructionist, Marxist, and feminist challenges, the New Critical aesthetic remains the dominant mode of teaching poetry in the English departments and creative-writing programs that support the anthology industry. Frank Lentricchia points out that

> the American New Criticism, the critical movement which made formalism famous in this country, whose death has been periodically announced since the late 1950s, remains in force as the basis (what goes without saying) of undergraduate literary pedagogy. . . . The ideological effect of the New Criticism in the United States is to sustain, under conditions of mass higher education, the romantic cult of genius. (323)

For poetry that seeks to start from scratch and rethink its function altogether, the anthologies have no sympathy. The anthologies represent a profoundly conservative retreat from the new—not just the new of today, but the new of the past half-century.

The canonical imperative exercised by many anthologists reinforces the notion in our students that there is such a thing as timeless, universal literature and that there is a need to read "classic" texts to the exclusion of others. The notion of literary permanence is self-deceptive, however; there is no fixed paradigm for literary greatness, and canonical contexts change dramatically. The question of permanent value and eternal modernity is still open. It is instructive to remember, for example, that William Carlos Williams didn't achieve literary notoriety until he died, with a posthumous Pulitzer Prize for *Pictures from Brueghel* in 1963. At many universities Williams was not even taught as a major figure until the early 1970s. Williams (who, by the way, was a part of Louis Zukofsky's 1930 *'Objectivists' Anthology*, which included Pound, Eliot, Oppen, Reznikoff, and many other poets in the objectivist tradition) was a formal innovator of revolutionary impact whose technical originality is still being digested. Canonized poetry, then, cannot be seen as existing outside political, social, academic, *and* pedagogical contexts. We see, however, that the anthologies tend to muffle the roar of political and artistic revolution in their selections and in their omissions. And they reinforce modes of teaching poetry in a basically New Critical, formalistic way, defining the central work that we perform.

The omission of Oppen and other poets in the objectivist tradition is, I think, not an accident of taste but a systematic exclusion, aimed not at scattered poets but at an alternate tradition of writing which fought off the petrification of poetic forms through an opening up of formal boundaries. Like the Imagists before them, the objectivists aimed to disrupt poetic traditions in order to keep poetry alive. What Pound called poetry's "revolution of the word" never quite made its way into the academies. By excluding such poets as Oppen (whom Pound early on considered a distinctive voice and a highly original poet) and other objectivist poets, those academies do, however, ultimately falsify the nature, evolution and intellectual urgency of poetic creation.

Notes

1. I prefer to use the lower-case "objectivist" because the group of poets associated with the designation never really took part in a poetic program

and their poetic styles are so varied that they could hardly be said to have formed a literary movement. The term describes a philosophical disposition as much as it does a "school" of poetry. Zukofsky, Reznikoff, and Oppen are further linked, significantly, by the fact that they are New Yorkers, Jewish, and politically leftist, all crucial dimensions of their poetry (and part of the reason for their exclusion from the anthologies?).

2. Four collections of essays and many articles by a wide range of critics have emerged over the past decade or so, and since Oppen's death in 1984 several articles have surfaced. Critics such as Kenner (*The Pound Era* and *A Homemade World,* 1975), Hatlen (*George Oppen: Man and Poet*), and Heller (*Conviction's Net of Branches: Essays on Objectivist Poetry and Poetics*), along with many British and American poets, realized the significance of Oppen's poetry, especially after he won the Pulitzer Prize in 1969 for *Of Being Numerous.*

3. All poems cited are from Oppen's *Collected Poems.*

4. It is interesting that the word "text" in one of its many meanings means "worker in wood, carpenter, joiner; generally: any craftsman or workman; metaphorically: maker, author" (Scholes 142).

5. Oppen takes issue with H.D.'s poem "Oread" when he says, "I never really forgave her for giving advice . . . or orders to the sea. The poem is a distortion of the senses which seems to me intolerable." Such use of metaphor and "strained images" is "very seldom valid" ("Oppen on Literature" 132–33).

Works Cited

Altieri, Charles. "The Objectivist Tradition." *Chicago Review* 30.3 (Winter 1971): 5–22.

Bachelard, Gaston. *The Poetics of Space.* Trans. Maria Jolas. Boston: Beacon Press, 1958, 1969.

Carruth, Hayden. *The Voice That Is Great within Us: American Poetry of the Twentieth Century.* New York: Bantam Books, 1983.

Ellmann, Richard and Robert O'Clair. *The Norton Anthology of Modern Poetry.* New York: W.W. Norton and Co., 1990.

Hatlen, Burton, ed. *George Oppen: Man and Poet.* Orono: U of Maine P, National Poetry Foundation, 1981.

Heidegger, Martin. *An Introduction to Metaphysics.* Trans. Ralph Mannheim. New York: Anchor Books, 1961.

———. *Poetry, Language, Thought.* Trans. Albert Hofstadter. New York: Colophon Books, 1971.

Heller, Michael. *Conviction's Net of Branches: Essays on Objectivist Poetry and Poetics.* Carbondale: Southern Illinois UP, 1985.

Kenner, Hugh. *A Homemade World: The American Modernist Writers.* New York: Knopf, 1975.

———. *The Pound Era.* Berkeley: U of California P, 1971.

Lentricchia, Frank. "In Place of an Afterword—Someone Reading." In *Critical Terms for Literary Study*. Ed. Frank Lentricchia and Thomas McLaughlin. Chicago: U of Chicago P, 1990.

Olson, Charles. *Selected Writings*. Ed. Robert Creeley. New York: New Directions, 1966.

Oppen, George. *Collected Poems*. New York: New Directions, 1975.

———. "George and Mary Oppen: An Interview by Michel Englebert and Michael West." *American Poetry Review* 14.4 (July/August 1985): 11–14.

———. "The Little Hole." *Collected Poems* 81.

———. "The Mind's Own Place." *Kulcher* 3.10 (Summer 1963): 1–7.

———. "The 'Objectivist' Poet, Four Interviews." With L. S. Dembo. *Contemporary Literature* (Spring 1969): 159–77.

———. "Of Being Numerous." *Collected Poems* 147.

———. *Of Being Numerous*. New York: New Directions, 1968.

———. "Oppen on Literature and Literary Figures and Issues." With David McAleavey. *Sagetrieb* 6.1 (Spring 1987): 129–44.

———. "Parousia." *Collected Poems* 83.

———. "Psalm." *Collected Poems* 78.

———. "Route." *Collected Poems* 184–86.

Pevear, Richard. "Poetry and Worldlessness." *The Hudson Review* 29.2 (Summer 1976): 317–20.

Poulin, A. *Contemporary American Poetry*. 5th ed. New York: Houghton Mifflin, 1991.

Reznikoff, Charles. "The 'Objectivist' Poet, Four Interviews." With L. S. Dembo. *Contemporary Literature* (Spring 1969): 193–202.

Scholes, Robert. "Canonicity and Textuality." *Introduction to Scholarship in Modern Languages and Literatures*. 2nd ed. New York: MLA, 1992. 138–58.

Shaw, Peter. "The Modern Language Association Is Misleading the Public." *The Chronicle of Higher Education* 27 Nov. 1991: B3.

Taggart, John. "George Oppen and the Anthologies." *Ironwood 26* 13.2 (Fall 1985): 252–62.

Vendler, Helen. *The Harvard Book of Contemporary American Poetry*. Cambridge: Harvard UP, 1985.

———. *The Music of What Happens: Poems, Poets, Critics*. Cambridge: Harvard UP, 1988.

Williams, William Carlos. *The Autobiography of William Carlos Williams*. New York: New Directions, 1967.

Zukofsky, Louis. " 'A' (Seventh Movement)." *Poetry* 37.5 (1931): 242–46.

13 The Recuperation of Canon Fodder: Walter Scott's *The Talisman*

Caroline McCracken-Flesher
University of Wyoming

Canonization, we have learned, "authorizes" a text. To be canonized, a text must to some degree express the dominant ideology; canonization thus constitutes an ideological recognition of conformity, and a concurrent assumption of "quality." And once canonized, a text will operate as "quality control," denying authority to less culturally conformist works. The canonized text obscures and forces out the texts of otherness—indeed, as our recent professional/political battles have demonstrated, it can be launched like a literary cruise missile to obliterate them.

As generations of schoolchildren have discovered in Britain and the Empire (more recently the Commonwealth), Walter Scott is one of the English canon's biggest guns, and his works make up a large and heavy pile of ammunition. Salvoes of Ivanhoe have been loosed at hoards of trembling teenagers with deadening—one might even say deadly—effect. Legions of Ivanhoe's shell-shocked victims have gazed down the twin barrels of *Waverley* and *The Heart of Midlothian* and acknowledged the novels' firepower by surrendering to their greatness without reading them.

But I would suggest that Scott himself is the primary casualty of the canonical bombardment in which he figures so prominently. How can this be? The answer lies in the criteria that loaded Scott into the canon. When the canon's architects included Scott in their pantheon of novelists, they did so grudgingly and for all the wrong reasons. Their choice had nothing to do with avowed criteria such as aesthetic quality or realism—it didn't even have anything to do with Scott himself. Time and again, we find these self-conscious builders of novelistic tradition invoking Scott as a naive, flawed, yet authorizing precursor for some "better" novelist. For instance, ever digging for the roots of his own genius, Henry James declares after a visit to Scott's home at Ashestiel: "I took up one of Scott's novels—*Redgauntlet*; it was years since I had read one. They have always a charm for me—but I was amazed at the badness of [it]: *l'enfance de l'art*" (James 37). Similarly, although less sympathetically, as he gathers the Pole, the American, the Englishman, and the (manly) Englishwoman from whom he will oddly constitute the "Great Tradition" of English novelists, F. R. Leavis takes a moment to install Scott in the canon—and summarily eject him from it. He writes, significantly in a footnote, "Out of Scott a bad tradition came. It spoiled Fenimore Cooper. . . . And with Stevenson it took on 'literary' sophistication and fine writing."[1] Leavis and James imply that Scott's successors, while owing him some vague degree of provenance, succeed in spite of him, or fail because of him. The hapless Walter Scott is tamped down the canon as a kind of primitive wadding for the really important (Anglocentric) weaponry.

Perversely, then, we might consider Scott not just as canonical ammunition, but as a kind of canon fodder. Although fed into the canon to enhance the ballistic power of superior English authors, the Scottish novelist is there digested into England's cultural stew. However centered in the canon he may appear, Scott resides there for his service to other authors and texts, and to interests not his own. Even though this grudging canonization empowers him, it constitutes him as unremittingly English. He thus languishes disempowered as what he really was, a Scottish Other. To be fair to James and Leavis, however, this process of canonization and consequent homogenization gained momentum along with Scott's popularity as a writer, and it affected even his compatriots' view of his work. In 1838, with Scott only six years dead, his countryman Thomas Carlyle wrote: "So bounteous was Nature to us; in the sickliest of recorded ages, when British Literature lay all puking and sprawling in Werterism, Byronism, and other Sentimentalism tearful or spasmodic (fruit of internal *wind*), Nature was kind enough to send us two healthy Men [Cobbett and Scott], of whom she might still say, not without pride, 'These also were made in *England* [my emphasis]; such limbs do I still make there!' " (qtd. in Hayden 350). Carlyle goes on to discuss Scott's national origins in his next paragraph, but the Freudian slip has been made; however Scottish their shared background, Carlyle sees and celebrates Scott in an English context. From its inception, then, Scott's canonization transformed him into an indistinguishable servant of the Empire, even for fellow Scots.

This is the more ironic because, as I will argue here, not only is Scott's work in many respects specifically Scottish, it is actively and aggressively so. Moreover, it is constructed in opposition to precisely the kind of cultural cannibalism inevitably exercised by England's dominant culture over Scotland's national literature, and under which Scott's own novels have suffered. Indeed, Scott's novels, once disgorged from the canon and recoded according to their Scottish cultural matrix, might join with those "other" texts marshaled under the banner of world literature that seek to deconstruct the canon as oppressive instrument, and to open in its place a discursive space.

To the canon's harshest critics, and to the staunchest advocates of world literature as a literature of difference, this may appear an unlikely case. It is to combat such criticism that I have chosen here to argue from an unlikely text, *The Talisman*. This novel, first published in 1825, of all Scott's works seems thoroughly and uncritically to participate in the discourse of Empire; to all appearances, it little deserves to be snatched from the canon's mouth. Despite the fact that it comprises the elements of an oppositional text, it seems to offer no critique of English mores or even of colonial subjection. For instance, although in *The Talisman* as in nearly every Scott novel the supposedly central character is Scottish, in Sir Kenneth we find no resistant figure; a Scottish prince in disguise, Sir Kenneth serves anonymously but supportively in Richard the Lionheart's crusading army. Further, although while guarding the English standard Sir Kenneth commits a sin of omission that results in the standard's theft, his crime cannot be seen as even a momentary gesture of resistance, for he immediately subjects himself to English justice, effectively putting his neck under the executioner's axe. Then, although Sir Kenneth escapes subjection/death, he is saved not by his own actions but rather over his objections and by "the enemy," Saladin. Finally, when rescued, Kenneth returns to the camp to find the thief, redeem the honor of England, and marry a Plantagenet. Not surprisingly, even the canon's advocates have viewed this apparently simplistic romance suspiciously, but perhaps because of their formal reservations *The Talisman* has achieved what is sometimes a dangerous kind of canonization: it has become exclusively a high school text. Not sophisticated enough to warrant more advanced study, it has nonetheless indoctrinated generations of younger students, in Britain and throughout the colonies, with the romance of Empire.

Understandably, then, Edward Said considers Scott a logical target for his critique of Orientalism. Said focuses on the first encounter between Sir Kenneth and Saladin, the conjunction between Occident and Orient. Here, Sir Kenneth comments to Saladin:

> I well thought that your blinded race had their descent from the foul fiend, without whose aid you would never have been able to maintain this blessed land of Palestine against so many valiant

soldiers of God. I speak not thus of thee in particular, Saracen,
but generally of thy people and religion. (39)[2]

Taking predictable offense at Sir Kenneth's sweeping generalization
and his blindness to specific difference, Said writes: "What is truly
curious is the airy condescension of damning a whole people 'generally'
while mitigating the offense with a cool 'I don't mean you in particular'"
(101). For Said, *The Talisman* clearly functions as part of England's
arsenal of oppressive, imperialist texts.

Yet the sin of thoughtlessly dismissing cultural difference for which
Said chastises Scott can equally be identified in Said's own text. Just
as Sir Kenneth diminishes Saladin by sweeping him into the category
of undifferentiated Arabs, when Said seeks to validate Middle Eastern
culture against the imperialist dynamic he diminishes Scott by sweeping
him into a similarly general but dominant category, "the English." He
writes:

> Scott, Kinglake, Disraeli, Warburton, Burton, and even George
> Eliot are writers for whom the Orient was defined by material
> possession, by a material imagination, as it were. *England* had
> defeated Napoleon, evicted France: what the *English* mind sur-
> veyed was an imperial domain which by the 1880s had become
> an unbroken patch of British-held territory. (169; my emphases)

And again:

> *English* writers . . . had a more pronounced and harder sense of
> what Oriental pilgrimages might entail than the
> French. . . . Romantic writers like Byron and Scott consequently
> had a political vision of the Near Orient and a very combative
> awareness of how relations between the Orient and Europe would
> have to be conducted. (192; my emphasis)

Said sees Scott as English even in a comparative context that necessarily
foregrounds terms like "British" and "French" in a way that proble-
matizes his assumption. Ironically, this advocate for otherness is fooled
by Scott's canonization into committing that cardinal sin within his
own system—failing to recognize difference.

And in fact, if we read *The Talisman* by Said's own criteria, not by
his interests, it appears a quite other tale. Despite the text's apparent
Englishness and endorsement of English imperialism, when subjected
to the light of *Orientalism, The Talisman* stands forth not as a quisling
imperialist romance, but as a resistant Scottish tale—as exactly the
kind of ethnic and oppositional text Said might celebrate.

Scott wrote *The Talisman* at a moment when he was becoming
deeply concerned with the effects of anglicization in Scotland. In 1707,

Scotland had joined in parliamentary Union with England to avoid economic penalties—but also for financial gain. After a slow start, in the early years of the nineteenth century, she finally began to achieve her monetary desires. Scott, however, realized that whatever the financial benefits of Union, Scotland's assumption of her neighbor's bourgeois economic goals inevitably subjected her to England's imperialist narrative; Scots stood to lose their remaining national institutions, and even their national identity. In his early novels, therefore, Scott painstakingly constructed two types of narrative for Scotland, one within which she could enjoy the gains of Union, while refusing to bring herself unduly under English scrutiny and losing nothing of her own identity, and another wherein she might retain a separate subjectivity protected from England's colonizing impetus. (As I have argued elsewhere, these narratives are marked by Jacobitism and gender, on the one hand, and socialized Calvinism on the other.)[3] By this strategy, Scott himself managed to remain outside the colonizing economic narrative while yet participating in it. Although he narrated a space for Scottish difference, in so doing he made English money. Indeed, he wrote himself into a knighthood (gazetted 1820).

Around 1825, however, Scott began to realize that even this cautiously played game was not worth the candle. First, the financial gains of Union suddenly appeared ephemeral, as bubble corporations began to burst. The predicament of the small joint-stock companies that Scott parodied in his introduction to *The Betrothed* and *The Talisman* (published together as *Tales of the Crusaders*)[4] was about to overtake him in his own ill-advised association with publishers and printers.[5] Equally important, perhaps, through his son's service in an English regiment in Ireland Scott was becoming aware that Scotland had other comparator nations than England, and that—for worse and for better— she might stand categorized with the lowly Ireland.[6] Both these perceptions bear most obvious fruit in Scott's 1826 *Malachi Malagrowther* letters. Here, Scott responds to a projected English encroachment on the Scottish banking system that he considered would prove financially and nationally damaging by at last arguing openly and vigorously for Scotland's own financial rights, and by appealing to Ireland for support in his opposition. He writes:

> What is our case to-day will be [Ireland's] the instant you have got a little tranquillity... I see you grasp your shilela at the very thought! Enough; we understand each other: Let us be friends. Patrick aids Saunders to-day; Saunders pays back Patrick to-morrow.... But what do I talk of to-day or to-morrow? The cause of Ireland is tried ALONG WITH that of Scotland.[7]

The Talisman, then, was written at a moment when financial circumstances were beginning to bring home to Scott that however successful
his nation, from England's perspective she was still inevitably Other
and inevitably less. Scott, moreover, was beginning to understand that
Scotland had chosen her friends ill-advisedly, and that her most effective
alliance might be with equally othered nations, like Ireland.

It is perhaps his growing awareness of Scotland's status as Other
that causes Scott to struggle in *The Talisman* not to diminish or dismiss
difference, but to recuperate and empower it. Indeed, I suggest that
through Scott's novel, Scotland as Other stands empowered both in
itself and through its conjunction with similarly obscured nations and
persons. The distorting light of canonization refracts *The Talisman* to
Said as a text wherein Saladin can be seen only momentarily as an
individual, but persistently as a relatively insignificant Saracen Other.
Said consequently argues that Sir Kenneth and Scott, themselves
representative of the Occidental cultural bloc, together see Saladin as
"*first* an Oriental, second a human being, and *last* again an Oriental"
(102). But viewed from a less canonically driven and more culturally
conscious perspective, Scott's novel works to demonstrate, through the
racially, religiously, and geographically distinct Saladin, and for a
specifically Scottish Sir Kenneth, the positive value of otherness.
However Saladin enters the text, he exits it as no mere "Oriental," but
rather as a celebrated, highly visible leader, and one who significantly
owes his effectiveness to his difference. He shows, in fact, that otherness
may have operative force, that difference may comprise not diminution,
but agency, and that Others may work successfully as brothers. Thus
Scott looms from *The Talisman* not as an imperialistic oppressor, but
as a visionary opening a space for colonized nations, as one who
transforms otherness from a position of weakness into an oppositional
position of strength.

In *The Talisman,* far from establishing Sir Kenneth as an unprob-
lematic representative of England, or even of Scotland, Scott uses him
to explore the conditions of Scotland's contemporary subjection; he
takes a long, cool look at Scotland as she stands othered by the English
perspective. Committed to the Crusade, Sir Kenneth nonetheless vigorously denies Saladin's suggestion that he serves Richard or England.
He insists on his separate, Scottish identity when he noisily declares,
"One of [Richard's] followers I am, for this expedition . . . and honoured
in the service; but not born his subject, although a native of the island
in which he reigns" (35). And in response to Saladin's suggestion that
Richard might better have served the cause of Christendom by subduing
his Scottish neighbors before turning his ambitions to Palestine, Kenneth

exclaims: "No, by the bright light of Heaven! If the King of England had not set forth to the Crusade till he was sovereign of Scotland, the Crescent might, for me, and all true-hearted Scots, glimmer for ever on the walls of Zion" (36). But whatever the vehemence of Sir Kenneth's protest, and perhaps because he constantly emphasizes his Scottish otherness, he stands effectively elided by the English court. Kenneth's assertion of national difference has led his English allies to assume in him that primary marker of otherness, bodily difference. Thus, Richard's right-hand man, Sir Thomas de Vaux, when first he notices Sir Kenneth on his return from a desert encounter with Saladin, cannot immediately identify him, but can categorize him as "a Spaniard or a Scot" (82). Like the Christian Spaniard, Sir Kenneth can serve in the English cause, but like the racially distinct Spaniard, he cannot be considered English. For Sir Thomas, Kenneth verges away from Occidental and toward Oriental. Once located as Other, moreover, the Scot stands voiceless, deprived of his function as speaking subject. Kenneth, in fact, is returning from a mission where he has unwittingly served as an empty vessel bearing the words of conspiratorial forces, and now, de Vaux's first instinct as an Englishman and consequently one of the Crusade's elite is to pass Kenneth by without speaking to him. Scott writes: "Loath to ask even a passing question, he was about to pass Sir Kenneth, with that sullen and lowering port which seems to say, 'I know thee, but I will hold no communication with thee' " (82). Given that Sir Kenneth turns out to be a Prince of Scotland—David, Earl of Huntingdon, serving anonymously in the crusading forces—Scott offers no optimistic picture of the contemporary Scot's rehabilitation within the Union; even the primary representative of Scottish difference cannot maintain his identity, his role as speaking subject, inside the orbit of English power.

But Scott interestingly takes care to emphasize that Scottish subjection does not arise simply as an inevitable effect of England's hegemony. Instead, he suggests through Prince David/Sir Kenneth that the Scot shares responsibility for his own subjection. Kenneth, after all, has joined the Crusade, and taken the role of follower (wherein, as Saladin points out, he may be confused with "subject" [35]), by choice. Further, as the story proceeds, he takes on the values of the colonizer to the extent that he willingly gives over not just his voice but also his body to English purposes. As a reward for bringing to Richard a Saracen doctor (Saladin) who cures him of fever, Kenneth receives the task of guarding the English standard. When he proves derelict in his duty and the standard is stolen, his punishment is death. Yet far from recognizing his failure as a necessary expression of Scottish resistance,

Sir Kenneth covers himself with remorse, and subjects himself to English punishment. As Alexander Welsh notes, when Kenneth declares, "I have deserted my charge—the banner intrusted to me is lost—when the headsman and block are prepared, the head and trunk are ready to part company" (170), "not only is Richard prepared to execute the hero, but the hero is prepared to die" (Welsh 217). Kenneth cannot, and despite Saladin's promptings will not, step outside the English system even to save his own Scottish life; he subjects himself unquestioningly to the terms and processes of English power. By accepting England's honor code, Sir Kenneth accomplishes his own erasure as a Scottish subject—with relatively little help from England. And in so doing, he casts a critical light on contemporary Scots who sought the gains of Union and thereby subjected themselves to English power.

Moreover, Scott stresses that such unthinking subjection to a foreign code achieves little honor for the Scottish subject. When Sir Kenneth worships before a fragment of the true cross at Engaddi, he conjures up two oddly substantial visions. First, a parade of veiled women circles the shrine. As they pass Sir Kenneth, one drops rosebuds at the knight's feet. This, Sir Kenneth acknowledges, is Edith Plantagenet, his one true love, and he forgets the one true cross in order to worship speechlessly—as befits a Scottish Other—at her English feet. After this vision retires, another takes its place. From the floor erupts a misshapen creature, which eagerly displays itself to Sir Kenneth. Scott writes:

> a long skinny arm, partly naked, partly clothed in a sleeve of red samite, arose out of the aperture, holding a lamp. . . . The form and face of the being who thus presented himself, were those of a frightful dwarf, with a large head, a cap fantastically adorned with three peacock feathers, a dress of red samite, the richness of which rendered his ugliness more conspicuous, distinguished by gold bracelets and armlets, and a white silk sash, in which he wore a gold-hilted dagger. This singular figure had in his left hand a kind of broom. So soon as he had stepped from the aperture through which he arose, he stood still, and, as if to show himself more distinctly, moved the lamp which he held slowly over his face and person, successively illuminating his wild and fantastic features, and his misshapen but nervous limbs. (65)

With his tawdry accoutrements and his deformed body, the dwarf parodies knightly nobility, but when he very deliberately reveals to Sir Kenneth his red samite rags, his peacock feather *fleur de lys,* and his trusty broom, he stresses his similitude to the Scottish knight particularly. Scott here suggests that the Scottish knight, functioning in an English army, can be only a thing deformed, a thing showing grotesquely through the knightly signs to which he has subjected himself. But Scott goes further. When Nectabanus, the dwarf, is followed from the depths by "his lady and his love," an equally deformed apparition named "Guenevra," Scott mocks both courtly romance and Kenneth's aspirations, as Scottish Other, to the unattainable Edith Plantagenet; an alliance between Englishwoman and Scot can occur only in Sir Kenneth's dark dreams or in the persons of these deformed representatives (67). Most incisively of all, when Nectabanus lures Sir Kenneth from his post guarding the English standard to fulfill a supposed assignation with Edith, Scott brings into question Sir Kenneth's very commitment to the crusade he espouses. The dwarf demonstrates that Sir Kenneth makes only a deformed, an ineffective, and perhaps even an insincere knight, a knight with a secret, self-serving agenda. For Scott, then, the Scotsman in part subjects *himself* to outside standards, but without much visible gain and at considerable risk. He will not accomplish the alliances he desires, he will prove derelict in his duties to his adopted system, and he will lose, or severely deform, that which he is.

So in *The Talisman* Scott carefully maps the conditions of Scottish subjection to England's colonizing power, not omitting to detail the naivete and complicity of the colonized Scot. Then, with equal deliberation, he offers a way for the Scottish Other to step outside England's malforming concerns, to escape England's dominance, a way, indeed, to convert Scottish otherness into agency. How does Scott accomplish this? When we meet Sir Kenneth, he rides by the Dead Sea, an almost anonymous knight. Years of blows suffered in the course of the Crusade—in his subjection to the English-dominated cause—have practically wiped out his identifying heraldic device. Moreover, the design that looms uncertainly from his shield is that of a couchant leopard, underwritten by the words, "I sleep—wake me not" (14). (Scott thenceforward refers to him as "The Knight of the Sleeping Leopard.") As a Scot, Sir Kenneth is asleep, with the result that his identity as a separate Scottish subject has been practically obliterated. But Scott now begins to wake the Sleeping Leopard. He starts the long process of Sir Kenneth's reeducation as a speaking subject by confronting him with Saladin. This most alien of Others can teach the Scottish knight that he must neither hide his otherness, nor subject it to English power, but embrace it and use it, voice himself across it.

In the heart of the land, at a fountain of clarity and truth called "The Diamond of the Desert," Sir Kenneth meets Saladin (here Sheerkohf, the warrior; later El Hakim, the doctor). As a Scot in the matrix of England, and a soldier in the Crusades, Sir Kenneth has studied to suppress difference in himself and in Palestine, so now, not surprisingly, he fails at first to recognize his kinship with this epitome of otherness, and the two men do battle before becoming friends. But once Scott has established the friendship between Kenneth and Sheerkohf, he carefully aligns his characters. The narrator compares the way the two men fight, judge horses, and eat, and, in a series of conversations, they themselves compare the way they believe and love. In every case Kenneth and Sheerkohf stand parallel: each fights well in battle, rides a horse perfect for him, eats appropriately to his needs, is sincere in his religion, respects women. The Scot and the Saracen can be equated. But, interestingly, in every case, they are also distinguished from each other. Kenneth, for instance, appears the perfect type of a soldier— from the North. He is "a powerful man, built after the ancient Gothic cast of form, with light brown hair, which was seen to curl thick and profusely over his head. . . . His nose was Grecian. . . . His form was tall, powerful and athletic. . . . His hands . . . were long, fair, and well proportioned." Similarly, Sheerkohf perfectly represents the warrior— for the Middle East. "His slender limbs, and long spare hands and arms, though well-proportioned to his person, and suited to the style of his countenance, did not at first aspect promise the display of vigour and elasticity which the Emir had lately exhibited. But, on looking more closely, his limbs seemed divested of all that was fleshy or cumbersome; so that nothing being left but bone, brawn, and sinew, it was a frame fitted for exertion and fatigue" (24). The men, Scott stresses, while similar, are not the same; their every similitude comprises a difference. That is, Kenneth and Saladin are the same only insofar as they are systematically different; they are brothers in their otherness.[8]

As the warrior more racially and geographically distinct from the English, and consequently as the more experienced and self-accepting Other, Saladin has a series of lessons to teach Sir Kenneth. First, he demonstrates that if one is delineated by dominant powers as inevitably and inalienably different, the best strategy may be not to resist or repine at one's designation, but to use it. Because he is racially other, Saladin is almost invisible to the crusaders. Just as Sir Thomas de Vaux couldn't distinguish a Scot from a Spaniard, neither can the invaders individualize Middle Eastern Muslims. Indeed, Sir Kenneth himself initially takes Sheerkohf/Saladin for an Arab, although he is in fact a Kurd. Sheerkohf/Saladin has to inform Sir Kenneth: "For me, I am no Arab, yet derive my descent from a line neither less wild nor less warlike. . . . I am Sheerkohf, the Lion of the Mountain. . . . Kurdistan, from which I derive my descent, holds no family more noble than that of Seljook" (33). But far from being subjected by his erasure, Saladin turns it to his advantage. If his body renders him indistinguishable from the Arabs, and effectively invisible to the crusaders, then he can play different roles without drawing attention to himself. Thus, in the course of the novel, Saladin appears first as the warrior Sheerkohf, then as the physician El Hakim, and finally as himself. In these roles, he manages to negotiate a treaty, cure King Richard, and set the crusading camp to rights. That is, Saladin transforms his bodily difference and its accompanying erasure into mutability and mobility; he uses his body like a cloak of invisibility under cover of which he can direct the course of events.

Second, Saladin shows that there are advantages in accepting one's otherness, as well as in making strategic use of it. Sir Kenneth asserts his national difference, but does not live up to it, instead subjecting himself to English codes; Saladin, by contrast, fully embraces his otherness. Most obviously, he acts in the apparently mutually exclusive capacities of warrior and doctor. As he explains to Sir Kenneth, the roles are necessary if opposite elements in the multiplicity that consti-tutes the complete man. He comments:

> Doth it so surprise thee . . . and thou an approved warrior, to see that a soldier knows somewhat of the art of healing?—I say to thee, Nazarene, that an accomplished cavalier should know how to dress his steed as well as how to ride him; how to forge his sword upon the stithy, as well as how to use it in battle; how to burnish his arms, as well as how to wear them; and, above all, how to cure wounds as well as how to inflict them. (242)

And as the complete man, Saladin manages both to kill crusaders, and to cure their leader, in each case directing events toward a treaty in the Saracens' favor.

Third, Saladin reveals that one can use not just one's own otherness, but the very principle of otherness. The dominant King Richard cannot moderate his Englishness toward otherness even so far as to negotiate with his own allies. When Scott first introduces the English monarch, he notes that the Crusade is already in decline because of "the jealousies of the Christian princes and the offence taken by them at the uncurbed haughtiness of the English monarch, and Richard's unveiled contempt for his brother sovereigns" (69). By contrast, Saladin embraces even the otherness of death. As a doctor, he acknowledges death and consequently gains the power of life; as a ruler, he accepts his own death, and thus uses his power more advisedly and effectively. In his tent, Saladin reclines under a spear, a shroud, and a banner that simultaneously proclaims his power and its transience. It reads: "SA-LADIN, KING OF KINGS—SALADIN, VICTOR OF VICTORS—SALADIN MUST DIE" (308). Saladin brings this awareness to play in his crucial closing scene with Richard. He hosts for Richard the tournament in which Sir

Kenneth disciplines the real thief of the English standard, and afterwards he himself disciplines the Crusade's conspirators. In the celebrations that follow, not recognizing the possibility of death for himself, Richard challenges Saladin to a duel for Jerusalem or, failing that, to a friendly bout in the lists. Saladin refuses for a number of reasons, but one is of particular interest here. He argues: "The master places the shepherd over the flock, not for the shepherd's own sake, but for the sake of the sheep. Had I a son to hold the sceptre when I fell, I might have had the liberty, as I have the will, to brave this bold encounter; but your own Scripture sayeth, that when the herdsman is smitten, the sheep are scattered" (313). The monarch, in the knowledge of death, must preserve himself as governor. So Saladin lives in death's shadow, and works with it; he realizes that death comes even to kings, but on his awareness he builds careful action. Thus he derives his power from accepting what others fear or—in Richard's case—lack the sense to fear.

And finally, if Saladin shows how to turn otherness into agency, he also demonstrates how to convert its forced silence into speech. Scott repeatedly emphasizes that one of the colonized subject's inevitable and most damaging losses is that of the right to speak. In the context of imperial power, the Other cannot voice himself in a way that may be heard. Richard, as English monarch, on the other hand, fully enjoys the right and the power of speech; his loud voice constantly echoes around the camp. In fact Richard's speech is so effective an instrument that it works not just to establish his dominance, but to fragment the crusading alliance—it unavoidably "others" even England's friends. Richard's words indeed, are too powerful; he must constantly call them back. In one crucial scene, he apologizes for his English, monarchical, and overbearing voice, on the grounds that it is an untutored, military one. He cajoles his offended royal brothers:

> Noble princes, and fathers of this holy expedition, Richard is a soldier—his hand is ever readier than his tongue, and his tongue is but too much used to the rough language of his trade. But do not, for Plantagenet's hasty speeches and ill-considered actions, forsake the noble cause of the redemption of Palestine—do not throw away earthly renown and eternal salvation. . . . because the act of a soldier may have been hasty, and his speech as hard as the iron which he has worn from childhood. (202)

With these words, apologizing for his dominance by self-deprecatingly allying his word with his sword, Richard hints at the terms of his power, and once more establishes it. The word of English governance, even when retracted, inevitably asserts English control. Saladin acknowledges this when Richard declares, in response to pleas from his women and from Kenneth's confessor that the delinquent knight's life be spared: "Ladies and priest, withdraw, if ye would not hear orders which would displease you; for, by Saint George, I swear—" "Swear NOT!" Saladin intervenes (183). A word of kingly power must not be lightly uttered, for such a word has performative force. As for Kenneth, his word has no power; he serves as a vehicle for the crusading voice and cannot speak even his own name, David, Earl of Huntingdon.

By contrast, though even more othered than Kenneth, Saladin enjoys the power of speech. If Saladin is overborne by crusading voices, he has not, nonetheless, given up his own culture's modes of speech; at different points in the story, he speaks as warrior, as doctor, and even as muezzin.[9] Furthermore, he has found ways to speak as ruler within his own system; he has but to send a sign to accomplish real effects. He tells Sir Kenneth, who is bemoaning the desertion of his own troops: "When I send one [eagle-feathered arrow] to my tents, a thousand warriors mount on horseback—when I send another, an equal force will arise—for the five, I can command five thousand men; and if I send my bow, ten thousand mounted riders will shake the desert" (33–34). Saladin's speech is so powerful that he doesn't have to open his mouth. More important, if Saladin has found alternate forms of speech, he also, unlike the garrulous Richard, understands the power even of *no speech*. When Richard challenges him to fight for Jerusalem— or even for fun—Saladin withholds consent. Two of his reasons are of interest here. First, he refuses the challenge because he already holds Jerusalem, and would stand only to lose in the encounter. Second, he refuses the contest because, Other though he may be, he can yet resist the lure of inclusion in the dominant culture that lies behind Richard's invitation to participate in the discourse of English chivalry. It is not, then, that Saladin cannot say yes, but that he *will* not say so. So Saladin demonstrates how to assess a situation dispassionately, and how to take control of it; he shows how to exercise and assume power by remaining silent, remaining Other.

Sir Kenneth, however, constitutes for Saladin no promising pupil. He steadfastly refuses to recognize his own otherness, holding instead to an English culture which has already rejected him as alien. On the one hand, he insists on his similarity to his fellow knights—against even their indications to the contrary. Despite the fact that he is so constantly othered by crusaders like Thomas de Vaux, Kenneth constitutes his body as English when he subordinates it to Richard's punishment. A further index to his failure to recognize and act upon his own difference occurs even after he has been saved from death by

Saladin. In the desert, they meet a troop of Templars. Kenneth refuses to flee men he calls "my comrades in arms—the men in whose society I have vowed to fight or fall" (236). Despite Saladin's observation that these same Templars are the least honorable of the crusaders, and that they will certainly slaughter him along with the Saracens, Kenneth again has to be forced to flee, to separate his Scottish body from men who espouse the crusading code of honor but do not in fact adhere to it. Kenneth would prove a martyr to an adoptive code whose own proponents ignore it. At the same time, as Kenneth insists on his similarity with the crusaders, he is equally insistent that he cannot be compared with the Saracens. When he meets Saladin at the Diamond of the Desert, his first instinct, based on Saladin's appearance, is to fight him. Then, when Saladin urges him to flee death, and to recognize the Saracens as his friends, Kenneth makes no bones about declaring that such an alliance would be a dishonor. For him, as for the crusaders, the Saracen seems immutably and negatively Other. Saladin has humanely and practically argued: "Man is not a tree, bound to one spot of earth, nor is he framed to cling to one bare rock, like the scarce animated shell-fish. Thine own Christian writings command thee, when persecuted in one city, to flee to another; and we Moslems also know that Mohammed, the Prophet of Allah, driven forth from the holy city of Mecca, found his refuge and his helpmates at Medina." But Kenneth replies, churlishly: "I might indeed hide my dishonour . . . in a camp of infidel heathens, where the very phrase is unknown. But had I not better partake more fully in their reproach? Does not thy advice stretch so far as to recommend me to take the turban?" (158). Kenneth is so thoroughly colonized by crusading ideas that he cannot step outside them, and cannot even begin to accept a brotherhood based on the Scot's and the Saracen's distinctive otherness. Small wonder, then, that Saladin has to drag him first from the camp, and then from the Templars, to initiate his recuperation as Scottish Other and Saracen brother.

In the course of *The Talisman,* however, Saladin does finally teach Sir Kenneth to embrace his otherness. The Saracen Other who is yet a brother teaches the Scottish knight not simply to succumb to or adopt the crusading culture's view of the world, but rather to act expediently, across his othered body; he teaches him to speak across silence. In the depths of his despair, Kenneth asserts that rather than become a Muslim, he would wish "that my writhen features should blacken, as they are like to do, in this evening's setting sun" (158). Saladin recognizes in this death wish an opportunity both to separate Sir Kenneth from his false brothers, and to connect him with his own body, his otherness; thus he transforms the Scottish knight into a Nubian slave. Judith Wilt considers Kenneth's transformation "one final humiliation" (182), but Scott makes very clear that it is not loss, but gain of identity that is at stake. Saladin stresses that in this black body, "not thy brother in arms, not thy brother in blood, shall discover thee" (247). Kenneth will be separated, by the barrier of his racially distinct body, from his false brothers; what is more, in this othered body, he will finally attain agency: he will be able to explain the events surrounding the theft of the standard. All he has to do is accept himself as Other, and model his behavior on that of his brother. As Saladin tells him: "Thou hast seen me do matters more difficult; he that can call the dying from the darkness of the shadow of death, can easily cast a mist before the eyes of the living" (247).

But in this blackened body, Kenneth will be voiceless. His blackness itself will render him thoroughly other, and as such he will become functionally invisible, for all intents and purposes, mute. Further, Saladin insists that as Nubian slave, Kenneth lacks not just the ability to make himself heard, but also the basic power to articulate. Sir Kenneth, of course, has been subsiding into voicelessness in the course of the text, but now Saladin offers him an opportunity to influence events and achieve identity once more. All he must do is voice himself out of the silence of subjection, by means of that which renders him most visibly subject, his othered body. And this he accomplishes. With a certain ingenuity, Kenneth communicates in writing, and with the help of man's best friend, his dog Roswal. However, it is his body that initiates the train of events leading to the discovery of the thief and to his own recuperation as a distinct, Scottish entity. A Marabout makes an attempt on Richard's life; Kenneth, in his role as slave, sees the fanatic approach mirrored in the shield he is cleaning, and aborts the attack, but in the scuffle he sustains a possibly poisoned flesh wound. Predictably, Richard's courtiers refuse to suck the poison from such a visible Other—however his actions have served their purpose, and whatever they might cost him. Long Allen protests, "Methinks I would not die like a poisoned rat for the sake of a black chattel there, that is bought and sold in a market like a Martelmas ox" (223). But when Richard himself sucks the poison, he sucks away some of Kenneth's black dye, and realizes that this is no Nubian, but some other Other, perhaps even to him a sort of brother. Although of course Richard, as prime mover in the dominant culture, cannot yet quite grasp Sir Kenneth's situation, after the tournament wherein Sir Kenneth begins the rout of evil, and reestablishes himself as Scot, Richard opines: "Thou hast shown that the Ethiopian *may* change his skin, and the

leopard his spots" (303). Kenneth has not so much changed his skin
and his spots, however, as acknowledged them and learned to use them.
Sleeping no longer, and speaking loudly through his (Scottish) knightly
body, he is now, truly, the "Knight of the Leopard" (303).

According to *The Talisman,* then, the subjected Other has two
obvious options: like the early Sir Kenneth, he can accept his subjection,
and effectively die as a distinct self; or, like the Marabout who is
mirrored in Richard's shield as Kenneth's inverse, he can openly resist,
and be killed. But Scott recommends Saladin's more complex and
creative strategy. Saladin teaches Kenneth to accept his own otherness,
and thus neither to reject the boundary between himself and the
crusaders, nor to transgress it. Indeed, Saladin insists on delineating
boundaries clearly: he lives under the sign of death; he welcomes
Richard to his camp with a shower of arrows that clearly demarcates
the English monarch's acceptable space, since if the crusaders exceed
the room Saladin allows them they risk death; and even to Kenneth,
to whom he claims he is a brother (230), Saladin presents himself not
as slavemaster, or physician, or friend, but "as your ancient foe . . . a
fair and generous one" (241). Why all this emphasis on recognizing
one's difference? First, as Saladin stresses to the resistant Sir Kenneth,
"Knowledge is the parent of power" (158). To him, difference realized
constitutes the subjected Other's only locus for agency; bodies and
boundaries are to be recognized for what they are—and used. Second,
if Others can honor one another for their difference, they can truly
become br/others; they can multiply their agency against colonial
subjection across their varied bodies. And, as Scott demonstrates in
his novel, the strategy works. Through his br/other Kenneth, Saladin
manages to negotiate a treaty with Richard; through his br/other Saladin,
Kenneth manages to operate within the crusading system without
sacrificing his identity. The knight who first appeared with arms effaced
now blazons forth on his shield a leopard with collar and broken chain;
Kenneth has learned to control and exploit his difference, and can now
acknowledge and cut the leading string that bound him to Saladin.

And within *The Talisman,* Scott makes it clear that this is his
preferred strategy for the contemporary, subjected Scot. At the end of
his novel, he projects the talisman, the occulted symbol of Saladin's
mobility, into Scotland. Using this little stone in a net bag, Saladin has
penetrated the crusading camp, and persistently seized life from death.
But the talisman's "plop plop, fizz fizz" must be administered according
to the movements of the heavens; if the stone is not used enough, or
not used aright, the last patient and the physician both will die. Now,
Scott casually mentions that Saladin has given the talisman to Kenneth

as a wedding present. How do we read this remarkable gift? The talisman requires its operator to recognize death, but to live to heal. The Scot is to flee the death of accepted subjection, but to recognize himself as Other, to deal with death, and accomplish life. Moreover, Sir Kenneth, as Prince David, is to perform a kingly cure on his people.

But as I suggested earlier, in 1825 Scott was just beginning to grasp the limitations and the potential in the contemporary Scottish situation. In the years immediately following *The Talisman*'s publication, he learned that his country's problems were more acute, their solutions more urgent, than he had recognized. It is perhaps for this reason that after his own financial collapse and the Scottish banking crisis, and after he appealed openly to the Irish for support, he hedged his text about with rather strange supplements. For the 1832 edition of his works, he loaded the novel with prefatory and closing material, some of which is worth particular note. First, in his "Introduction," he links the talisman to a curative stone brought back from the Crusades, and held by the Lockharts of Lee (3–4). Then, in a footnote, he recounts that the Lee-penny, as it is now known, serves to cure cattle, and that the ungracious Presbyterian Scots have rejected even these cures as potentially diabolic (316). That is, Scott indicates paradigmatically for those who have missed the message that his countrypeople need to regain their talismanic power, to accept and to use otherness, to fight for life in the context of death, and to be agents of their own destiny. Second, in an appendix to the 1832 "Introduction," he quotes George Ellis's retelling of a tale in *Richard Coeur de Lion* (Ellis 233–46). Here, suffering from fever like the King in Scott's own novel, Richard craves pork. With none available, his cooks slay and serve a Saracen, instead (a bitterly ironic choice given the Islamic proscription of pork in any form). When Richard discovers the substitution, far from resenting it, he uses it to intimidate the Sultan's ambassadors: rather than negotiate with them, he invites them to a banquet at which he serves and eats their relatives. Needless to say, they are only too happy to forget their ambassadorial duties, and to escape with their lives. In this appendix, Scott adds a new urgency to his text; he stresses as far as he can the risks to the unresistant Other: to a voracious, dominant culture, the Other looks a lot like dinner. Just a little cultural cookery will make it digestible.

If Scott's supplements make him seem paranoid, if his text's rein-scriptions indicate desperation, the history of his own text reveals that he didn't worry without reason. As we have seen, even *The Talisman*, Scott's carefully modulated consideration of the dynamics of ethnicity subjected to colonial power, has slipped easily down the English canon's open maw. But perhaps this essay's Saidian Heimlich maneuver can dislodge it, can make the canon cough it up, and into the discursive space of world literature—or at least, perhaps it can give the canon a case of cultural indigestion.

Acknowledgments

My thanks go to Ric Reverand, University of Wyoming, for the careful reading and thorough comments that have helped me to limit this paper's controversy to its content, rather than its form.

Notes

1. Leavis began more complimentarily, describing Scott as "primarily a kind of inspired folk-lorist.... a great and very intelligent man; but not having the creative writer's interest in literature, he made no serious attempt to work out his own form and break away from the bad tradition of the eighteenth-century romance" (14).

2. As we await the Edinburgh Edition of Scott's works, I have chosen to refer to the most easily accessible current edition (Everyman 1991).

3. See McCracken-Flesher, "Thinking Nationally, Writing Colonially? Scott, Stevenson and England"; and "A Wo/man for A' That? Subverted Sex and Perverted Politics in *The Heart of Midlothian.*"

4. This introduction seldom prefaces *The Talisman* when the novel is published separately, but it appears in any complete edition of Scott's works.

5. Scott's son-in-law J. G. Lockhart sounded the alarm in November 1825, although the crash did not occur until 1826. (See Scott's November 18 letter to Lockhart in Grierson, 291–95).

6. See, for example, Scott's letter of 4 April to his son, Walter. He writes, shifting blame for Ireland's problems from her poor, Catholic population to her rack-renting and absentee landlords, "The Catholic question seems like to be accomodated [sic] at present. I hope though I doubt it a little, that Ireland will be the quieter & the people more happy. I suspect however it is laying a plaister to the foot while the head aches & that the fault is in the landholders extreme exactions not in the disabilities of the Catholics or any remote cause." Parts of *The Talisman* were in press by May 15 of the same year. (See Grierson 63, 113).

7. Scott wrote three letters, each headed "To the Editor of the Edinburgh Weekly Journal, from Malachi Malagrowther, Esq. on the Proposed Change of Currency, and Other Late Alterations, as they affect, or are intended to affect, the Kingdom of Scotland." He addresses "Patrick" in the second (23–29).

8. In his recent book, Bruce Beiderwell adds his voice to those stressing that here Saladin and Sir Kenneth represent the East and the West. He calls

Sir Kenneth and Saladin "the two best representatives of their respective cultures' virtues" (85). He misses, I think, the fact that each is also encoded as Other.

9. When Kenneth is saved by Saladin/El Hakim from death, their ride through the desert is interrupted for prayer. Scott writes: "The sonorous voice of El Hakim himself overpowered and cut short the narrative of the tale-teller, while he caused to resound along the sands the solemn summons, which the muezzins thunder at morning from the minaret of every mosque" (233).

Works Cited

Beiderwell, Bruce. *Power and Punishment in Scott's Novels.* Athens: U of Georgia P, 1992.

Ellis, George, ed. *Specimens of Early English Metrical Romances.* Vol 2. London: Longman, Hurst, Rees, Orme, and Brown, 1811.

Grierson, H. J. C., ed. *The Letters of Sir Walter Scott: 1825–1826.* 1935. New York: AMS Press, 1971.

Hayden, John O. *The Critical Heritage.* New York: Barnes and Noble, 1970.

James, Henry. *The Notebooks of Henry James.* Ed. F. O. Matthiessen and Kenneth B. Murdock. 1947. Chicago: U of Chicago P, 1981.

Leavis, F. R. *The Great Tradition.* 1948. Harmondsworth, Middlesex: Penguin, 1980.

McCracken-Flesher, Caroline. "Thinking Nationally, Writing Colonially? Scott, Stevenson and England," *Novel* 24 (1991): 296–318.

———. "A Wo/man for A' That? Subverted Sex and Perverted Politics in *The Heart of Midlothian.*" In *Scott in Carnival.* Ed. J. H. Alexander and David Hewitt. Aberdeen: Association for Scottish Literary Studies, 1993. 232–44.

Said, Edward. *Orientalism.* New York: Random House, 1979.

Scott, Walter. *To the Editor of the Edinburgh Weekly Journal, from Malachi Malagrowther, Esq. on the Proposed Change of Currency, and Other Late Alterations, as They Affect, or Are Intended to Affect, the Kingdom of Scotland.* Edinburgh: William Blackwood, 1826.

———. *The Talisman.* 1825. London: Everyman. 1906, 1991.

Welsh, Alexander. *The Hero of the Waverley Novels.* New Haven: Yale UP, 1963.

Wilt, Judith. *Secret Leaves: The Novels of Walter Scott.* Chicago: U of Chicago P, 1985.

14 A Different Kind of Hero: *The Tale of Genji* and the American Reader

Charles B. Dodson
University of North Carolina at Wilmington

In my sophomore-level course surveying world literature through the seventeenth century, I emphasize the theme of heroes and heroic codes. But in addition to such Western classics as *The Iliad, The Odyssey, Don Quixote,* and *The Song of Roland,* I also include *The Ramayana,* one of the great epics of India, and *The Tale of Genji,* a fictional account of an idealized Japanese courtier and gentleman, written in the late tenth or early eleventh century A.D. by the court lady Murasaki Shikibu, and often considered to be the world's first novel. Although the attitudes and behavior of Rama in *The Ramayana* depart in certain respects from the Homeric and chivalric warrior codes that my students are familiar with, they see in him many parallels with Achilles or Odysseus or Roland, although they of course find Rama and his milieu much more exotic. However, in Genji they find a "hero" who is not only different from the classic Occidental figure, but in many respects almost diametrically opposed to it.

The values and standards of behavior that Genji embodies and that are perceived in him by the author and the other characters (especially the female ones) often astonish, even offend, many of my students, steeped as they are in the ethos of a culture that, having evolved from its roots in the Homeric warrior code, continues to prize violent or at least aggressive behavior, Marlboro-man virility, materialism, athletic vigor, and an aesthetic sense that doesn't go much beyond sports-car styling. Nonetheless, I begin the course with the Homeric poems not only because they are the earliest works on our reading list but because my students will easily recognize many facets of the warrior code that underlies them. We read *The Song of Roland* next, comparing the Homeric and early chivalric codes and discussing among other matters how Roland and other characters do or do not manifest traditional heroic traits.

The Ramayana not only introduces the students to a new and different set of cultural and religious constructs, with its exotic locale, bizarre supernatural events, and polytheistic Hindu context; but also Rama himself serves as a transitional heroic figure between the violent, relatively crude Homeric warriors and the refined, gentle, aesthetic Genji. Rama possesses many of the usual traits of a Western heroic protagonist: aristocratic birth, piety, courage, great skill at arms, endurance, singleness of purpose. But to these are added traits not often associated with the Western heroic figure: courtesy, humility, modesty, self-denial, learning, a highly developed ethical sense, and especially compassion. The latter takes many forms, including a desire to help others (e.g., Sugreeva, who has been unjustly persecuted by his brother Vali, and Ahalya, who has been changed to stone after being seduced by Indra). In fact, as the incarnation of the great god Vishnu, Rama exists to "abolish fear from the hearts of men and gods, and establish peace, gentleness, and justice in the world" (Narayan 67). His compassionate nature is particularly revealed by his treatment of his arch-foe, Ravana, for he wants to save rather than destroy him (Narayan 154), and he finally does destroy him only when Ravana has refused Rama's final plea to free Sita and end his evildoing. Rama does not respond to Ravana's death with jubilation, nor does he gloat over a fallen opponent as would a warrior in *The Iliad*; his reaction instead is regret that Ravana's great powers had been so grossly misused, and he urges that Ravana's soul, now purged of its destructive hostility, concupiscence, and egotism, "may go to heaven, where he has his place" (Narayan 160).

Rama both differs from the Homeric warrior hero and anticipates the soft-spoken, introspective Genji in other ways as well. He strives to embody his father's teaching that "humility and soft speech" are limitless virtues and that "anger or meanness" can have "no place in a king's heart" (Narayan 38). Homeric heroes have little time or inclination for speculation; Rama has fourteen years for it during his exile (Genji will likewise spend several years in lonely exile). In seeing life "as a bondage from which one should escape," Rama is much closer to Genji's outlook than to the Greek warrior's belief that "human existence is a gift [from the gods] which must be enjoyed" (De Bary 112).

Having briefly reviewed the traditional Western heroic figure and code of behavior along with an Asian work—*The Ramayana*—which shares some of its characteristics but also, as students soon realize, has some affinities with Genji and his world, students will be better prepared to take up their study of the latter. They are somewhat surprised, I think, when they learn in the opening chapter not only that Genji is (by our monogamous standards, anyway) illegitimate but that this fact is of no real importance in other characters' attitudes toward him.

Other surprises soon follow. Although there are vague references to military matters in the novel, arms and warfare play no significant part in the story, nor in Genji's characterization (*The Tale of Genji* takes place during a peaceful and isolationist era in Japanese history). Genji is indeed good-looking, but the author speaks not of a square jaw or rugged physique but rather of his beauty. He is indeed so beautiful even as a child that many at court fear he will not live long, great beauty (like other personal accomplishments) being, for them, an omen of potential disaster. As he matures into a young man, the other characters often perceive a sort of radiance in his beauty—he comes to be referred to as "the shining one"—and during one moment of great sorrow we are even told that "he was so handsome in his grief that Koremitsu [his servant] wanted to weep" (Murasaki 53). When he visits his father-in-law's social gathering during the festival of cherry blossoms, his combination of personal beauty and exquisite taste in selecting and blending the colors of his robes "quite overwhelmed" even the cherry blossoms themselves (143).

Indeed, his refined aesthetic sensibility is one of his most notable traits. Genji is keenly attuned to the delicate beauty of the natural world; he not only responds to it emotionally but is most adept at capturing and expressing it through his great skill as a painter and poet. Like the other court ladies and gentlemen he composes poems spontaneously and publicly and is admired for the flowing delicacy of his calligraphy and his ability to choose just the right shade and texture of paper for the poems through which he not only seduces women but *literally* converses with them and others. As do all court gentlemen, Genji perfumes his clothing with a delicate scent of his own devising. His singing and his grace as a ceremonial dancer are such that they can bring tears to the eyes of an entire assembly, even the emperor himself:

> Genji and To no Chujo danced "Waves of the Blue Ocean." To no Chujo was a handsome youth who carried himself well, but beside Genji he was like a nondescript mountain shrub beside a blossoming cherry. . . . Genji scarcely seemed of this world. As he intoned the lyrics his auditors could have believed they were listening to the Kalavinka bird of paradise. (107)

Genji is moreover an accomplished player on both the Japanese and Chinese kotos, and is moved by the playing of others.

A scene early in the novel epitomizes the almost obsessive pervasiveness of Genji's aesthetic sensibility. As he departs one morning from a secret romantic liaison, he pauses "to admire the profusion of flowers below the veranda." His mistress's lady-in-waiting follows him out, and he is so struck by her aster robe ("which matched the season pleasantly") and by the elegance and grace with which she wears it and her "gossamer train" that he asks her to sit with him for a while. "The ceremonious precision of the seated figure and the hair flowing over her robes" strikes him as being "very fine." When a "pretty little page boy" then appears among the flowers and breaks off a morning glory blossom to present to Genji, the set piece is complete and so perfect that Genji feels the urge to capture it on canvas (37).

Another of Genji's differences is his mind. The classic Western hero is not known for his intellect. Even the wily and resourceful Odysseus is essentially a man of action rather than contemplation, and his mental faculties are largely devoted to outwitting enemies and responding to life-threatening situations. But Genji is not only an accomplished poet: he is likewise a scholar of Chinese literature and history who, on the occasion of a Chinese rhyme-guessing contest, dazzles even the university professors who are present (223).

Even more important is his sensitivity to *mono no aware,* the pervasive sense of the transience and essential sadness of life, which can be found in even the most ordinary of events. Frequently translated as "the evanescence of things," *aware* is perhaps the major thematic motif in the novel. All of the characters possess *aware,* but Genji does so to the utmost extent. Thus sadness is an inseparable facet of Genji's response to beauty, whether the beauty emanates from a melody on the koto, a woman, or a natural scene. Once, as Genji travels to a shrine to plead with one of his mistresses not to go into religious seclusion, he traverses "a reed plain of melancholy beauty," where "insects hummed sadly" among plants bereft of their flowers by winter. Moreover, "more perceptive men saw how beautifully the melancholy scene set him off" (187). There is sadness in the beauty, but there is also beauty in the sadness. At the end of the tale Genji, after a period of disgrace, has not only been restored to his former rank and offices but is even more influential than before and has emerged triumphant over his rivals in a painting contest that has considerable political implications. Yet instead of exhilaration or even satisfaction, he is only more convinced than ever that "men who rise to rank and power beyond their years cannot expect long lives" and that further "glory could only bring uncertainty. He wanted to withdraw quietly and make preparations for the next life," and so he begins making arrangements to move to a remote mountain village (359–60).

Other traits that set Genji above his peers include his polite respectfulness to all, even to his political and social opponents, and an often self-effacing modesty, especially when contemplating or admitting his weakness for women. He frequently displays generosity and spontaneous concern for others, especially those who have suffered as a result of his actions—a far cry from Achilles' petulant demand to Thetis that many Achaians must fall to Trojan blades while he remains sulking in his tent. For example, in spite of Genji's shock and fear at the sudden and unexplained death of his mistress Yugao, "his confused thoughts centered upon the girl. There was no room for thoughts of himself" (50), and he even gives the now rootless Ukon, Yugao's lady-in-waiting, a home and employment in his own household. When he is scandalously discovered in Oborozukiyo's bed, "the immediate business was to comfort the lady" (228), and he is empathetically aware of the suffering of the Rokujo lady and others who have come to grief, frustration, or embarrassment as a result of the vagaries that inevitably come with the passing of time. Perhaps Margaret Berry best sums up the positive qualities of Genji when she says that

> Genji's life is devoted to an exploring of his world for beauty; his search is solely to give, to receive, to bring into being as much creative affection, . . . as much psychological delight in perfection of form as possible. In his long series of amours—despite impetuosity and irresponsibility—the Heian prince basically pursues only beautiful and enduring, though not exclusive, relationships in which he can promote the well-being, the capacities for beauty of the beloved while himself savoring union with that which is beautiful. (5–6)

The matter of his amours is probably, for my students, Genji's most distinctive departure from the traditional heroic role, whether Western or Eastern. They accept Achilles' relationship with Briseis and, presumably, others; the Mycenaean age, after all, was a primitive one, and students can understand the concept of women as war booty without endorsing it. They are even willing to accept Odysseus' long liaison with Calypso and, somewhat less readily, his year with Circe. After all, he does have as his ultimate goal reunion with his wife and son, his relationships with Calypso and Circe are essentially at the behest of the gods, and he turns down Nausicaa. Rama is unhesitatingly and completely faithful to his wife Sita, and Roland is an essentially sexless figure.

But my students have a great deal of difficulty with Genji, right from the opening chapter, when he conceives a childhood yearning for his stepmother Fujitsubo which, as he grows up, becomes a consuming and compulsive passion that is only partly satisfied when she bears him a son. He has affair upon affair, often simultaneously, sometimes with older women like the Rokujo lady (who is also his aunt by marriage) and the nearly sixty-year-old Naishi; sometimes with women of his own age; and even with Murasaki, whom he abducts and installs in his household when she is ten, then raises for several years like a younger sister or daughter, and then, in effect, rapes as a way of signaling to her that their relationship is now to change from filial to sexual. My students are unconvinced by the author's rather pro-forma criticism of Genji at such times, and they resist her constant insistence on how devastatingly attractive everyone finds him. Nor are they impressed by his servant Koremitsu's rationalization that because women find him so attractive, "to refrain from these little affairs would be less than human. It was not realistic to hold that certain people were beyond temptation" (35). I remind the students that in Heian tenth-century court society, promiscuity was common, even encouraged, among men and women alike; that it was a polygamous society to begin with; that marriages, like those among European monarchies, were arranged for political and economic purposes, not for love (hence Genji's indifference to his wife Aoi during most of their marriage); that social judgments were more often made on aesthetic rather than moral principles; and that the author was too elegant and reticent herself to provide any specific, let alone lurid, erotic detail. Nonetheless, my students' reactions to Genji's usually refined but inexhaustible sexual adventuring tend to vary from astonishment to disapproval to indignation to outright disgust, and I sometimes find myself in the rather awkward position of defending him by reiterating all his other, clearly admirable (if, by Western standards, rather unorthodox) traits as a "hero."

I should point out that whatever resistance my students show to Genji does not seem to come from any prejudicial hostility to him for being either nonwhite or specifically Japanese. None of the contemporary resentment that perceives Japan as a trade opponent, a cause of the loss of American jobs, or our bitter enemy in World War II seem to enter into this resistance. If anything, the students (many of whom are from rural or small-town North Carolina) are curious about the culture and customs of Japan during the tenth century, just as they were receptive to and curious about the "foreignness" of Rama and his world earlier in the course. Perhaps it is not just Genji's sexuality, but his promiscuity and its tacit endorsement by the author that they find unacceptably "foreign." They are of course aware of the sexual revolution that has been taking place in American culture for the past several decades; and I have no reason to doubt that they endorse it—at least in theory—as much as would any other group of students their age on other campuses. But what they have trouble accepting seems to be that, first, Genji's promiscuity is carried to an extreme that, in Rokujo's and especially Fujitsubo's cases, verges on incest, and, second, his obsessive sexual adventuring is presented as an important and essentially acceptable personality trait—almost a *sine qua non*—in a character that the author clearly considers to be paradigmatic. Their aversion to incest is of course attributable to our cultural taboo on it; and even Murasaki Shikibu's sophisticated audience no doubt considered Genji to be perilously close to violating cultural limits in his relationships with Fujitsubo and Rokujo (McCullough 135).

"But how can such a sexual athlete be a hero?" my students ask. After all, the heroes of their literary tradition are essentially monogamous and sexually conventional. Thus *The Odyssey* presents Penelope as Odysseus' bravely persevering wife and a mother, not as Odysseus' sexual partner. Their reunion in Book 23 probably has its (unstated) physical manifestation, but the reunion primarily represents the restoration of domestic order in Odysseus' household just as the killing of the suitors leads to the reestablishment of civil order in Ithaca. In *The Iliad* Hector is movingly presented as a family man: the scene in Book 6 with Andromache, and especially the poignantly humorous incident when their son Astyanax is frightened by the bristling horsehair crest on his father's helmet, underscore the portrayal of the Trojans as a coherent community defending home and family, in contrast to the bickering, belligerent invaders from across the sea. Achilles does avail himself of his female battle prizes, but my students realize that fighting and glory, not sex, are what really matter to him. Roland's world is almost exclusively male. Rama behaves like a properly lovestruck American teenager when he first sees Sita, and they marry early in the story. Not only does he remain faithful to her but in a sense his final conflict with Ravana is precipitated by his quite firm yet polite refusal to be seduced by Ravana's sister, Soorpanaka. Don Quixote is of course very much aware of the beauty of women, but he is placed beyond sexuality by both his age and his derangement: Dulcinea is mostly an idealized figment of his imagination, and the other women he meets are vaguely and safely abstracted into court ladies or damsels in distress for whom his feelings, those of a chaste knight, are protective and paternal, not sexual.

One might expect that the sexual revolution would make students more receptive to a hero so sexually precocious as Genji and even make them at least willing to tolerate his attraction to his stepmother (and her evidently mutual attraction to him, though she resists it much more than he does). But such seems not to be the case. In class discussion, students do not mention either Don Juan or contemporary popular figures famous for their supposed sexual conquests (e.g., Warren Beatty, Magic Johnson, Wilt Chamberlain, the Kennedys, Prince, and so on) as counterparts—admirable or not—to Genji. They seem to want their heroes' sexuality to be conventional, in both quality and quantity.

All of the foregoing is not to say that Genji has nothing in common with the traditional heroic figure of Homer or the chivalric epic. There are parallels. He is of course an aristocrat. He has the charisma of a Hector or a Roland. Like the classic Western hero he is larger than life in personality and in attainments, different in kind from those of an Achilles or an Odysseus as these might be. In fact, in the diversity of his accomplishments we can even see the Homeric ideal of *arete,* which Kitto translates as all-around "excellence" (171–72).

And particularly, like the Homeric heroes, like Roland, like the protagonists of Greek tragedy, he is flawed. Achilles' initial withdrawal from the Trojan war was acceptable to his peers; but he puts himself in the wrong when in Book 9 of *The Iliad* he refuses Agamemnon's exceedingly generous compensatory offer and this decision leads to the death of his dearest friend Patroclus. Odysseus has to learn the hard way that when he gives in to the warrior's impulse to boast over a victory, he gets himself and everyone else in serious, even fatal, trouble. Roland is blinded by his arrogant conviction that as a Frenchman and a Christian he is immeasurably superior to the heathen Saracens.

Genji too is guilty of excess, of his own kind of *hamartia.* This excess grows out of his sexual drive, but it is more a matter of *whom* he chooses to pursue than how many. As he himself admits, "it was his nature to be quickened by danger" in matters of love (225). This can explain his attraction to the volatile Rokujo lady, who directly if unintentionally causes the death of his wife Aoi and his mistress Yugao, and immeasurable grief to Genji. He is fascinated not only by the ten-year-old Murasaki herself but by the challenge of spiriting her away before her father comes to take her, hiding her away in his Nijo palace and molding her over the years into his ideal woman. Oborozukiyo's undeniable charms merely augment the danger of carrying on a forbidden liaison with a woman who is at once the intended wife of his brother (the emperor) and the sister of his bitterest enemy, Lady

Kokiden; he even beds her in Kokiden's own house! Their discovery there by her father leads directly to his eclipse at court and several years of lonely, painful exile at Suma and Akashi, and like the errors of Hector, Achilles, Odysseus, and Roland, it is entirely his own doing.

But Genji's most excessive act, because it is the most severely forbidden of all, is his relationship with Fujitsubo. That she is his own stepmother makes their affair, though technically not incestuous in a Heian reader's view, nonetheless highly improper. But there is more: she is the favorite mistress of Genji's father, who is also the emperor himself. When it becomes clear to Genji and Fujitsubo that her son is Genji's and not the emperor's, her resulting anxiety is so intense and unrelieved that it ultimately, even after the emperor has died unaware of the truth, leads her to sever her ties with the world by becoming a nun. As for Genji, he must suffer not only the fear of discovery, but also the guilt of knowing he has terribly deceived his father (whom he genuinely loves) and the frustration of having a son he can never acknowledge, even after the son himself becomes emperor.

My students are quick to perceive Genji's similarities to the traditional hero, but they insist, and I agree, that Genji differs from the Western heroic figures we have studied far more extensively and dramatically than he resembles them. As Earl Miner has said,

> The dance, music, poetic composition, painting, the beautification of one's environment, a sensibility that is both touched by nature and able to convey its beauties to others—these no doubt seem tame accomplishments set beside the wrathful greatness of Achilles or the thirty-man-power grip of Beowulf. And the concern with love—which enables the novel to develop Genji's fullness of personality—is apt to make him seem either 'effeminate' or altogether profligate. (7)

The sharp contrast that Genji thus provides with the classic figure of the warrior hero they have inherited from the European cultural and literary tradition forces students to reconsider and perhaps even modify their response to that traditional figure. Some of them even end up admiring Genji.

Works Consulted

Berry, Margaret. "The Meeting of the Twain: Japanese and Greek." Unpublished essay, 1986.

Cervantes, Miguel de. *Don Quixote*. Trans. Samuel Putnam. Mack et al. 1176–1329.

De Bary, William T., ed. *Approaches to the Oriental Classics.* New York: Columbia UP, 1959.

Goldin, Frederick, trans. *The Song of Roland.* Mack et al. 679–736.

Homer. *The Odyssey.* Trans. Robert Fitzgerald Mack et al. 172–227.

——. *The Iliad.* Trans. Richmond Lattimore. Chicago: U of Chicago P, 1971.

Kitto, H. D. F. *The Greeks.* Baltimore: Penguin, 1951.

Mack, Maynard, et al. *The Norton Anthology of World Masterpieces.* 5th Continental ed. Vol. 1. New York: Norton, 1987.

Maki, J. M. "Lady Murasaki and the *Genji Monogatari.*" *Monumenta Nipponica* 3 (1940): 480–503.

McCullough, William H. "Japanese Marriage Institutions in the Heian Period." *Harvard Journal of Asiatic Studies* 27 (1967): 103–67.

Miner, Earl. "Some Thematic and Structural Features of the *Genji Monogatari.*" *Monumenta Nipponica* 24 (1969): 1–19.

Morris, Ivan. *The World of the Shining Prince.* New York: Knopf, 1964.

Murasaki Shikibu. *The Tale of Genji,* translated and abridged by Edward G. Seidensticker. New York: Random, 1990.

Narayan, R. K., trans. *The Ramayana.* Harmondsworth, Middlesex: Penguin, 1977.

Rimer, J. Thomas. *Modern Japanese Fiction and Its Traditions.* Princeton: Princeton UP, 1978.

15 "Singing in the Seams": Bharati Mukherjee's Immigrants

Ranee Kaur Banerjee

I see myself in an article on a Trinidad-Indian hooker; I see myself in the successful executive who slides Hindi film music in his tape deck as he drives into Manhattan; I see myself in the shady accountant who's trying to marry off his loose-living daughter; in professors, domestics, high school students, illegal busboys in ethnic restaurants. It's possible, with sharp ears and the right equipment—to hear America singing even in the seams of the dominant culture. In fact, it may be the best listening post for the next generation of Whitmans. For me, it is a movement away from the aloofness of expatriation, to the exuberance of immigration.

—Bharati Mukherjee, Introduction to *Darkness*

The twentieth century is best characterized as that of the postcolonial, the migrant, the refugee, the exile, and the immigrant, of all those who are cultural nomads. As our world becomes increasingly a-cultural, as the number of tribes traveling across traditions grows, as Bombay and New York become boroughs of the same moving city, itinerants like Bharati Mukherjee are creating their own nomad literature. Here is, finally, a literature that no national boundary can hold in and claim; a literature that reflects fragments from distant parts of the globe that have come together and collected within the nomad's body; a literature of kaleidoscopic rather than mirrored images.

Bharati Mukherjee, like her "lady from Lucknow," knows that "the traveler feels at home everywhere because she is never at home anywhere" (31). A Western-educated postcolonial woman, Mukherjee has always been aware of the fragmentation of her identity, of the unbridged gaps between her missionary school education in Calcutta and her indigenous heritage, between her affluent, cosmopolitan upbringing and her conservative Bengali beginnings. After three decades of living in different parts of North America with her Canadian husband,

Mukherjee would like to be considered an American writer "in the tradition of other American authors whose ancestors arrived at Ellis Island." But she has to admit that

> when you are from the Third World, when you have dark skin and religious beliefs that do not conform to those of Judaism or Christianity, mainstream America responds to you in ways you can't foresee. (Interview 650)

Mukherjee's Third World immigrants "have different gods" and come to America for "different reasons." Her fiction, therefore, "has to consider race, politics, religion, as well as certain nastinesses that other generations of white immigrant American writers may not have had to take into account" (651). As one of Mukherjee's characters describes the process of her immigration to the United States,

> At first you don't exist. Then you're invisible. Then you're funny. Then you're disgusting. Insult, my American friends will tell me, is a form of acceptance. No instant dignity here. ("A Wife's Story" 27)

Mukherjee describes her fiction as an investigation into the myriad "remarkable, often heroic" tales of the survival of the Third World immigrant in the new world s/he has adopted out of choice or necessity. Of course, the figure of the Third World immigrant does not consist of a single, homogenous, coherent composition. The picture is actually more like a three-dimensional jigsaw puzzle made up of a conglomeration of many nationalities, races, classes, religions, and political systems, many histories and traditions, many "broken identities and discarded languages" (Interview 654). As Mukherjee further explains in her introduction to *Darkness,* each piece that makes the picture has its own unique story of survival to tell, and the pieces are joined together only by a common "will to bond" themselves "to a new community against the ever-present fear of failure and betrayal" (3). Thus, what at first glance may seem like a very limited fictional world is actually one with an endless treasury of untold stories, each unlike any other in the world.

Yet there are similarities that become evident to an immigrant intellectual like Mukherjee. The Third World is not geographically contiguous—the nomenclature itself is a First World construct—nonetheless, certain sections of the world merit a common name because of certain shared experiences and conditions, which, though few and superficial, are enough for the formulation and expression of a bond that underlies all the differences. It is inevitable that Western-educated postcolonials, whatever their origins, will identify with other peoples

of the world who share with them an experience of economic deprivation, of belonging to a traditional, agricultural society and culture,
a similar history of colonial subjugation and exploitation and a common
postcolonial crisis of identity.

The narrator of "A Wife's Story" has left her home and her husband
"to get a Ph.D. in special ed." Her mother, she says, was beaten by
her mother-in-law, the protagonist's grandmother, "when she'd regis-
tered for French lessons at the Alliance Française." Her grandmother,
the daughter of a rich zamindar, was illiterate. The protagonist, Panna
Bhatt, has been "trained . . . to behave well" by "expensive girls' schools
in Lausanne and Bombay." Her "manners are exquisite, [her] feelings
are delicate, [her] gestures refined, [her] moods undetectable" (28–29).
She tries to explain the postcolonial crisis of identity:

> It's not my fault; it's the *situation*. Old colonies wear down.
> Patels—the new pioneers—have to be suspicious. Idi Amin's
> lesson is permanent . . . I know how both sides feel, that's the
> trouble. The Patels sniffing out scams, the sad salesmen on the
> stage: postcolonialism has made me their referee. It's hate I long
> for; simple, brutish, partisan hate. (27)

Hate is an emotion Third World immigrants like Dr. Supariwala and
J. M. Persawd ("Isolated Incidents"), Gupta the cook, and the illegal
busboys of Mumtaz Bar B-Q ("Tamurlane") have to face often in the
First World. But it is not an emotion Third World immigrants like:
Nafeesa Hafeez ("The Lady from Lucknow"), for whom lines from
Donne and Urdu verses carry equal significance; Ratna Clayton ("The
World according to Hsu"), whose "Europeanness" lies submerged just
below her skin waiting to be discovered; Vineeta Kumar ("Visitors"),
who majored in French literature at Loreto College, Calcutta—or even
"Angela," who grew up learning poise and piano at a Christian
orphanage in Bangladesh, can reciprocate easily. For Western-educated
postcolonials, the First World is too much a part of them even before
they have entered it; the New World has penetrated their Old World;
its ways have been imposed upon them through colonization. In time,
they have internalized the lessons taught to them by colonial masters,
learned their "masters' " languages, become part of their traditions and
cultures, histories and literatures and philosophies, learned to partially
comprehend their own worlds through the perceptions of the Other.

Thus, to Western-educated Third World immigrants, coming to the
New World is at least in part a homecoming. They are not total strangers
to it. But they are, unfortunately, perceived as such. And their survival
as a loosely integrated identity, a hybrid-species that incorporates two

or more cultural strains, is threatened. An imbalance is automatically created when they, who carry this world everywhere within them, are taken to be strangers the moment they set foot within it. An identity crisis becomes inevitable with the awareness that the Other who is so familiar, so much their own self, perceives them to be alien, incomprehensible, inscrutable, undesirable.

For Western-educated postcolonials, the traditional and colonial coexist without any overt need for analysis, explanations, or apologies. It is not anybody's fault, "it's the *situation.*" One can be a hybrid, be aware of the fact without taking sides, without needing to explain to society why one is that way, *what* one is, how one is combined. But as a Third World immigrant in the New World one is immediately made aware that one is an anomaly, an absurdity or, at the very least, an aberration. And one is forced to take sides, one way or the other, forced to explain, analyze, apologize; forced to privilege one part of this hybrid identity over the other, forced into a crisis of identity. Thus Mrs. Bhowmik ("A Father") goes out of her way to seem "Americanized" to the point of reading pop psychology books in order to improve her relationship with her husband; she tries out new, American cuisine from her cookbook of "Eggcellent Recipes"; she wants her husband to give up his Old World beliefs in his pagan goddess, Kali, and become a fashionable atheist like herself. Thus, Mr. Bhowmik feels obliged to keep a firm hold on his religion and his superstitions. As his physical association with India fades with the years, his morning prayers to Kali become longer and more devout, his adherence to old superstitions becomes more desperate, and his fantasies about his life in India become more vivid. Thus Ratna Clayton ("The World according to Hsu"), presumed to be Indian because of her looks, is compelled to assert her Canadian nationality with more force than necessary.

At first you don't exist. The Third World victims of First World wars, like Eng ("Fathering"), Tran ("Saints"), and Kim ("Angela"; *Jasmine*), as well as the children of the Vietnam War and Third World refugees of First World politics, like Angela, Ro ("Orbiting"), and "Jasmine," do not exist, as it were, in the eyes of the American dream. Neither does the Western-educated postcolonial. While Angela was learning the religion, language, and culture of the First World, while Eng was growing up in a refugee camp, while people like Maya Sanyal ("The Tenant"), Leela Lahiri ("Hindus"), and Blanquita ("Fighting for the Rebound") were attending classes taught in English, the First World was effectively oblivious to their presence. It is not until they physically inflict their scarred bodies and minds on the American landscape and start affecting American lives—when "Jasmine" becomes Jane Ripplemeyer, when the Patels ("A Wife's Story"; "Loose Ends") own and run popular motels, when Dr. Manny Patel ("Nostalgia") becomes a millionaire—that the First World starts reacting to them in any real way. And the reactions range from unprovoked hate and violence (J. M. Persawd, "Isolated Incidents"; Gupta, "Tamurlane"; the young Gujrati woman in "Loose Ends"), to suspicion (Hernandez, "Isolated Incidents"; Eng, "Fathering"), to job discrimination (Dr. Supariwala, "Isolated Incidents"), to governmental neglect ("The Management of Grief"), to awkward, parochial incomprehension (Ro, "Orbiting"), to polite dismissal (Nafeesa Hafeez, "The Lady from Lucknow"), to making a particular community the butt of stand-up comedy ("A Wife's Story").

Then you're invisible. The major difference between European immigrants and immigrants from the Third World is that the latter, because of their physical appearance, cannot hide in a crowd. And it is because they are so physically "visible" that they become invisible as individuals. Judged by their physical presence alone, they become stereotypes. Leela Lahiri ("Hindus") is thus commended on the lack of a sing-song accent. Nafeesa Hafeez ("The Lady from Lucknow") is thus mistaken for a Palestinian. In most traditional, Third World societies, a person's name instantly transmits the entire surface of his or her identity: the origin and meaning of the name, the region of its origin, the person's mother-tongue, sex, religion, caste, perhaps even the social status of his or her family. All the necessary preliminary information about a person is taken care of with the sounding of his or her name. So when Nafeesa Hafeez's name becomes a-signifying, when it becomes merely "musical," and when Panna Bhatt's name ("A Wife's Story") is mispronounced even after she has spelt it and corrected the pronunciation many times over, Nafeesa and Panna themselves become invisible, a-signifying, and have to begin groping for other ways to define themselves. Perhaps that is why the words "Hindu" and "Brahmin" appear infinitely more often in Mukherjee's smaller corpus than they do in the work of Indians writing in English in India. Perhaps that is Mukherjee's way of defining, in no uncertain terms, the "givens" of her protagonists and endowing the words with more significance, character, and "meaning" in the First World than they would merit in their home environment. In Mukherjee's fiction, the physical "visibility" and the loss of any signifying power affects the second generation of immigrants even more than it does their parents. When Detroit, the only home a young girl named Babli Bhowmik ("A Father") has ever known, is both "native to her" and yet "alien"; when she has to explain Hinduism to her school friends as "neat" and "like a series of super graphics"; when the "cosmos balanced on the head of a snake" has to be equated to "a beach ball balanced on the snout of a circus seal" (65), she is herself juggling the different pieces of her identity in a desperate effort to survive intact, to fit in with her American friends and at the same time, to be different, mysterious, "visible." For Babli it is a losing battle and at age twenty-six, she lives with her parents like an Indian daughter, seems to have no real friends outside the Indian community, and is almost killed by her father for getting herself artificially inseminated. Shawn ("Saints"), whose cross-cultural parents are divorced, lives with his American mother and doesn't remember his Indian father "in any intimate way" (155). But Shawn's last name is Patel, and he does not, cannot, consider himself a "real" American. Some nights, Shawn looks for an Indian name in the phone book, and "at midnight," disguised as a woman, he "float[s] like a ghost through other people's gardens," looks into "other boys' bedrooms" and becomes "somebody else's son" (156).

Then you're funny. As Panna Bhatt ("A Wife's Story") rants against "communal, racist, antisocial" (26) humor directed against the Latinos and the Chinese and Indian immigrant communities, she knows "we've made it. Patels must've made it. Mamet, Spielberg: they're not condescending to us. Maybe they're a little bit afraid" (29). Humor is one First World way to subvert the threat of Third World immigrants and undermine their survival as legitimate citizens. Franny ("Orbiting") smirks as she watches Ro, and his girlfriend Renata cannot help but see her Afghan boyfriend through Franny's eyes:

> I see what she is seeing. Asian men carry their bodies differently, even these famed warriors from the Khyber Pass. Ro doesn't stand like Brent or Dad. His hands hang kind of stiffly from the shoulder joints, and when he moves, his palms are tucked tight against his thighs, his stomach sticks out like a slightly pregnant woman's. . . Ro, hiding among my plants, holds himself in a way that seems both too effeminate and too macho. I hate Franny for what she's doing to me. I am twenty-seven years old, I should be more mature. (70)

And "foreignness" becomes embarrassing, awkward, "freaky," as "visible" and "abnormal," as "crippling" as a man with no arms:

> She has never slept with a man without arms. Two wounded people, he will joke during their nightly contortions. It will shock her, this assumed equivalence with a man so strikingly deficient. She knows she is strange, and lonely, but being Indian is not the same, she would have thought, as being a freak. ("The Tenant" 112)

For the children of immigrants, it is once again, more difficult to deal with the overt "foreignness" of their parents over and above their own physical handicap of skin color or facial features. Shawn Patel's ("Saints") only intimate memory of his father is that of embarrassment at Manny Patel's "overstated black Mercedes" and the "hugging and kissing in such a foreign way" (156).

Then you're disgusting. After a certain degree of familiarity, old-fashioned contempt proves most effective. The trusted weapon of colonial masters, it is a natural tool to kill any sense of security and self-worth the immigrant might have garnered. With a withering glance and a few well-chosen words Kate Beamish ("The Lady from Lucknow") can annihilate the well-traveled, sophisticated Nafeesa and turn her into a"shadow-person," an intruder who is too disgusting, too inconsequential to worry about. One mentally ill Horowitz ("Nostalgia") in Manny Patel's successful, "mainstream" life calling him " 'Paki scum' in exquisite English" (98) is enough to ruin Manny's patriotic American identity. Disgust and contempt, whether aggressively overt like Jeb Marshall's ("Loose Ends") for the motel-owning Patels, or couched under governmentalese like Ann with Hernandez ("Isolated Incidents") or the social worker ("The Management of Grief"), kill the immigrant in body or mind, and either way the immigrant is prevented from appropriating and securing any First World space for himself.

No instant dignity here. "And in spite of everything the Supariwalas wanted to stay on. That was what amazed Ann" ("Isolated Incidents" 79). Ironically enough, for the victims, refugees, and postcolonial misfits created by the First World, the home of the ex-colonizer is the only asylum. Mukherjee's stories tell of two classes of immigrants. The first group consists of the survivors of wars or of racist and terrorist attacks and those who have been driven to America by poverty or physical necessity. Angela, the product of a war resulting from Britain's creation of two Pakistans hundreds of miles away, is given refuge by American "parents." Left for dead by her own race, she is rescued, given a new name and a new identity by a nun and given a home and another name, a brand new lease on life, by the Brandons in Iowa. Tran ("Saints"), one of the "boat people," made that long journey to survival hiding from pirates and "having to chew on raw fish just to stay alive" (150). In America, Tran might be lonely, unhappy, "a freak," but he is alive. Eng ("Fathering"), Kim ("Angela"; *Jasmine*), Ro ("Orbiting"), Jasmine, and the fifteen-year-old Ugandan-Indian narrator ("Danny's Girls") are all survivors who might not have lived through prison camps, terrorist attacks or Idi Amin's politics if they hadn't made the illegal journey to America. Here they do not have dignity or understanding. Self-inflicted scars on Eng's child-body make her seem monstrous and horrify her would-be mother. Tran's story embarrasses his teacher. Ro's war-scars, mapped on his body, make Renata's parochial parents uneasy. But in America they have found a refuge, legal or illegal, that their own countries could not ensure for them. The legal refugees like Angela, Eng, and Kim have it slightly easier. The underclass of illegal immigrants—like the busboys of Mumtaz Bar B-Q, Dinesh (who uses the alias "Danny") or Ro's cousins— hide in dingy, unsanitary holes and are hunted down. Looked at "through the wrong end of the telescope," America becomes "a police state, with sudden raids, papers, detention centers, deportations, and torture and death waiting in the wings" ("Orbiting" 66). And still they want to stay on, those "illegals," hunted, humiliated, stripped of all identity. Poverty provides the impetus. They cannot go back because they have sold everything they owned and have given all their money to the agents who provided them with forged identities and false papers ("Tamurlane"; "Buried Lives"). They cannot go back because they can earn more here even if they are illegal. Like Alfie Yudah ("The Middleman"), a hustler will always be able to find "something worth trading in the troubles [he has] seen" (21) to somebody in America. Like "Danny," an entrepreneur will always procure sellable merchandise, even if it happens to be women. Perhaps that is the tyranny of the American dream. It strips them of their identities and robs them of their dignity, but it promises them a money-order they can send home to starving families.

For the second group of Mukherjee's characters, the dream is more vivid, more accessible and therefore more treacherous. These are the "well-bred" Third Worlders: professionals, executives, aristocrats who are intellectually more at home in America than in their own countries. For these postcolonials, economic well-being is not the main concern. They are driven to the First World by ambition, a desire to excel in their chosen fields, a will to join the international community of professionals. Once here, they adapt faster, learn faster, succeed faster than the refugees. The edge is erased from their accents in no time (Leela Lahiri, "Hindus"; Panna Bhatt; "A Wife's Story"), they learn to downplay their looks (Maya Sanyal, "The Tenant"), many of them marry Americans and join, at least in a superficial way, the American mainstream (Manny Patel, "Nostalgia"; Ratna Clayton, "The World according to Hsu"; Maya Sanyal, Leela Lahiri, "Jasmine" a.k.a. Jane Ripplemeyer). Their struggle for survival in the New World is neither physical nor economic: it is one of maintaining their identity and dignity while at the same time achieving status and legitimacy as part of the majority culture—a task that few can accomplish. Manny Patel is betrayed by his own "nostalgia." Iqbaal ("The Lady from Lucknow") is haunted and driven by the knowledge that he will always be a "not-quite." Blanquita ("Fighting for the Rebound"), being an aristocrat in her native land, cannot take the ignominy of being ordinary. Ratna, Maya and Leela, for all their well-bred Westernization, are trapped within their brown skins. These women, who would in their own worlds be considered elite and command automatic respect because of their status and education, become ordinary second-class citizens in the New World. The American Dream has given them success and recognition, but it cannot give them the means to be themselves and to be American. And still they stay on, juggling pieces of their identities in a constant personality crisis.

And among the "well-bred postcolonial" immigrants to Britain and America are the ever-increasing numbers of writers and intellectuals like Mukherjee herself. The First World is increasingly becoming the home of the Western-educated, Third World intellectual. At home only in the languages of the First World, these intellectuals are best heard in the West. This is where they are published, where their work is appreciated, where they can get international exposure and recognition, this is where they *want* to be heard. It is the best place, says Salman Rushdie, from which the Third World intellectual can enter the over-determined, "orientalist" discourse and "wail and whine" in public and thus oppose "notions about history which must be quarrelled with, as loudly and embarrassingly as possible" (qtd. in Needham 611). It is the best position from which a postcolonial writer can challenge popular myths and misrepresentations about his or her culture and oppose "neo-colonial modes of thought and action which continue to pervade most . . . post-colonial societies" (Katrak and Radhakrishnan 581). Here Maya Sanyal can try to change the perceptions of mainstream America by introducing sophomores to the fiction of Narayan and Achebe. Here Mukherjee can try to introduce Americans to her immigrant story which is "replicated in a dozen American cities" (Introduction, *Darkness* 3).

All Mukherjee's characters—even the white, fourth-generation Amer-icans—mirror the fragments of her own identity. Mukherjee's characters are created out of the pieces of her own "fractured" self. Thus, even though the facts of her characters' lives might be far removed from her own, each one of Mukherjee's characters is, in fact, autobiographical in so far as (s)he reflects Mukherjee's own experiences in the New World, her desires, the "shape of [her] feelings," her politics and her philosophies. The kaleidoscope of shifting "voices" that makes up Mukherjee's fiction is actually the ever-shifting composite Mukherjee creates of the varied, many-colored, multitextured shards of her own personality.[1]

A chronological review of Mukherjee's characters, from Tara Banerjee Cartwright (*The Tiger's Daughter*) to *Jasmine* reveals what we may postulate as the progressive fragmentation of her own personality, her own journey from the certainty of an inviolate "expatriate" identity to a surrender to the notion of "a set of" constantly shifting, kaleidoscopic, "immigrant" selves that make up her personality. From a desire to have an impact on the American landscape and a frustration in not being able to enter "mainstream" America, her characters have begun to forge for themselves other Americas—where differences teem, skin colors vary, and languages babble. From complaints about the difficulties (perhaps the impossibility) of being a Third World American, Mukherjee's fiction, since *The Middleman and Other Stories,* has begun to assert the Americanness of those other, underground Americas of people like herself who retain their "unpronounceable" names, speak with "outsize Yankee accent[s]," wear their sarees awkwardly and seem, to the Indians back home, "very much the occidental at odds with the native dress" (Varughese 60).

"Continents slide, no surface is permanent," Mukherjee says in "The World according to Hsu" (38). The statement is especially true of her own self as well as her characters since *The Middleman.* Once she, and therefore they, have stopped struggling against the "triple disruption of reality" that all migrants suffer (the loss of "place," language, and society), and once they have surrendered to the total disintegration of an identity that is no longer possible to define, Mukherjee and her characters begin to find new ways of describing themselves, "new ways of being human." They begin to realize

> that reality is an artifact, that it doesn't exist until it is made, and that, like any other artifact, it can be made well or badly, and that it can also, of course, be unmade. (Rushdie xiii)

Instead of seeing their identities as "permanent designs" that they were born with and bred into, Mukherjee and her characters begin to perceive themselves as kaleidoscopes made up of multiple identities, a shifting composite of little, fragmented, brilliantly colored pieces of all their experiences, all the "cities" they have found and lost, all the diverse lives they have lived. With every movement of Mukherjee's kaleidoscope, a new pattern is formed out of those individual multiple fragments of her own life and the possibilities of "becoming" are so infinitely rich and endless.

Thus Nafeesa Hafeez ("The Lady from Lucknow"), born into a conservative Muslim family "of soft, voluptuous children," raised in purdah by a father who "wanted to protect us from the Hindus' shameful lust," can, after passing through "Lebanon, Brazil, Zambia and France," become in Atlanta, Georgia, an inconsistent conglomeration of personalities: traditional wife to her husband, Iqbaal, an American mother to her children, a gracious host to international students, a practiced adulteress, an irresistible temptress and a pathetic Third World shadow-person in America, all at the same time (23–24). Thus Manny Patel ("Nostalgia") can be a patriotic, Republican American with an American wife and a son at Andover and still count his millions in rupees. He can be a respected psychiatrist in love with all that America has offered him and still wish "he had married an Indian woman, [one] that his father had selected," wish for "any life but the one that he had chosen" (111). He can instantly fall in love with a woman who looks like an Indian goddess, be conned by her and turn from a perfect, sophisticated gentleman into a crude, vengeful creature:

> Then, squatting like a villager, squatting the way he had in his father's home, he defecated into the sink, and with handfuls of his own shit—it felt hot, light, porous, an artist's medium—he wrote WHORE on the mirror and floor. (113)

Manny Patel is at once, schizophrenically, upstanding patriot, nostalgic expatriate, loving husband, adulterous "slum lord," suave man of the world, crude avenger, and anyone else he needs to be at any given moment. Inconsistencies abound in Mukherjee's characters and in the stories they tell. Brash, crude, sophisticated, cynical, naive, legal, illegal, erudite, and illiterate, the one trait common to all Mukherjee's characters is the elasticity of their personalities, their ability to restructure their identities according to the situations and environment in which they find themselves. A coy, shy, typically Indian beauty, as in "Nostalgia," can, in the space of a moment, transform herself into a dirty-talking whore and be part of a gang that scams wealthy, unsuspecting Indian immigrants like Patel; a mild-mannered professor ("The Tenant") can turn into a Bengali patriarch and then a sexual pervert in the space of an evening, while a blasé, cynical woman who has seen it all can become a freak or an outraged maiden according to the circumstances.

Inconsistencies, the blatant disregard for facts, the callous remaking of histories, these are qualities and characteristics not only of Mukherjee's characters but of the author herself in her occasional disregard for accurate detail in her rendering of a fictional world. In Mukherjee's fiction a Sikh grandfather ("The Imaginary Assassin") can blithely offer tobacco to his grandson, the author apparently oblivious to the fact that tobacco is taboo to the followers of Sikhism. Whereas a writer like Ruth Prawer Jhabvala takes into careful consideration the different accents and idioms, the various registers of Indian-English, in Mukherjee's fiction "Indianness," whatever region or class it belongs to, is characterized simply with an exaggerated overuse of the present continuous made "Indian" to America by Peter Sellers ("I am knowing so little about shaking cocktails and pouring jiggers, I'm afraid" ["Visitors" 175]). In Mukherjee's fiction a Punjabi villager (*Jasmine*) addresses her grandmother by the Bengali name "Dida"; a Sikh adolescent ("The Imaginary Assassin") remembers being born in the month of "Sravan" again, a Bengali word, while Gandhi is reportedly assassinated on the second of October (his birthday) instead of the correct date, the thirtieth of January. The list is long.

It is not a simple matter of ignorance. Facts, histories, localized truths are easily researched and verified. But they are just not important considerations for Mukherjee and her characters. Facts don't matter. Continents slide. Realities and identities are artifacts to be made and unmade, over and over again. What is all-important is the essential transfigurative yet tenacious nature of the migrant and the fascinating, compelling stories (s)he has collected on the way; what is all-important is that America listens to the sound of the "energetic voices of the new settlers in this country" (Interview 654) and to the songs being sung in its seams.

Note

1. It is relevant here to note Knippling's critique of Mukherjee's method of characterization: According to Knippling, Mukherjee "ignores the role that representation (of the Other) plays in the textual production of her writing and, second, . . . she homogenizes her ethnic minority immigrant subjects, instead of calling attention to the [their] actual heterogeneity. . . ." (144). [Ed.]

Works Cited

Katrak, Ketu H., and R. Radhakrishnan. "Introduction." Special issue on Asian literature. *The Massachusetts Review* 29.4 (1988–89): 580–82.

Knippling, Alpana Sharma. "Toward an Investigation of the Subaltern in Bharati Mukherjee's *The Middleman and Other Stories* and *Jasmine*." In

Bharati Mukherjee: Critical Perspectives. Ed. Emmanuel S. Nelson. New York: Garland, 1993. 143–59.

Mukherjee, Bharati. *Darkness.* New Delhi: Penguin Books (India), 1990. Includes the following stories referred to in the text: "Angela," "A Father," "Hindus," "The Imaginary Assassin," "Isolated Incidents," "The Lady from Lucknow," "Nostalgia," "Saints," "Visitors," "The World according to Hsu."

———. Interview with Alison Carb. *The Massachusetts Review* 29.4 (1988–89): 645–54.

———. *Jasmine.* New York: Grove Press, 1989.

———. *The Middleman and Other Stories.* New York: Grove Press, 1988. Includes the following stories referred to in the text: "Buried Lives," "Danny's Girls," "Fathering," "Fighting for the Rebound," "Loose Ends," "The Management of Grief," "The Middleman," "Orbiting," "Tamurlane," "The Tenant," "A Wife's Story."

———. *The Tiger's Daughter.* New Delhi: Penguin (India), 1990.

Needham, Anuradha Dingwaney. "The Politics of Post-Colonial Identity in Salman Rushdie." Special issue on Asian literature. *The Massachusetts Review* 29.4 (1988–89): 609–24.

Rushdie, Salman. Introduction. *On Writing and Politics: 1967–1983.* By Günter Grass. New York: Harcourt, 1985. i–xv.

Varughese, Suma. "Bharati Mukherjee: Writes of Passage." *Gentleman,* 31 Aug. 1989: 58–62.

Index

Editor

Photo: Steve Davis

Michael Thomas Carroll (Ph.D., Temple University) is associate professor of English at New Mexico Highlands University. His publications include "The Bloody Spectacle: Mishima, the Sacred Heart, Hogarth, Cronenberg, and the Entrails of Culture," "Agent Cooper's Errand in the Wilderness: Twin Peaks and American Mythology," and "The Cyclic Form of [Milan Kundera's] *Laughable Loves*." He was a participant in a 1992 National Endowment for the Humanities Seminar on Realist Fiction, and currently serves as a faculty consultant for the Educational Testing Service, Princeton, New Jersey.

Contributors

Aron Aji (Ph.D., Southern Illinois University at Carbondale) is associate professor of comparative literature at Butler University in Indianapolis. He is the editor of *Milan Kundera and the Art of Fiction: Critical Essays,* and has published and presented work on Achebe, Rushdie, Kundera, Seifert, Soyinka, Césaire, and Alkali.

Ranee Kaur Banerjee received an M.A. in English literature from the University of Calcutta and a Ph.D. in comparative literature from the University of Georgia in 1992. She has read papers at several international conferences and her published work includes poetry and book reviews. She has also contributed critical essays to the five-volume *Critical Survey of Mystery and Detective Fiction* and to Katharina Wilson's *Medieval Women Writers.*

Mackie J. V. Blanton is associate professor of linguistics at the University of New Orleans and a pro bono advisor to the New Orleans/New York Gestalt Psychotherapy Institute. Having written essays in linguistics, poetics, scientific and technical discourse, Louisiana dialects, and Sufi and Hasidic sacred language, he is currently doing research in subtle body mysticism and in sacriture, i.e., sacred discourse.

Paulo de Medeiros is assistant professor of English and comparative literature at Bryant College. His publications include "Simian Narratives at the Intersection of Science and Literature," "O Som dos Buzios: Feminismo, Posmodernismo, Simulacao," and "Eating (with) Nietzsche: Reading as Devouring in Die Froehliche Wissenschaft," as well as essays on Miguel Torga, Sa-Carneiro, and Clara Pinto Correia.

José J. de Vinck (Ph.D., State University of New York at Binghamton) has two books forthcoming: *Allegories of Exchange* and *Exchange Theory.*

Charles B. Dodson is professor of English and director of graduate studies at the University of North Carolina at Wilmington. His publications include an edition of three novels by Thomas Love Peacock and contributions to *Nineteenth-Century British Periodicals* and the *Directory of Victorian Journalists.* He is currently compiling an annotated bibliography on alcoholism in twentieth-century fiction.

209

Howard M. Fraser (M.A., University of New Mexico; M.A., Harvard University; Ph.D., University of New Mexico) is N.E.H. Professor of Modern Languages and Literatures at the College of William and Mary in Williamsburg, Virginia, where he has been teaching both Spanish and Portuguese for the past twenty years. He is the author of two books, over two dozen articles, and twenty reviews covering a variety of subjects in the field of Spanish and Portuguese and Latin American literature.

Sharon Hileman is chair of the Department of Languages and Literature at Sul Ross State University. She has written articles on cross-cultural autobiographical fiction and serial life-writing. Currently she is working on an N.E.H.-sponsored project investigating postcolonial narratives from Africa and the Caribbean.

Sarah Lawall is professor of comparative literature at the University of Massachusetts at Amherst. Her research interests are literary phenomenology, the history of reading practices, modern poetry and poetics, and the concept of world literature. Her publications include *Critics of Consciousness: The Existential Structures of Literature,* a co-authored translation of and commentary on Euripides' *Hippolytus,* "René Wellek: Phenomenological Literary Historian," "Bonnefoy's *Pierre Écrite*: Progressive Ambiguity as the Many in the One," and *Reading World Literature: Theory, History, Practice.* She is on the editorial board of *Comparative Literature* and is assistant general editor and editor of the modern sections of *Norton World Masterpieces.*

Caroline McCracken-Flesher (M.A., University of Edinburgh; Ph.D., Brown University) is assistant professor of English at the University of Wyoming. Her research interests include the literary formulations of cultural marginalization, particularly in nineteenth-century Scotland, and cinematic renarrations of novels. She edited *Why the Novel Matters: A Postmodern Perplex* with Mark Spilka (1990), and she has published articles on Scott, Stevenson, and Dickens.

Erskine Peters (Ph.D., Princeton University) is professor of English and African American studies at the University of Notre Dame. His books include *William Faulkner: The Yoknapatawpha World and Black Being, African Openings to the Tree of Life,* and *Lyrics of the Afro-American Spiritual.* He was the recipient of a Lilly Endowment Faculty Open Fellowship, 1994–95.

Marilyn Gaddis Rose, Distinguished Service Professor of Comparative Literature, is the founding director of the Translation Research and Instruction Program (TRIP) of the State University of New York at Binghamton, which shared the Alexander Gode medal of the American Translators Association in 1981. Founding editor of the annual *Series* of the American Translators Association, she herself received this medal in 1988. Her translations include *Axel* and *Eve of the Future Eden* by Villiers de l'Isle-Adam and *Lui: A View of Him* by Louise Colet. She is also the editor of

Translation Perspectives and the Women Writers in Translation series for the SUNY Press.

Katrina Runge is currently an English major at Butler University, Indianapolis, Indiana.

Ismail S. Talib is a senior lecturer in English language and literature at the National University of Singapore. He has published studies in a number of journals, including *The Journal of Narrative Technique, The ELT Journal, The Journal of Multilingual and Multicultural Development,* and, in the Malay language, in *Dewan Sastera* and *Dewan Bahasa.*

Dennis Young teaches writing and literature at George Mason University. His scholarly writing focuses on the politics and philosophy of teaching. He has published articles in *The Iowa Review* and has recently completed a book on teaching writing.

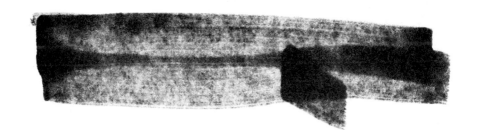

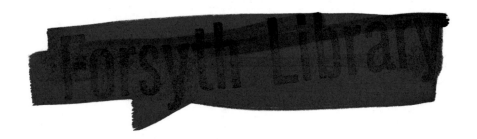